BY LINCOLN KIRSTEIN

Ballet: Bias & Belief

By With To & From: A Lincoln Kirstein Reader

The Classic Ballet

Dance: A Short History of Classical Theatrical Dancing

Elie Nadelman

Flesh Is Heir: A Historical Romance

Four Centuries of Ballet: Fifty Masterworks

Memorial to a Marriage (with Jerry L. Thompson)

Mosaic: Memoirs

Paul Cadmus

Pavel Feodorovich Tchelitchev

The Poems of Lincoln Kirstein

Portrait of Mr. B

Quarry: A Collection in Lieu of Memoirs

Thirty Years: The New York City Ballet

Mosaic

MEMOIRS

Mosaic

MEMOIRS

LINCOLN

KIRSTEIN

FARRAR, STRAUS & GIROUX

NEW YORK

Copyright © 1994 by Lincoln Kirstein
All rights reserved

Published simultaneously in Canada by HarperCollinsCanadaLtd
Printed in the United States of America
First edition, 1994

Library of Congress Cataloging-in-Publication Data
Kirstein, Lincoln.
Mosaic : memoirs / Lincoln Kirstein. — 1st ed.
p.   cm.
Includes index.
1. Kirstein, Lincoln. —Childhood and youth.   2. Authors,
American—20th century—Biography.   3. Ballet—Biography.
I. Title.
PS3521.I74Z47 1994   818'.5209—dc20   [B]

Parts of chapters 8 and 9 first appeared in different form
in *The Hound & Horn Letters*, edited by Mitzi Berger Hamovitch,
published by the University of Georgia Press.
Quotation from *Ulysses*, by James Joyce, reprinted by permission of
Random House, Inc. Copyright © 1934 by Random House, Inc.,
renewed 1962 by Lucia and George Joyce. Quotations from "The
Hurricane" and *The Bridge* by Hart Crane, from Crane's letter to
Waldo Frank, and from Frank's introduction to *The Bridge* all re-
printed from *Complete Poems and Selected Letters and Prose of Hart
Crane*, edited by Brom Weber, with the permission of Liveright
Publishing Corporation, copyright © 1927, 1933, 1958 by Liveright
Publishing Corporation. Quotations from Hart Crane's letter of Dec.
21, 1923, from *The Letters of Hart Crane and His Family*, edited by
Thomas H. Lewis, copyright © 1974 by Columbia University Press,
New York, reprinted with permission of the publisher.
Photograph of George Gurdjieff courtesy of the Bettmann Archive,
New York. Photographs of Romola Nijinsky with her husband and
their daughter and of George Balanchine courtesy of the Dance
Collection, The New York Public Library for the Performing Arts,
Astor, Lenox, and Tilden Foundations. Photograph of Lincoln
Kirstein in Cambridge, ca. 1928, copyright © by the Estate of
Walker Evans. Reprinted by permission. Photographs of Carl
Carlsen and of Lincoln Kirstein with his father courtesy of the
Estate of George Platt Lynes.

For Siri Huntoon and Nicholas Jenkins

Contents

Illustrations

Chronology

1907 Born in Rochester, New York, second child of Louis Edward and Rose (Stein) Kirstein.

1911 Kirstein family moved to Boston.

1919 Visited Chartres with mother and brother George.

1921 Completed elementary education at Edward Devotion School, Brookline, Massachusetts.

1921–1922 Briefly attended Phillips Exeter Academy.

1922 *Summer* Visited London for the first time.

1923–1924 Attended Berkshire School.

1924 *Summer* Visited Bayreuth with mother.

1925 Worked in Connick stained-glass factory in Boston.

1926 *Fall* Entered Harvard.

1927 *Spring* Started *Hound & Horn. Summer* Traveled to Marrakesh. Visited George Gurdjieff at Fontainebleau. Met T. S. Eliot in London.

1928 Started Harvard Society for Contemporary Art.

1929 *Summer* Saw first Balanchine ballet, *Prodigal Son*, in London, and Diaghilev's funeral in Venice.

1930 Graduated from Harvard.

1931 Moved, with *Hound & Horn*, to Manhattan. Met Romola Nijinsky. Began
work with her on biography of Nijinsky.

1933 *Summer* Visited Paris and London. Met
Balanchine, persuaded him to come to
America. *October* Balanchine arrived in
New York.

1934 *January* School of American Ballet
opened.

mosaic: originally, pertaining to the muses; also to music and museums. Later, the process of producing pictures or patterns by cementing bits of glass, stone, or wood. A *mosaic* of cones and rods is the basis for clear human vision. Also *Mosaic*, laws issuing from the divining rod of the prophet Moses.

•

Spinks and ouzels sing sublimely
"We too have a Saviour born";
Whiter blossoms burst untimely
On the blest Mosaic thorn.

—CHRISTOPHER SMART
"The Nativity of Our Lord and Saviour"

•

In writing my life in 1835, I make many discoveries about it. These are of two kinds; they are like great fragments of fresco on a wall, which, long forgotten, reappear suddenly, and by the side of these well-preserved portions there are great gaps where there's nothing left but bare bricks on the wall. Plaster, upon which the fresco was painted, has fallen; the fresco has gone forever. There are no dates beside the pieces that remain, and now I have to hunt for them.

—STENDHAL
La vie de Henri Brulard

Mosaic

MEMOIRS

Rochester, New York

1907–1911

THE PEAR WAS plump, ripe, juicy, pale jade—no need to have its silken skin peeled away. Late afternoon: my nurse, an hour before bedtime, carefully sliced my supper. Abruptly, my father appeared from work. Kissing me, he bid: "Go, run. Tell your Uncle Mart that DOUBLE-YOU-OH-OH-DEE-ARE-OH-DOUBLE-YOU, WILL-SON has been elected President . . ." Uncle Martin Wolfe, Aunt Jane, and my first cousins Nat and Margaret lived two houses away, toward one end of Portsmouth Terrace, a quiet, tree-lined, residential street in Rochester, New York.

I swallowed my piece of pear on our back-porch steps, facing a wide yard which stretched, unfenced, down to the Wolfes'. Their place was separated from ours by another, similar house, where dwelt Aunt Molly, a widow, with Simon, her bachelor brother. Catty-cornered, across our common sward, stood the firehouse, a Gothic castle of red brick with yellow turrets. Here Big Ben, its captain, would hoist me piggy-back from his second-story dormitory, and together we would plunge down a greased brass pole, through a square hole and onto the driver's seat of his scarlet-and-gold fire wagon, already harnessed to a thumping pair of grey-and-black dappled horses primed for their morning rehearsal.

The iteration of the letters-as-words spelling the new President's name I hardly remembered to repeat, yet they were to strike recurring echoes in my early life. Eight or nine years later, in Boston, Massachusetts, waiting in a crowd at the corner of Commonwealth Avenue and Dartmouth Street, I watched a motorcade conveying Wilson, already defeated, on the last stage of his journey back from the Versailles peace conference, his crusade for a League of Nations barely begun, yet doomed. He was slumped under a grey blanket on the back seat of a long, black, open Packard, his face hidden. As he rolled past, my father tweaked both my ears, hard. I was not to forget I'd caught a glimpse of "the greatest president since Abraham Lincoln." I dimly sensed Dad's awe and sadness for a paladin of peace and world-unity who was battling cosmic threats and happenings past rational expectation. For me, it was a first raw buzz of current events, which, certified by my father's apprehension, may as well serve as a basis (*intonaco*) for the plaster-ground of these memorial tesserae.

Uncle Martin Wolfe owned and managed the Lyceum Theater, a provincial opera-house with balconied auditorium in a red-and-gilt sublimity of Wilhelmine taste. Lit by electrified candles in pink silk shades, furnished by frail, gilded chairs, a stage-box was always at the disposition of our family. From it, I viewed *Kismet* by Edward Knobloch, my first theatrical vision. Its climactic scene, the drowning in an open, square stage-trap of Mansur, the villain vizier, by Haj, the hero-beggar, my mother judged too grisly for my virginal eyes. However, her loose, inefficient fingers failed to blind me entirely to a fair view of the phoney mayhem. Immediately after vague excitement came disappointment at the poverty of performance, for both leading actors re-appeared, smiling wanly, to bow before the curtain and accept applause from their unenthusiastic audience.

Far more exciting were the spotlights haloing Harry Lauder, the famous Scottish balladeer, who sang "A Wee Drop and Doris," "Coming Through the Rye," and "The Blue Bells of Scotland." There were also Pathé and Edison newsreels with their shots of corseletted cuirassiers and knights in full armor. The scarlet-and-gilt of Big Ben's fire wagon, the red-and-gold of the Lyceum Theater, inflamed in me an inborn greed for artificed splendor which could be brought into being by hands like my own.

The three comfortable, adjoining homes on Portsmouth Terrace housed the progeny of Nathan Stein and his wife Mina. Forty years before, he had helped found a firm which became well-known as Stein-Bloch, purveyors of men's clothes. Contracts came for uniforms for the Union Army in our Civil War. Then litigation followed shortly, the details of which I never learned, but this seemed to shade my father's reluctance to join the firm after he married my mother. There also lurked dubious, familial residues, clouding the reputation of Louis and Simon, her elder brothers. Neither married. Simon was not nice to his female "help," while Louis lived in a palatial cottage-bungalow at Charlotte, on the border of Lake Ontario, designed by Claude Bragdon, a progressive local architect responsible for Rochester's handsome tiled railroad station. Bragdon was an innovative builder influenced by Frank Lloyd Wright's Prairie-style long, low houses, touched by semi-mystical notions of "Dynamic Symmetry." Uncle Louis was believed to be under the malign influence of Percy Miles, his chauffeur, and worse, of Ella, his wife, a cook. My mother was convinced that Percy and Ella were conspiring to ruin their boss and benefactor. My first breath of mortality came when I was four or five and our world waited for Uncle Louis to "pass on." It was a relentlessly tardy performance. Time passed, but he didn't. I would be put to bed with a sure expectation that he couldn't last the night; for weeks he did. The smothering atmosphere of medical business, its aura of deathly gossip, was thrilling. Finally, Uncle Louis died and Percy and Ella Miles inherited the "cottage." Bragdon's house on the lake is now memorialized in a small, handsome, expensive brochure illustrated by pencil sketches.

My mother's parents celebrated their half-century's marriage in 1905, two years before I was born. They then "passed on." At Charlotte, under a bell-glass on a stand in the balcony over the living-room, was a dinky, lasting relic of golden observance, a miniature tree, which I was led to believe was cast from pure gold but was probably plated-silver. Its tiny, crisp, gilded leaves bristled as prickly foliage, among which nestled seven big plums of polished cabochon sapphires, inscribed "Jenny," "Louis," "Abraham," "Simon," "Birdie" (Bertha), "Molly," and "Rose" (my mother).

This tree, ten full inches of it, pushed up through a midget eruption of cattails which sprang stiffly from a solid slab of "gold." Compared to the masterworks of Fabergé or Tiffany, it was provincial handicraft, but to me, a piece of perfection, the single object in all the rich catalogue of heirlooms in which I had any interest. Inherited by Rose, the youngest jewel, it descended to me. Subsequent careers of other sapphires: my aunts, Molly and Birdie, my uncles, Abe and Simon, stay vague. Many affluent German-Jewish families, like the Steins, could be stuff for nostalgic fiction. But my father harbored a patient disdain for this tribe, and neither my sister nor myself ever felt tempted to trace its origins.

Jenny, the eldest daughter, married Martin Wolfe, a beefy bully. His wire moustache grazed my cheeks each time he bestowed a wet, perfunctory smack. He systematically thrashed Nathaniel, his only son, in order to "make a man of him." In this, according to his own terms, he failed. Nat Wolfe, as a Harvard sophomore, took me three nights running to watch Anna Pavlova dance on the stage of Boston's Symphony Hall. The first ballet I remember was her *Syrian Dance* in which she wore transparent trousers and a tall, conical hat. Later, Nat was dropped from college in a hushed scandal. He took his M.D. from McGill University and never practiced. I once visited him in his quarters at Bellevue Hospital, where he interned. The room was filled with volumes of *Klassiker der Kunst*, and Japanese prints of mysterious indecency. He appears briefly in the journals of Harry, Count Kessler, companion of Hugo von Hofmannsthal, Richard Strauss, and Sergei Diaghilev. He exiled himself abroad and died in Mexico. His small, pretty sister, Margaret, hoped to become an actress or playwright. She encouraged my ambitions toward theater and married a courteous Sicilian of papal nobility whom my father called "the count of no account." She, in her turn, exiled herself to Switzerland (for tax reasons?), where she became a companion to Princess Mafalda, the daughter of the King of Italy. Her residual fortune passed to Rochester University's excellent hospital, where she and her husband returned annually for check-ups.

My father's people had come to America in the aftermath of the 1848 revolutions. His father had been a lens-grinder in Jena and found a job soon enough in the great Bausch & Lomb optical works in Rochester. Foster children of the Enlightenment, both Steins and Kirsteins were loyal, if non-observant, Jews, attending synagogue at least once a year, on the Day of Atonement, and subscribing to charities as they were able. The elder Steins became rich; the elder Kirsteins did not. There was a class difference separating the two families and they stayed apart. My father was a bit of a maverick, schooled mainly by commercial travel; for a while he sold eyeglasses with special metal cases for tortoise-shell frames. When I first knew him, he had been a rich man for five years, but he had previously gone through three bankruptcies and the loss of his baseball team. He rarely spoke of his youth, but once slyly boasted of being sprung from a Saint Louis hoosegow by the madam of a pleasure-house he had known from earlier rounds.

In Rochester he met George Eastman, who became a friend. This inventor of a hand-held, boxed camera called the "Kodak" offered him a share in its original patent. The ultimately fantastic tender was rejected; my father prophesied it could never be popular, since it was but a toy for the idle rich. This failure in foresight was probably sparked by inverse class prejudice. In later life there were many proofs of his shrewdness: among them, advice to the treasurer of Smith College anticipating the stock-market crash of 1929 (perhaps via counsel from Bernard

Baruch), which kept Smith's endowment intact. I sometimes attributed my father's extraordinary liberality with myself to his memory of the refusal of the Kodak offer. It was less a matter of money, although I was never in need, than his tolerance, if not his support, of my mercurial, diverse ambitions, none of which aimed me toward becoming an eminent merchant. From my earliest memory of the meaning and use of money, I knew he considered me either a wastrel or retarded about the nature and value of coin. How, then, did he take my odd notions which succeeded one another in volatile whirligigs—to be a painter, a poet, an editor, or, Heaven forbid, a ballet dancer? Every facet of fantasy was given its fair consideration; the most hindrance was a quiet hearing. "Have you really *thought* about it?" "What leads you to suppose you can really *do* it?" But he was always generous; I never recall being in want, though I was always to have great difficulties with him about the cost of my tastes until I started working with George Balanchine, of whom he was very fond.

Grandma Kirstein, his mother, long widowed, had been "artistically" photographed in the profile of Whistler's mother. The result was framed in large format by brass and fumed oak. Father installed her in a small ground-floor apartment far across town, where she taught my sister Goethe, Schiller, and most of all Heine. She never spoke English easily, but I was taught to repeat, parrot-wise, Heine's "Die Lorelei":

> Ich weiss nicht, was soll es bedeuten
> Dass ich so traurig bin;
> Ein Märchen aus alten Zeiten,
> Das kommt mir nicht aus dem Sinn.

I would be taken by Father to visit Grandma, where there were always waiting small delicious treats of marzipan shaped like strawberries, almond cakes, and honey for lady-fingers. Also, there was *apfelstrudel*, black licorice sticks, and thin, knotted and seeded pretzels. In between bites, I tried to recite the few bits of poetry I'd been given to remember from a last occasion. Once, after terminating a recitation, when I needed a bathroom, I noticed next to the toilet a neat pile of newsprint clipped off the Sunday "comics" from the *Democrat & Chronicle*—"Foxy Grandpa," "Max & Moritz," and "The Katzenjammer Kids." My father, extremely upset, scolded the woman who looked after his mother. When later I pondered over this unaccustomed anger, I sensed it was guilt at his own inattention or thoughtlessness. On our next visit, proper paper was provided.

My mother was not fluent in German, but her mind held tags of quotations clipped from her girlhood. Returning from a meagerly attended matinée, she complained that "there wasn't a *Hund in dem Haus.*" Some actors or dancers were, alas, "*ohne Talent.*" A silly woman had the habit of "*fantazieren ohne Hitze,*" rambling on without brains, or "heat." Mother, a tailor's daughter, had an inbred devotion to certain crafts: dressmaking, interior decoration, and, more incidentally, painting and music. In my teens, when I began to try to paint on a more or less serious basis, I made a careful watercolor of the black, columnar telephone that stood on the night-table between my parents' twin-beds. She recognized the effort and attention involved but was disappointed in the choice of subject. It was monochrome, utilitarian, unlovely. She did not wish to be discouraging and so she suggested, smiling as she uttered her own name: "Why don't you paint something lovely—like a single *rose.*"

Infancy held its hazards. A week and a day old, I was circumcised, due to what lingering atavistic compulsion, I wonder? Septicemia set in and almost did for me. Sweat glands on both sides of my groin were excised. Naturally, I recall nothing firsthand of this, but there were scars, organic and fictive. My mother developed a panic fear of any infection, real or suspected. Cancer, at the least, must follow discovery of a brown birthmark under my chin the size of a blueberry, which, though it never burst, for years threatened to. Constant, unprovoked attention by a surgeon who never shaved, and who stank of iodine and garlic, made me query the sources of my putative manhood. Was I becoming a "sissy," like my unfortunate cousin Nat? Castration nightmares precipitated me into self-testings: holding my breath till I almost passed out, crossing streets ignoring traffic. I wrecked a new bicycle trying to see if I could fly over a low hedge down the embankment of a park path. Fear of more surgery was at the root of it all; my mother's fathomless apprehension determined more of my character than was necessary.

Helen Crevlin Bodine, my one and only nurse, was a farmer's daughter from Elmira, New York. Fresh-faced, bone-thin, gray-haired near to baldness, virginal, plain-spoken, and wise, she delighted my father, who loved to quote her aphoristic comment: "As Bodie says, your mother is a lousy housekeeper but a damn good provider." As a counter-balance to my mother's dire warnings, she was a source of solid information as to the part bodily functions play in young humans. Aged four, I shared a vacation with her on her family's Elmira farm. A hushed, vast, aromatic barn smelled dreamily of velvet cows and friendly horses who were far more welcoming than her tribe of hooligan nephews and nieces. As a citified intruder, I attracted less than love from them. At a ceremonial dinner one Sunday midday, I had the ill-chance to ask for a "pusher," or bit of bread to sop up gravy. I'd been taught to make clean sweeps, since it was wicked to waste a drop that "starving Armenians" might want. How this accursed race of unfortunates might benefit was not clear, but awareness of their dismal plight was very fashionable at this time. Here on the farm, though, it was assumed that what I demanded must be a special arcane tool, costly and rare, used only by the idle rich. I'd been entirely misunderstood. My shy appeal, however automatic, inspired a spurt of hatred around the table where we were sitting, and I quaked helplessly as I experienced a first tremor of the fear of awesome injustice, absolute, without redress.

Sometime later, Bodie took me for a saunter across a deep-green pasture bestrewn with rotten apples, each fallen with an unspoiled red cheek upward but nary a one fit to eat. Here, I reasoned, was a profligacy of natural overproduction that might feed the starving Armenians. At the field's edge grew ripe corn in full tassel; we pushed aside a thick wall of head-high stalks, penetrating into a tiny cleared square of dusty earth. Within this poor, secret place, a bent, wizened dotard scraped his hoe laboriously over dead weeds, hardly marking our intrusion. The dry sod mocked his raking. It was Grandfather Bodine, exiled or relegated to his desert patch—by whose will, his own or his heirs? It was pointless and unfair, like the children's response to my plea for a "pusher." His arms and claws seemed healthy enough; he handled his hoe firmly, working with urgent, rhythmical pressure. He was not "sick," nor yet exactly "well." Often in future years, between sleep and waking, Grandpa Bodine raked my worry into the furrows of unproductive labor which were his meager salvation. Dead, inexplicable repetition, locked in this corn patch, was all that was wrong with a world.

On another shared vacation, Bodie took me by small coastal steamer to visit a brother who farmed an orange plantation near Orlando, Florida. Our boat anchored briefly outside Savannah, where, on a bright, early morning, the fog-horn began to boom resounding blasts. These were neither warnings nor complaints, but memorial homage to a lighthouse keeper, long deceased, honoring a widow who now lived in his light-house. This sign of ritual ceremony struck me as more full of personal meaning than any celebration I had seen at Temple Israel in Boston.

On this trip, Bodie wore on her breast an oval, ceramic brooch, three inches across. Blazoned upon it in frail transparency was a grove of feathery palms which glowed in the reflected glory of a couchant sun. Arriving at Robert Bodine's Orlando grove, I saw through tall, huge, fernlike fronds, an identical landscape to the one limned on her brooch. I was so exhilarated by recognition of the power of paint that I had to express my excited recognition of beauty. Standing by the gate was one late rose, in full bud; I tore it off, thorns and all. Nearby, on the ground, providentially lay a scrap of ribbon, metallic red and gold, with which I bound the plucked blossom. This I gravely presented to "Uncle" Robert Bodine. With a half-suppressed, snarling grin, he seized it, tossed it over his shoulder and spat out: "Oh, thank you, *little girl!*" I looked down and noticed that I was bleeding slightly, nicked by a rose-thorn. Art, sexuality, nature, death, the mysteries of the human psyche, as I watched, oozed drip by drip from my bloodied finger.

Boston

1911–1918

TOWARD THE TURN of this century, my father had transferred briefly to Boston with my mother and sister, who was ten years older than I. He was employed there by a venerable firm of Scottish opticians, Andrew J. Lloyd & Company. I might connect his job with a suggestion from George Eastman, or with remnants of his contacts through my grandfather with Bausch & Lomb. It must also have been due to my father's gifts as a salesman of eyeglasses. He never had the chance to study optics, but a considerate manner pushed him onward and upward. My parents rented a small apartment, the fourth floor of a walk-up on Marlborough Street, where my mother salvaged her diminished state by installing a "Turkish corner." A prayer rug hung from a brass rod. Cushions were heaped beside a small, mother-of-pearl-encrusted tabouret which supported a heavy brass dish holding an authentic hookah, or water-pipe. The family soon returned to Rochester at the bidding of the Stein-Bloch clothing business, but any ultimate proposition for my father to join the firm collapsed. For whatever good or bad reasons, the constraints, geographic or moral, of a small town pushed him back to Boston.

When I was brought there in 1911, the Turkish corner

had vanished; only the hookah survived. Boston this time marked my father's re-birth and he rapidly became a partner in the department store of Filene's. How he met Lincoln and Edward Filene, sons of William, I never knew. For their growing retail business, preparations were headily advanced toward a noble new emporium, designed by Daniel Burnham, the famous Chicago engineer, city planner, and architect. A general belief developed that I was named after my *"Uncle"* Lincoln Filene; the middle name given me was Edward, his brother's, but neither were blood-uncles, nor in fact was I called after either. Father told me privately, so as to hurt nobody's feelings, that my name was strictly derived from the speaker of the sacred oratory of the Gettysburg Address and Second Inaugural. But names were numinous, and echoed onto faces, like masks attached. Woodrow Wilson, Big Ben, Martin "Woof-Woof" Wolfe, EFF-EYE-ELL-EE-EN-EE. When an immigrant family reached Ellis Island, or wherever their port of entry was, a recording officer, bemused by the moniker Katz, transposed it to Feline, but wrote it down Filene—or so the story went. To me, both foster "uncles," Lincoln and E. A., bore the aspect of benign, house-trained pets. They wore rough, fuzzy gray suits, had neat moustaches, and were as self-sufficient as happy cats.

I reconstruct a two-dimensional tableau of our arrival in Boston. In a chill, late February dusk, my mother, sister, brother, nurse Bodie, and myself were bundled into a horse-drawn cab that was waiting for arrivals at the old Trinity Place railroad station, now long gone. A sad horse stumbled up cobbles onto the street across Copley Square. Tiny lamp-lights twinkled from a procession of identical windows up the lengthy ride to 373 Commonwealth Avenue, where we unloaded at the Hotel Ericson. Here, for two years, we inhabited a long suite of almost blanked-out space, lit only by two large, bowed windows, front and back. The walls were hung in coarse brown buckram with big sepia photographs of the Roman Forum, Louis D. Brandeis (my father's lawyer), my Whistlerian grandmother, and Abraham Lincoln with his son, Tad.

Across from the broad front window, on a park strip splitting the avenue, stood a green-bronze effigy of Leif Ericson, who had landed on Vinland centuries before Christopher Columbus. This was the first sculpture of which I was conscious as metal cast from modeled clay. It was by one Anne Whitney. Shy of working from the male nude, she had evidently equipped a breasty girl with Viking attributes. It was my real initiation into the difference between girls and boys. The fact that he-she was clad in smothering costume was a small metaphor for the silence, shame, and secrecy protecting me from what, for much too long, I had wished most to know.

Visually, my appetite and curiosity were thus fixed on sculpture, and there were many public monuments at hand for discovery and comparison. At the front gates to the Public Gardens at the footing of Commonwealth Avenue pranced a formidable equestrian General George Washington, brandishing a strongly detached saber, with clanking spurs. His horse proffered one sharply shod, raised hoof. My father (on what evidence I don't know) reported that its sculptor, Thomas Ball, discovering he'd forgotten to include a tongue in the mount's mouth, had committed suicide. Opposite, looming like the figure-head of a clipper ship, was a stone Alexander Hamilton, by Dr. William Rimmer, who believed himself to be the Lost Dauphin, Louis XVII. Up the long double avenue of tree-lined promenade stretched cross streets, named in alphabetical order: Arlington, Berkeley, Clarendon, Dartmouth, Exeter, Fairfield, Gloucester . . . on to Massachusetts Avenue, which led to the Charles River Bridge, Cambridge, and Harvard.

At the center of each block stood memorials to local worthies, notably William Lloyd Garrison, firebrand editor of the abolitionist *Liberator*. He sat enthroned in an easy chair overstuffed in puffed, metal velvet, books and papers crammed underneath in astonishingly inclusive detail. On the tall campanile of Richardson's handsome Brattle Square Church, four trumpeting angels blew their brass psalms against the sky in arresting silhouette. These angels were from the workshop of

Bartholdi, who set the Statue of Liberty in Manhattan harbor. The three-dimensional presence of molten metal made permanent, eternal, unchanging, granted a quality of magic to handicraft: and I knew that somehow I wished to share in such alchemy. Unchangeable, defying weather and opinion, the silent life of sculpture stocked my imaginary museum in which the common element among all the athletes and generals was a full, muscular plasticity by which I have ever since tended to judge all figurative art.

But my mother's enlarged ambition soon outgrew her present horizons. As a young girl of the late Eighties, she'd been dispatched from Rochester to Manhattan's lower Madison Avenue, near Gramercy Park, where a Madame Meares (Myers?) kept a modestly genteel finishing school. Here, provincial damsels were instructed in what passed for Parisian deportment, speech, and chic. She was taught the hierarchy of *haute couture*: Worth, Doucet, Marcel et Armand, the roster of fashionable dressmakers. She learned to disdain her mother's tarnished German silver, furniture miniatures, and a dust-gathering collection of Dresden and Meissen figures with their ceramic, fretted ballerinas' skirts. As a prize for "improvement" in French, she won a red-morocco volume of Madame de Staël's *Corinne*, which descended to me, its shiny gilt fore-edge uncut.

In Mother's maturity, she gained a passion for dress which had little to do with self-adornment. Her own apparel was often peculiar. She adored fancy hand-work for its own sake—layered silks, glittering sequins, the contrast of woven textures, most of all lace or embroidery. And although she had a weakness for peacock plumage, birds-of-paradise, and egret feathers, she disapproved of reckless pillage. She never owned much jewelry, save for a necklace of authentic pearls. Each one of the Stein daughters received her string on a seventeenth birthday. On successive occasions, a new pearl, perhaps larger, would be added. In 1921, on my first sight of Oxford, we encountered, billowing down the High, a magnificently upholstered lady with a dazzling choker of pigeon-egg pearls. As she passed, I heard my mother gasp: "Those are REAL!" Later, we were told this was the Lady Ottoline Morrell, Egeria of Bertrand Russell, D. H. Lawrence, and Aldous Huxley.

After quitting Rochester in 1911, my father never owned real estate. However, with his elevated status as a partner in big business with obligations and emoluments, a railroad flat in the Hotel Ericson grew inappropriate. He rented 506 Commonwealth Avenue, which landed us about a mile up from 373. While our new address rang with an honorary glamour, it actually numbered a last single, private domicile on the street which faced the Kenmore subway station, where trains constantly emerged from the tunnels of a pioneer underground. Our location symbolically signified the tail-end limits of Back Bay affluence and elegance.

Number 506 was a featureless limestone mansion with a three-story bay window, put in the shade by its cornering neighbor, a chateau whose crisp detailing recalled Blois or Chambord. Here dwelt Simon Vorenberg, business rival and competitor in charitable giving, but no friend. I sensed definite isolation in our new venue, as not quite worthy of its boast. The house had been built in the late Eighties by a Mr. Whitney, whose family or whose first name we would never know. Whoever he may have been, he had seldom slept in his house, existing instead as a virtual exile in Rome, Venice, or Madrid. This was odd, since 506 was completely and tastefully furnished, even with an elevator. It was solidly constructed, with an air of dowdy luxury, and advanced facilities for cooking, plumbing, and lighting.

A small, mosaic-paved vestibule led six steps up to an entrance hall hung with sea-green watered silk, whose centerpiece was a marine-green marble fireplace, never lit. Upon a massive mantel stood, at attention, twin gilt-bronze torchères, each sprouting five electrified candles, from Thomire's foundry. Their strict severity enthralled me. These militant silhouettes were in contrast to a more than life-size marble bust of Jean-Baptiste Colbert, Louis XIV's great minister of finance and patron of the arts. He stood on a stout, gilt-wood pedestal, a fancy octagon which nevertheless betrayed its mean material—thin plywood. There was an excessive daintiness in Colbert's florid details: the finicky precision of wig; sunburst medallions; punctured, curly carving thumbed rather than cut, as if from clotted cream or warm snow. The Colbert smirked in robust, narcissistic complacency, more flagrant for its skill in craft than for any insight into a showy personality. My father conceived inexplicable contempt for it, pointing out the coarse, lumbering fraudulence of its pedestal. But my mother and I prevented its relegation to a big basement storeroom.

Under a turn in the flight of stairs leading to a second floor, or *piano nobile*, lurked a hidden, cupboard-sized closet, housing a telephone and a monstrous, black, steel safe with secret combination locks. I often painfully watched as it tested my mother's memory for numbers, and saw the safe release its secrets: a nest of trays, lined in red plush, snugly protecting the full panoply of Tiffany's "mythological" dinner service. Knives, forks, slim pincers for cracking lobster claws, coral-handled toothpicks, scimitars for roasts, small shovels, and sauce spoons—each was smartly modeled with a classical deity, the amplitude of whose full form corresponded to the plentitude of provender it serviced.

On a wall above the stairs hung a series of stubby, gilt-framed details from Velázquez's Prado masterpieces, each with a clear signature: "*José Villegas y Fornér.*" Themselves copies, these were my first sight of "hand-painting." Detached bits of heads, hands, hound, and horse, they must have been commissioned by Mr. Whitney with real love. To me, they appeared as bits of a lost puzzle, awaiting re-assembly. On the second-story landing was a full-size copy of Titian's great *Bacchus and Ariadne*. Veiled in many layers of somber varnish, hints of a god's crimson cloak and blue sky filtered through; the scale and depth of its burnished frame lent it a solid presence in spite of its being a copy. In the living room, which it bordered, a range of glazed library shelves held complete editions of

Dickens, Thackeray, Robert Louis Stevenson, and Mark Twain. On top paraded a dozen electrotypes of Roman bronzes: "The Boy Removing a Thorn from His Foot," "Zeus," "Plato," "The Dancing Faun." I knew these were all "reproductions," like almost everything else in the house: my mother had given me several red volumes of *Klassiker der Kunst*, in which photographs of the originals *in situ* were shown.

Unique in Whitney's home was a genuine, gigantic seventeenth-century Dutch still-life which reigned over a buffet sideboard in the dining room. A grim and grimy masterwork by Melchior Hondecoeter, it gloried in fur and feathers of hunt and barnyard. His huge canvas in black-oak and tortoise-shell frame encroached on a tall space accommodating two floor-to-ceiling windows. These were crowned by contorted pelmets cloaked in red velour from which depended heavy plush curtains restrained by the tug of thick silk cords. Through the windows was a view of sad back streets and, beyond, Boston & Maine railroad tracks whose cars shunted through every meal.

I may have over-emphasized impressions of secondary handicrafts adorning my childhood. The immediacy of their presence, the effect of their tangible proximity, the enigmas of their shape, stuff, and origin, made me a partner in my mother's program of providing a suitable background for augmented inheritance. My father's future now looked fair and my mother decided to transform these borrowed lodgings into her own world. She had her dream of what befitted a merchant prince, while he was content to leave her free, however outlandish her whims might prove. With permission or indifference from our absentee landlord, she proceeded to redecorate the house. Affability, warmth, charm plus a generous spirit won a conscious campaign against the innate suspicions of ancestral Boston, which was largely unacquainted with the type and style of an ethnic intruder.

As a successful merchant and responsible citizen, even a candidate for civic honors, Father began to fill the role of one of Boston's housebroken, token aliens. A prevailing ambience

was exemplified for us by the wife of his friend Felix Frankfurter, already an ornament of Harvard's Law School. Mrs.
Frankfurter happened to be an adroit, personable Gentile, and
at an academic Cambridge dinner party she was idly asked by
an amusing faculty member who was seated next to her: "We
all have 'em;—who's your favorite Jew?" Sweetly she smiled,
without offense: "My husband."

Later, due to his part in establishing Harvard's innovative
business school, my father became a figure representing democratic integration. Membership was even proposed for the
Somerset Club, ancestral bastion of Cabots, Lowells, Forbeses,
and Higginsons. His refusal caused, he thought, less surprise
than relief. Later, a stillborn movement proposed that he run
for governor of the state. This he evaded by saying that he
would not file for office, but would accept it if popularly
acclaimed. In time he became a real friend to James Jackson
Storrow and a very few other Brahmin Bostonians.

Mother's redecoration of the Whitney house enlisted
professional counsel from Mr. Clarence Wilmerding, from the
old firm of Irving Casson and A. H. Davenport. For many Back
Bay householders, an unquestioned criterion was the stupendous mastaba of Isabella Stewart Gardner. Fenway Court had
a beautiful alternation of original, period rooms in their rich
complexity of paneling and paintings, crammed with Bernard
Berenson's formidable loot, her brilliant portraits by John
Sargent and Anders Zorn, and the earliest Matisse in America.

Mr. Wilmerding presented himself to us as a figure of fun;
he might have served as a tailor's clotheshorse or a barbershop
dummy. His hairpiece, patent-leather pointed shoes, spats, a
permanent boutonniere, oversize cuff links, together with
shameless cosseting of my mother and his aesthetic omniscience,
made me squirm. Wilmerding's comprehensive proposals included stripping Whitney's Napoleonic entrance hall, which I
fiercely opposed with all my midget expertise. Melchior Hondecoeter's magisterial trophies stopped him short in the dining
room, and in the end Whitney's whole first floor remained

untouched. What was denied here, he lavished in compensation on my parents' bedroom. Mrs. Jack Gardner had her French, Spanish, and Dutch rooms, as well as a basement Buddhist shrine. My father despised, my mother loved, and I (privately) adored Mr. Wilmerding's "Chinese" bedroom.

Gilt tea-paper in alternate squares clad walls and ceiling. He strait-jacketed beds and chaise longue in scarlet slipper-satin so tightly stretched that anyone tempted to recline would have skidded onto the floor. Heavily embroidered Ch'ien Lung court dresses were cannibalized for heaps of overstuffed cushions dripping in jade and crystal beads. Harsh necessity pitched a telephone between the bedsteads but it was crowned by a pagoda-shaped night light with translucent red silk shade, capped by a small brass phoenix. It was periodically my duty and pleasure to twist the bird tight, since the vibrations of constant telephone calls gradually undid it.

My sister's room was creamed up as a Tuscan peasant's parlor, the walls "wumpsed," or treated with rough-cast plaster, blistered a dark, thick omelette, plus coarse linen drapes. Where my brother and I slept held a suite of furniture, sole surviving relics from Rochester, now painted black, with stenciled fruit and flowers derived from "Pennsylvania Dutch" cupboards, colonial-American echoes of Hondecoeter. Bureau and armoire too were redolent of Rochester and reminded us of our distance from that old milieu. The scenario of semi-theatricalized backgrounds for our daily life made everything picturesquely alive. However much I bridled at details of Mr. Wilmerding's manners, I realize now that I owed him for sparks that would later ignite further pleasures.

The grand opening of a new store for William Filene's Sons was accompanied by boisterous confusion. Wax mannequins intended to display the latest fashions were delayed in transit and so huge glass windows facing main streets had to be filled with something suitable. This was solved by my father's friendship with a florist whose shop was around the corner from the Hotel Ericson. Burnham's richly framed windows were crammed with jungle-groves of hanging fern-baskets, potted palms, and lavish beds of cut flowers, so thickly packed that their vases were hidden. Their verdant overflow filled our apartment for weeks.

My father's office at Filene's, on the eighth floor of the new store, was guarded by Miss Effie R. Beverly, his secretary over twenty-five years. Its inner sanctum, which held his desk and files, was adorned by engravings of President Lincoln's cabinet, an autograph letter by Lincoln pardoning a deserter, and an illuminated scroll of Kipling's "If." Miss Beverly, for all the time when I was at school and college, administered my allowance, paid my bills, and took care, in the lives of his three children, of all the necessary boring bits that my father was often too busy to discuss. When I married, she presented me with exquisite twin pepper-and-salts from the shop of Paul Revere. His name was familiar, for my father had read to my brother and me from Longfellow's *Tales of a Wayside Inn* the ballad beginning "Listen my children and you shall hear / Of the midnight ride of Paul Revere," and of how, watching for lanterns hung from the steeple of Old North Church across Boston Bay, he learned redcoats were on their way, and rode to warn the militia of Concord and Lexington to save Liberty.

Filene's department store, its "bargain basement," and all ten floors became an extension of our daily life. On the top floor was a large, sky-lit restaurant, with a canopy of pendant, fern-filled baskets. One of the proven virtues of Daniel Burnham's engineering was that the roof, come hell or high water, rain, snow, hail, or storm, never leaked. My father always insisted on the cost and care of maintenance. Analyzing the vast difference between initial construction and constant subsequent repair, he drew a contrast between initiation—of a business or a friendship—and the expense of its perpetuation. From earliest youth, I knew I would find maintenance a drag and bore. Although I've spent much of my life seeking money to stay a variety of projects from foundering, I'm glad my father realized I was not one to whom he could entrust the continuity of his own work—or the maintenance of his impermeable roof.

Chef-in-chief of Filene's restaurant was Mr. Karl Friede, a Swiss, who, apprised of my mother's intended luncheons, would have ready on the centered table a bowl of chicken salad (white meat only) on its cushion of endive, celery, peppers, and tomatoes. New suits were supervised by friendly tailors, our hair was cut by knowing barbers. I refused the service of manicurists and pedicurists, which both parents considered indispensable. My father also took pleasure in indulging private pilfering from the general stock. He eagerly equipped a junior-league baseball team from Jamaica Plain led by its parish priest, Father Francis Spellman. In Rome later, as a secretary at the Vatican, Spellman arranged for my parents to be received by the Holy Father. Dressed in the formal black of protocol, my mother, veiled, had strung around her middle as many rosaries as would fit, all to be taken home as gifts for the salespeople.

My father never claimed to be a patron of art, but he had a lively feel for popular taste. The sculptor Jo Davidson, more a journalist than a talent of quality, had made one masterpiece, his portrait of Gertrude Stein squatting like the envelope of a heavy Buddha. And it was from Davidson that my father obtained two dozen heads of important participants at the Versailles Peace Conference. His less than monumental sketched heads of Lloyd George, Clemenceau, Pershing, Joffre, and Wilson for years remained on top of glass-enclosed cases holding men's clothing. I was puzzled that the features of such famous characters seemed weak and diminished, although I was assured they were precisely life-size. Later, when I posed for portraits by Gaston Lachaise and Isamu Noguchi, I learned the trick of a need for exaggerated scale in the transferring of flesh and bone to clay. Likeness, if merely literal, shrinks in the open air.

Over a long bank of elevators on Filene's ground floor was a series of murals by Arthur Covey, an able illustrator, depicting the history of fashion, masculine and feminine, through the ages. He gave my father his original watercolor sketches, amongst the first examples fresh from a real painter's hand that I had touched. It was partly as a result of these that I soon decided I wanted to be a painter, preferably—so energized was I by the identifications I felt for my heroes-of-the-moment—a portrait painter. Mr. Covey was sympathetic to my ambitions. He had a studio at Giverny, neighborly with Claude Monet's, and he invited me to spend a summer there, but I never went.

A key subsidiary avocation of my father's was his presidency of Boston's Public Library. Charles Follen McKim's and Stanford White's noble palace faces Richardson's Trinity Church across Copley Square, its dark, rough-hewn façade a brunette Romanesque older sister to the blonde Renaissance exterior. The fulfilled plan of the Library's decoration stayed with me as a reference point and criterion. When Lincoln Center for the Performing Arts was being planned in the early Sixties, I had hoped for a similar, overall coherent scenario for commissions awarded to the best artists of my time. While a number of secondary figures filled, almost by accident, a few vacant walls, there would be no commanding vision, and very few distinguished exemplars except for Elie Nadelman's twin giant ladies in the State Theater. As for McKim's and White's choices, Augustus Saint-Gaudens, our greatest American sculptor, was ill, so could not fulfill their expectations. He did, however, supply a handsome model of Boston's civic seal, supported by two healthy, nude youths, the public display of whose private parts caused offense. His brother Louis, an efficient craftsman, carved two large, crouching lions in golden Monte Riete Siena marble. These guard a splendid staircase, a memorial to the dead of the Massachusetts Union regiments. Daniel Chester French's bronze doors, his figure of Sir Harry Vane, the opulent brass zodiac inlay of an entrance vestibule, and the dignity of lettering on the exterior—all remain triumphs of caressing attention by visionary designers. Although Puvis de Chavannes was old and infirm, a model of the stair hall was sent to Paris and he was persuaded to undertake an elaborate scheme of "The Triumph of Electricity." Resembling tasteful, pale fresco, it is actually oil paint on canvas.

My father's office, as president of the Library, was in a large paneled room behind a delivery desk for books on outside loan. To me, this room was a paragon, an extreme of imaginative luxury carried through by lavish talent and unlimited means. Edwin Austin Abbey contributed a Wagnerian (or Tennysonian) mural sequence, "The Quest for the Holy Grail," enhanced by gilt, raised relief. The doorways are of blood-red *rouge antique* marble, with an eleven-foot-high carved fireplace. When the building was being constructed, McKim, the governing designer, needed for the steps to the main entrance some four hundred tons of Numidian marble from a quarry controlled by a religious order, who fortunately, at that moment, were in need. Royal Cortissoz documented the Library's construction: dimensions of the stone, he wrote,

were determined by McKim with the utmost care. He regarded these dimensions as essential to the ensemble but when the marble was delivered, it was found they had not been rigidly followed. Forthwith the sheets were rejected. The contractor argued at tremendous length and almost wept, but McKim was harder than the Numidian itself. He was dealing in marble as an artist deals in paint.

Individual stones had to be chosen carefully as regards color; the lightest is set at the steps' bottom, gradually darkening as one ascends, providing a golden blush and testifying to a visual virtuosity comparable to the subtlest colorist painters.

In the building's attic story, reached by an apologetic staircase of crisp slate, is a long vaulted gallery within which John Singer Sargent was contracted to depict a visual metaphor of world religion. Initiated by an end wall of Moses and Old Testament prophets, this took him thirty years to complete.

The immediate success of the initial stage was never to be granted again in the majestic panoply of a realized scheme. I have always thought Sargent's work grossly underestimated. It was as if Puritan contempt for divine revelation, an inheritance from Emerson's transcendentalism, counted this a barbarous relic. Sargent was known to have slight belief in any orthodoxy, but he was an erudite scholar and his conspectus of the sacred from Assyria through Byzantium does not deserve the disdain it has almost always gained. To me, it is infinitely richer, more thoughtful and dignified than those chapels decorated as holy cocktail lounges by Chagall or Matisse.

Completion of Sargent's decorations was scheduled for 1916, coinciding with my father's appointment as the Library's president. Two new large square paintings depicted "Synagogue" and "Church." They flanked a blank space double their size, intended for a later "Sermon on the Mount," which was never begun. Opposition to the two murals erupted at their unveiling. A Jewish community was outraged at Israel's personification as a strongly musculated female derived from a Sistine sibyl. She was seen as desolate, mantled in the richly textured, riven veil of the Temple, clutching the Tablets of the Law. In her stricken sanctuary Israel mourned fallen glory. And Roman Catholics were equally offended by seeing a Blessed Virgin envisioned as a young woman, between whose majestic knees slumped an all-but-nude figure of an athletic Jesus, no older than His Mother. Chief Rabbi Schindler, *The Boston Evening Transcript, The Boston Post*, and Cardinal O'Connell were not slow feeding fire to the controversy which burned on my dad's desk. He felt unequipped to render aesthetic, theological, or, what was probably primary, any political judgment. Steps were therefore begun to remove the murals, though Father was judiciously slow to comply with a public which had already forgotten its own protests against twin bare-assed boys supporting a civic seal.

In the meantime, Sargent was invited to justify his work.

My father was deeply impressed by the painter's professionalism, lack of vanity, historical logic. As for interpreting Israel in decline, this was not far from Father's own personal opinion. And as far as Catholicism went, like everyone else he knew the Boston Irish ruled with more political know-how in City Hall than did the Cardinal in his Bay State Road palace. Sargent explained to Dad that Church Fathers of the Christian apex held that Mary's essence in virginity stayed ageless, inviolate, unchanging. The Son died long before middle age. So Geoffrey Chaucer, in the Canterbury "Seconde Nonnes Tale," wrote: "Thow Mayde and Moder, doghter of thy Sonne, / Thow welle of mercy, synful soules cure."

Sargent's gravity, grace, lack of resentment, his acceptance of this world's Philistia, were convincing. He noticed that Puvis de Chavannes's murals were dirty. My father ordered them cleaned. Soon, talk extended to a family level: a young son was interested in painting. What could or should be done for him? Sargent had no vast opinion of local schools and a nine-year-old's future couldn't be fathomed. If I persisted, some apprenticeship in handicraft wouldn't hurt. He told my father that near the Library, just off Huntington Avenue, was the stained-glass shop of Charles J. Connick, who had made fine windows for Saint John the Divine in Manhattan and the National Cathedral in Washington. That, he averred, might be as good a place as any to begin.

APART FROM THE brothers Lincoln and Edward, and my father, there was still one other Filene partner. He was Mr. (first-name-unknown) Frost; also grey, fuzzy, feline. I caught glimpses of his vague, Wilsonian presence on my way to Father's office, which adjoined his. I doubt if they ever shared a formal meal, and Mr. Frost never visited our home. He was an expert and respected accountant and a keen analyst of present and futures, and his Gentile partnership may have helped remove particularization in a nominally Jewish firm. Stratification, class and ethnic, depended on hierarchies lacking any rational basis. I was conscious of such mysteries, yet never learned at the time why Mother didn't like Mrs. Ignatz Ratchesky, but often invited Mrs. Benjamin Cardozo, who seldom came. Bias was always present; social amity often absent. Still, one Christmas I received a glorious surprise from Mr. Frost, a large, painted tin top spun nonstop by a small battery. With help, I composed a first thank-you note, adorned with a crayon sketch of the top in its spin. Blue lines delineating its whirling blur made me proud. This was scarcely recompense, though; Mr. Frost in turn was presented with the ten volumes of Nicolay and Hay's biography of Abraham Lincoln.

A school chum, Jackie Payne, shared my hobby of stamp collecting and we began exchanging duplicates. After his first visit, Mother said: "Do you realize this must be the first Jewish home he's ever entered?" I had not and I'm sure it never occurred to Jackie. Yet here it was, dark, estranging, sad.

Aged seven, I'd been dispatched to Saturday Bible school. Our home was remote from real piety, but perhaps it was thought unjust or unlucky to deprive me of ritual habit as a cautionary discipline. Classes were held in the basement of Temple Israel, a white marble, mosquelike monument a mile up past 506. Pews and paneling were in silvery-olive, carved, grainy wood; the massive pulpit was flanked by twin seven-branched, electrified candelabra. I learned to draw maps of Palestine, and on Mount Carmel, a jagged bump on its western shore, I very neatly labeled "Jerusalem" from its salient location. But legends sparked no faith. When I was older, and conscience sought connection with scripture, there would be none. One Passover I was chosen to recite in public. Scared out of my wits, I negotiated the steps up to the pulpit, staring across to a merged blur of fearsome eyes and ears.

> Little drops of water,
> Little grains of sand . . .
> Make the . . . *something (or other)* . . .
> And (*oh, dear*) . . . the LAND!

Impact of an expectant audience, a blank fist in my face, coalesced in shame, and I wet my pants. After that, my parents relieved me of further attendance at Saturday school. However, I had there met Deborah Kallen, the mistress of mapmaking, who also taught primary courses at the Boston Museum school. She was an excellent analyst of decorative design, clarifying for me the organizations of pattern, forbidding mindless displays of easy meanderings, filling space rather with curves and branchings, echoing veins of leaf and artery.

Though I drew, I was also expected to play. My piano teacher was a Christian Science practitioner named Jane Russell Toland. In less than a week's time she enabled me to understand that notes printed in black, imposed on ruled lines, determined the sounds struck from black-and-white ivories. Immediately I grasped the root principle whole, and felt that in absorbing this mechanism I should at once be able to master contact between print, sight, and touch. An intermediary of conscious fingering was, to be sure, a hindrance to actual sound, but somehow I ecstatically believed that the blank impact of initial revelation ought to have implemented my sinews. I soon found that the gap between mind and muscle was infinitely mysterious. Doubt spread to all zones of judgment, and an incident which ended Mrs. Toland's lessons in helpless tears was an early shock full of hints of cosmic discrepancy.

I had no doubt of my father's humane consideration. Perfection of good manners, letting-ladies-go-first, hats-off-in-elevators, thank-you's, clean-hands-and-fingernails, ability-to-say-the-right-words-at-the-right-times—all were presupposed.

One afternoon, Mrs. Toland failed to appear and drastic news came instead. Her husband had jumped off a central span of the West Boston bridge. Mary Baker Eddy, the leader of the Christian Scientists, did not condone self-slayings, but there seemed no alternative explanation of this event. When a grieving widow resumed our piano lessons, Father felt obliged to acknowledge her loss. To my incredulous horror, I heard him vouchsafe: "Well, Mrs. Toland, since you were here last a lot of water has flowed under the bridge." An anguished widow emitted one agonized bleat, rushed from the room, and was never seen again.

I was not then aware of Father's agreement with Mark Twain over the verities in "Christian *Science*," or Mrs. Eddy's printed gospel of "Science and *Health*." A few families of my parents' provenance and generation had begun calling themselves Unitarians. As if this was not a sufficient transfusion for re-baptism, my father's friend Mr. Sidney Sinsheimer had become Sid Sinton, and Mr. Hyman Weisshacker, Hal Winton. "Christian Scientist" became their church affiliation. We discovered that Mrs. Toland had long been an official "healer" who preached that all evil, disease, pain, death were mere mental states, curable by simple faith. She had discovered Twain's polemic on Mary Baker Eddy on my mother's desk. This led to needless attempts at conversion so irritating to my father that he forgot his normal worldly compassion. Thus irony supervened, if indeed his tactless remarks had been unkindly meant. I had clearly understood that printed notes on linear bars proposed audible concord and measure, but Christian Science's denial of what I'd so far been granted as insight into our mortal condition seemed like sick black-magic. It was a cold fact that my piano teacher's husband had tossed himself from a stone bridge.

Around 1916, a Harvard Dean of Admissions with the Dickensian name of Pennypacker admitted that the college of which Charles William Eliot had been president, followed by A. Lawrence Lowell, kept a private quota of prospective students, calculated to discourage those of certain ethnic origins.* My father took this uncovery with catatonic fury. No meal was free from flurries of telephone calls to and from Justice Brandeis, Felix Frankfurter, Judge Julian Mack, or Rabbi Stephen Wise. "*Pennypacker*" took on the lurid resonance of "the Kaiser, Beast of Berlin," all but obliterating talk of the great battles going on across the broad Atlantic. And yet for my father, Judaism was no burden of belief, but an exercise of charitable obligation. For years he commandeered annual banquets at the Copley Plaza Hotel where by quaint, blackmailing exhortations he extracted from an affluent community competitive tithes. He never tried to push me toward any loyalty to divinity or race.

He was certainly no Zionist, despite the desperate urgency for enlistment. Chaim Weizmann, a prominent proponent of a reclaimed homeland, called on him once for support and cash. Weizmann was the distinguished chemist, inventor of TNT, an innovative high explosive. It was widely believed that, in exchange for its formula, Britain took over a mandate for Palestine, establishing Israel, despite the Arabs' historic claims, as a Jewish state. I was, aged nine, at their meeting in my father's suite in the Hotel Ambassador on Park Avenue, New York. A fairly big boy, I was still in short trousers, but Dr. Weizmann, in an ill-considered gesture of seduction, attempted to haul me

---

* President Lowell's (and Pennypacker's) quota proposal aimed explicitly at Jews was, in 1923, (publicly) rebuffed by his Board of Overseers. However, admission conditions were then altered to gain the same result. Entrance exams were suspended for a top 17th of secondary schools, in the hope of gaining applications from non-Jews outside the Northeast, where schools did not normally prepare for Harvard. In 1926, Lowell again begged his Board to deal with "a dangerous increase in the proportion of Jews." The Board created effective means by demanding photographs, and screenings through personal interviews. Applicants were forced to state their religion. The admissions office used this to extend geographical diversity, and as well, judgment of the "character" of individuals, irrespective of academic grades. Jewish applications radically diminished.

Perhaps I should add that, in 1934, my father was awarded a degree from Harvard University, *honoris causa*, which is the sole epitaph inscribed on his gravestone.

onto his lap. I scrambled off, resuming a proper filial position next to Father, who, I thought, was as much embarrassed as myself. He was an American patriot in the old Fourth-of-July, Stars-and-Stripes, Declaration-of-Independence style. Any appeal to dilute or exchange personal allegiance was treason. Any state founded on racist polity ran the risk of tyrannical usurpations; he would have none of it. While I had little comprehension of the subtlety, correctness, or failings in my father's refusal of so passionate a partisan, it filled me with the seeds of awe. While at the same time being alarmed by Weizmann's impetuous recklessness in this trivial social risk, I was impressed by a supersession of the politeness of ordinary decorum. But a fumbled appeal to this inconsequential infant sprang from selfless conviction. Courtesy had its place, but not on the fields of battle. My father's eleemosynary acts—gifts to Beth Israel Nurse's Home, the Public Library, or Harvard's Business School—were big, businesslike, and without political significance, except in a broad sense. It was a curious fact that after his death, neither my sister, my brother, nor I was ever listed for solicitation from a Jewish charity.

His public benefaction did of course have elements of public relations, though at the same time he thought to repay his city for the increase in his own good fortune. A first donation was a traffic-tower to front Filene's prime rival, the big department store of Jordan Marsh. It was a bronze box, raised off the street, in which a policeman switched off-and-on green-and-red go-and-stop lights. Intended to facilitate a flow of traffic along a narrow road developed from colonial cow-tracks, it caused further obstruction. Soon exiled to a harmless situation in emptier suburbia, it still bore a plaque modestly testifying to its crafty donor.

Father's economics branch-library borrowed its façade from the Tontine Crescent in Boston, an early, post-revolutionary housing project proposed in 1796 by the architect Charles Bulfinch and anticipating the circus and squares of Regent's Park and Bath. Bulfinch also built the Massachusetts State

House, crowning Beacon Hill with a golden dome. In World War I, there was a move to black out its gilding to disguise a landmark for German submarines that might penetrate offshore defenses. Part of the era's folklore, it prompted my first interest in the conservation of art, comparable to the cleaning of Puvis de Chavannes's murals in the Public Library. Vandalism of Bulfinch's golden dome seemed like rape. I felt personally relieved when war ended before its gold was defaced.

Slowly, though, I grew involved in the "war effort," if not directly, then at least in its long-range effect on the young men around me. Poor-folk were lacking food and fuel. Free distribution of both, in stout, double-paper brown bags, took place in a prefabricated hut at Cottage Farms Bridge, a further mile up past Temple Israel. In December 1917, aged ten-and-a-half, I had one intimate, elder buddy. Fred Rickson, a tall, handsome, pale mulatto, served our basement furnace. He was a first-rate plumber and electrician, black-polishing the huge old iron stove in our kitchen under the dining room and repairing the mechanism of the dumbwaiter that sent food up into the pantry. He also explained many mysteries to me, including those which engineered human bodies, lessening the terror of my gut by ready common sense and a workman's primitive familiarity with anatomy and psychology. Fingering chits obtained from some hidden source, I bundled up in Harris-tweed knickerbockers and heavy winter raglan to wait in long lines for him. I fought snow, rain, and frost at the distributing station, where I accepted canned goods and coal for Fred and his family. My mother must have known of this clandestine operation, but she trusted Fred: he was careful to borrow time which did not interfere with school.

My father's office boy helped Miss Beverly, the secretary. Peter Fitzgerald was a red-haired Irish kid, full of sweetness and fun, swathed in a rampant case of post-adolescent psoriasis. Father wished to recognize Pete's devotion to his country, since half a year before the declaration of war he had enlisted in the U.S. Navy. He was duly invited to Sunday dinner, and arrived, too early, in a smartly starched uniform, Navy whites with a bulging drop-fly. The immaculate laundering of his bell-bottoms contrasted with raw, blistered chin and cheeks. Conversation at dinner must have seemed as ragged for him as for the rest of us, the whole table worrying about gaps in our small talk and the condition of Peter's skin.

As a result, my fragmentary participation in World War I was mostly focused on Lieutenant André Morize. Father had somehow met this young, already wounded veteran who was at Harvard on a military mission preparatory to training Americans as future Allied officers. War with Germany became increasingly inevitable despite President Wilson's promise that we were "too proud to fight." I was at once captivated by Morize and his *horizon-bleu* uniform with its stiff, round, visored cap, encrusted with gilt piping. It was two times too big around for my head. One afternoon, he guided us to a review of Reserved Officers' Training Corps held in Harvard's football stadium in honor of Maréchal Joffre, "hero" of the battle of the Marne. On the way Morize told us how an entire flotilla of Parisian taxicabs had transported troops to the front, thereby saving Paris. The stadium march-past deployed a ragged mob of half-trained American undergraduates. Even I, early on, marked their feeble parade, broken ranks, and inability to keep step, as well as their tardy response to barked commands. Lieutenant Morize came back to 506 for tea and drinks. Everyone tried to be as encouraging as possible concerning the afternoon's exercise, which was nonetheless silently diagnosed as an unmitigated disaster. This professional Frenchman was courteously tolerant. After all, it was but a beginning and diplomatic good will was more useful than critical analysis. At his adieu, I handed him his stiff cap, fondling its sharp visor and gilt laurel. I was bold enough to demand his personal opinion, since all I'd overheard from my elders was short of what I'd seen for myself. Morize responded, as if he had had a mature interlocutor: "It is not real for them, yet. They marched across a football field. War is not that sort of game, yet there is no way to learn it, save as it is fought. They can learn." He gave me a short, sharp drill in the manual salute. What stayed with me from the shambles on the football field was the failure of order, strictness violated, gaps in merged, collective, massing movement. There was instead a vast immensity of individuals homogenized, robbed of their wills, dumb, all but blind, responding to some faceless threat, a gross, undefined thundercloud of menace.

Gradually the faraway war came to enfold everyone and, as it did, a subtle sense of awkwardness and anxiety settled on us. My sister had undergraduate boyfriends, met while she was at Radcliffe. A few enlisted some months before war was declared, parading sloppily across Soldiers' Field. I was particularly impressed by Cocky Kuhn, who had gained a second lieutenant's commission. My sister planned a dinner party as a celebration at the cottage my father had rented for the summer near Marblehead, north of Boston. Four girls and three boys (plus myself, who silently attended as an observer) waited for Cocky, who was detained, doubtless by critical martial business. Ordinarily, dinner need not have been postponed; everyone would have seated themselves. Now, though, in the wartime atmosphere, querulous airs prevailed. Very self-consciously, all remained uneasily standing. My sister tried to take up the slack, but there was awkwardness until Cocky appeared, in uniform, with decent, but by no means effusive, apologies. Curtly acknowledging the others, he seated himself. The rest of us followed. Arrival of food was too slow to fill another want of small talk, and consciousness of Cocky's rank took the edge off any friendly exchange. I was bemused by his assumption of status and authority, which seemed boastful. He was altered in his person while my ordinary routines of life seemed arranged by implacable events.

At around this time, my father told how, years before the war, he had been in Berlin, visiting a cousin. With him, he strolled along a pavement near the Brandenburger Tor. Cousin Leo sported a proboscis which might well be taken as tribal badge. Two "Death's-Head" hussars, smartly booted and spurred, felt impeded and shoved their two inferiors into the gutter, nor did they forbear to spit.

Father favored fat, strongly aromatic Havana cigars kept fresh in a brass-bound humidor, with its tiny ceramic cup for moistening. The cigars, each wrapped in gilt foil, nestled in a box of split cedar. On the lid glared an embossed portrait of Wilhelm der Zweite, bristling with imperial orders and angular, waxed moustachios, next to Kronprinz Friedrich and Kronprinzessin Cecile. Each evening before we kissed our parents good night, father would solemnly open his humidor and extract his choice. Before its tip was notched, first he, followed by my brother, then myself, targeted one of the tyrants with our thin saliva. Then Dad pulled from a breast-pocket his white linen handkerchief, heavily initialed "L.E.K.," and gravely wiped the Kaiser's face for next night's broadside.

The First War ended on November 9, 1918. Armistice was announced, but the German admiralty, loath to surrender an almost intact fleet, waited forty-eight hours before signing the final surrender. A false armistice finally turned true and my brother and I were bundled into the boot of my sister's Dodge runabout. With Mother brandishing small, silk Allied flags, we toured Boston's downtown, filled that night with boys wearing false moustaches and makeup, mocking the "Clown-Prince." We decided that Lieutenant Morize had won the war and he was awarded a congratulatory luncheon in Filene's restaurant, the tables decorated with tricolor ribbons and bouquets of blue-buttons, daisies, and rosebuds. He then joined Harvard's French faculty, but I was not forgotten: he gave me an album of Napoleon Bonaparte's career. The Emperor's visual taste was soon identical with mine.

Father had not fought in Flanders, but, shortly before the armistice, he enlisted in a mission, captained by Bernard Baruch, to plan the revival of European industry. Landing from a military transport at Cherbourg, he toured battlefields, interviewed businessmen, and brought back to Boston a Boche spiked helmet, gas mask, and bandolier with unspent cartridges.

Was this an end to wars, or just this one? For me, all it really meant was the Kaiser's abdication and the cords of wood he'd axe in Dutch exile. A spit-defiled cigar box was replaced by another, even more glossy—*"Antonio y Cleopatra"*—embossed with tragedians framed in a red-and-gold proscenium arch.

Camp Timanous,
Lake Sebago, Maine
1916–1917

IN 1916, NEARLY TEN, I was old enough to leave home. For a first summer alone, for the second with my brother George, I went to camp. This was directed by A. E. "Chief" Hamilton, son-in-law of Dr. Luther Halsey Gulick, a pioneer in pre-adolescent education. Ten years previously he had founded Camp Wohelo for young girls. When I heard that name, I assumed it belonged to an American-Indian princess, doubtless friend to the singer of Longfellow's *Song of Hiawatha*—"By the shores of Gitche Gumee, / By the shining Big-Sea-Water . . ." —already well-loved from my father's readings to us. Chief Hamilton had recently established Camp Timanous as a brother to Wohelo. Timanous meant "Great Spirit" and I identified him with Chief, my earliest genuine preceptor in art and life. His girlfriend (with marriage not a problem) was Christina Jurgensen, one of Isadora Duncan's "Isadorables," the California sisterhood which performed and promulgated her "method." Chris legitimized my passion for theatrical dancing while loathing classic ballet, which she estimated as sick, perverse, unnatural, deforming of our God-given human bodies.

At Camp Timanous, the smaller, less conditioned boys were persuaded to submit to hour-long dance sessions five days a week. Following Isadora's vocabulary, we flew like birds, bent like boughs, blossomed like buds, to wobbly gramophone records of Sinding's *Rustle of Spring*, the first movement of Beethoven's Pastoral Symphony, and Edward MacDowell's *Mud and Water*. Rapture in bodily movements ordained by metric obliterated all my self-doubts about sissiness. I wished to become a "dancer," like Chris. I *would* become a dancer. But organized motor-control had other, inferior outlets that for me were far less fun: swimming and diving. Flying like a bird, bending like a bough were easy enough, but swimming like a fish was a trial. Fish have no arms; with mine clamped close to my ribs, fishy writhing or wriggling was neither lovely nor fun. Still, I could swim. I knew I could never dive.

Chief Hamilton credited Order and his primary means of inculcating this metaphysic lay in ritual ordination. At Camp Timanous, less than a week after we'd arrived to pitch our wigwams, an initiation ceremony took place. Eighty youths encircled a heap of dried, resinous pinecones and birch-bark tinder, every right hand covering a heart. Chief lit a torch; captains of the four tribes—Bear, Elk, Eagle, and Fish—took his fire. Circumambulating the sacred blaze, we swore to become good scouts. Then Chris Jurgensen performed her "fire dance." It lasted just a little too long and lacked focus or climax. Maybe it meant more than we guessed but it seemed like some type of competitive event which nobody won. A similar rite was also observed at the end of the season. In place of the pinecone fire, Chief Hamilton awarded diplomas for the summer's achievements, proving to parents how well we'd all done. Neatly written on scrolls simulating birch bark, scores indicated progress at bow-and-arrow, tent-pitching, fire-making (without matches), swimming, diving. Dancing was not included.

With a degree of attention I'd not enjoyed before, Chief encouraged my interest in how my body might move. He recognized in unadulterated, energetic, mindless pre-adolescent innocence an unformed passion, which was also what, without formulating it, I felt for him. While he was experienced enough to keep kids at arm's length, sometimes he would let me hug him for a minute before tickling my ribs to let him loose. This was nearly eighty years ago, yet I feel again the stupendous surge of euphoria I experienced one particular evening, after an early supper, when the sun had not yet set. For a couple of recent, empty days I'd not exchanged a word with Chief, so I felt I must have been forgotten or abandoned. Suddenly, he came up to me and asked: "Would you like to go on an ADVENTURE?" Too astounded to believe my ears, I was told to get a blanket and mess kit, paddle and toothbrush; we'd meet by our springboard canoe dock.

Although I pulled only light-weight in a canoe, like everyone else I'd been given my own paddle, though this was still too big for me. Consequently my stroking fumbled. Chief sat me well in front, pretending I was half the crew. Crossing the lake under lowering clouds, we landed in a closed inlet. In pitch-black, starless darkness, I gathered sticks. Chief made us a fire with struck matches; then he laid out our blankets. There was no talk, until he said: "You've been in camp long enough; if you have any questions, I'll try to answer them." Such a ferment of unappeased curiosity, excitement, adoration boiled in me that I could hardly utter a sound. However, I was able to take refuge in the irrelevant, as if to throw the true current of my desire off track and make my ridiculous dwarf-self less suspect or vulnerable.

For some time I'd been preoccupied by the person of one of Chief's senior counselors, Karl Nicholson Llewelyn, known as "Kap." On vacation from Columbia's law school, while spending his summer "counseling" he stationed himself somewhat apart from the rest of the staff and carried on reading toward his bar exams. "Kap" derived from *Kapitän*; he was half-German, half-Welsh. He seemed well into middle age, at least forty; now I know he was not yet thirty. Lean, compact, gaunt, he had a trim black beard, a jet, bristling crew-cut thatch and a scar like a sabre slice branded around one cheek from chin to eye. Through last winter, we'd lived with a promise of war against the House of Hohenzollern. Sinister rumors passed around campfires: Kap had been a *U-Boat* Hun captain, and was now a German spy!

I felt free to ask Chief if Kap was indeed a traitor, like Benedict Arnold, or "The Man Without a Country," Edward Everett Hale's patriotic legend, a favorite of my father's. If so, why was Kap not in jail? With a trace of impatience, Chief answered with a firmness which implied that he'd heard my question before. I was told not to listen to all the rattlings around campfires. Kap was no spy. He was a poet. He had a romantic attachment to his maternal homeland. Since everybody was anti-Kaiser, Kap felt it was only fair to be pro-Kaiser and pro-German. Also, he was as much Welsh as German, and for centuries Wales had bred a race of poets against the British, our presumed allies.

Pine scent borne on a mild breeze, diminished lapping of still water, glimmering embers from Chief's fire, the tiny shot of brandy barely lining the bottom of my aluminum cup all soothed feverish curiosity. My throbbing body was filled with gratitude, love, peace; there was nothing more to ask. Chief indicated a hollow where he'd spread our blankets. As I lay in warm bliss beside him, I found I had one last question: "Who was Princess Wohelo?"

No noble lady, he said. Chief's father-in-law, Luther Gulick, was an ingenious teacher. He had baptized his girl's camp with an acronym from: WORK, HEALTH, LOVE. Chief started saying all good things come by number threes. "One" is the start, "Two" is what makes work work, "Three" is continuity, diversity, multiplicity. So, think of *work* as 1, *health* as 2, and . . . But by now I'd dozed off and this initiation into the doctrine of a Blessed Trinity sank gently into my dreamless slumber.

Chief Hamilton designed and colored with semi-professional skill in the style of Frederic Remington's Far-Western cowboys and the vignettes in Ernest Thompson Seton's scouting manuals. As a result, after we'd become acclimatized to camp schedules, every boy was encouraged to find his personal symbol, a coat of arms to paint on our blank paddles. Most of us bid for birds or beasts, allied to nicknames, blotching an animal's head—a fox, a wolf, or a bear—with help from a file of photographs torn from "nature" magazines. Chris Calkins was "Kit-Kat"; Bob Baird was "Birdy"; Ralph Rhodes, "Dusty"; Bob Robbins, "Red." Exceptionally, at my second but his first year at Timanous, my brother George chose an abstract hiero-glyph. His sign was a straight line attached to, but interrupted by, a half-circle: intention deflected and then resumed. As for myself, I thought I had settled on a five-pointed star to represent my five senses. Karl Nicholson Llewelyn had chaffed me, bestowing "Fimp," as my nickname, which was how he told me to pronounce "*fünf*," the German for "five." He knew this was an irritant, since I had already been told by other boys that *Kirstein* in traitor's German meant church-stone or cherry-stone.

Having selected our symbols, we were to inscribe them on our unvarnished blades. My elementary geometric star had been quickly executed by freehand stenography. But Chief advised against this. His criticism, a hindrance to my taste, hurt me. All the other boys had designed their birds and animals any way they pleased, and since very few had any talent for drawing, the general quality was a kindergarten vision. I shortly came to realize Chief's advice was not intended to undermine me. He simply favored absolute, Euclidean linearity and for the purpose he provided me with a metal compass holding a sharpened crayon. Birds and beasts may have suffered from infantile depiction, but my pristine star could hardly be im-proved upon. Yet to maintain selfhood, I then began to bridle at so simple a solution of this imposed pentagram. Chief allowed that there were other stars. Two triangles, superimposed, created a sextile Star of David, familiar to me from the beautiful silver, olive, and marble precincts of Temple Israel, but I hesitated to blazon a sacred sign upon the skin of a canoe paddle. It felt sacrilegious—or unlucky, as I must have analyzed it at the time. Chief said that I should be proud to be a Jew, and that this was a very nice choice, but I felt I needed something more personal. He drew for me a seven-pointed star—seven days of the week, seven ages of Man, also a very lucky number. But for me, seven was linked to games of chance. Fred Rickson, wagering with our chauffeur Tom O'Brien, had chanted: "Seven! Oh, man! Come eleven!" As Chief continued with further ideas about four seasons and twelve months, I saw number was an unlimited treasury, and of course the more points there were, the sooner the symbol would flare into a daisy, a chrysanthemum, the sun itself.

In discontent, I eventually went back and surrendered to the simple five-pointed star. Marking my hesitation, perhaps amused at how stubbornly I faced a choice, Chief took some crayons and colored in each point differently and arbitrarily, a concord without visible logic. What worried me as well was that while the five points were overlaid with red, blue, yellow, purple, and orange, the central, pentad space was left empty. What color was there left which would not seem to compete with or dilute the others? Chief said that was for me to choose. Why not leave this blank, white? Forswearing hasty, thoughtless decision over so deep a riddle, I took my paddle away to try to think out a design as appropriate to me as my brother's "interrupted path" was to him.

I couldn't stop worrying. Having learned the trick of tooling a compass to inscribe a perfect star in a circle, I sketched a pageful of possible variants. Finally I decided to junk the idea of the star: there was something boring about the repetition of the five identical triangles, and I didn't know what to do with the center. Karl Nicholson Llewelyn happened to pass by as I was scratching on my stupid pad. I hated the beam of his sardonic glance scanning over my rejects. I felt he held the time against me when, knowing of my interest in runes and rhymes, he had shown me a first draft of an official hymn commissioned for our campfire rituals. I pointed out to him that each one of his hymn's three stanzas commenced with: "*T is for Timanous, trusty and true,*" something, something, something . . . "*We'll try to be true to you.*" Repetition, I asserted, was *boring.*

Now my series of star shapes was *boring*. My admission of defeat apologized to Kap for any "freshness" I had shown. (When I'd been regrettably fresh at home, my mother would reprove my *Frechheit*.) However, Kap proved himself a friend: he seemed pleased at my trying to improve what I had to do.

He said straight lines were *always* tiresome. My brother had found this for himself when he brought a bump to his straight-and-narrow. But where were the alternatives? *Curves*—stupid! But what can curves describe as significant for my symbol? Apples, tomatoes, melons, pumpkins, pigs? The twisty curves in fire? To me, both crescent moon and circular sun read as zero. However, circles indicated a solution. With my compass I created five balls, stacked against one another, leaving a centered space which hinted at a curvaceous star. Five (*fünf*) senses left room for a sixth, although at the time I don't think I even knew the idea. Still, my paddle got painted.

Chief Hamilton seemed pleased by my dogged pursuit and he showed me how to brush in shadows on the periphery of my five globes. These not only proposed raised plasticity, but suggested a third dimension rising up from the plane surface. There remained the question of color. How about shades of sky-blue? Or a range of leaf-green? Chief again advised no color, plain black-and-white—the presence and absence of every color. But I felt I needed chromatic luxury. As if to prove his point, Chief, in his office studio, told me to open a closet door.

I did. Inside, I beheld half-a-dozen man-size paddles. As I accepted the subtle curvature of their softly sandpapered shapes, I counted seven. On each blade shone a very detailed black-and-white drawing in sharp ink, each representing a day of the week, each annotated with single lines of a rhyme, quite easy to read:

> Monday's child is fair of face,
> Tuesday's child is full of grace,
> Wednesday's child is full of woe,

[*44*]

Thursday's child has far to go,
Friday's child is loving and giving . . .

Instead of pictures, or portraits of seven children, each figure, fully clad as girl or boy, wore the mask of a bird or animal. I forget most of their particulars, but Wednesday was a wolf, Friday a fish. Friday's body had been left blank, untouched by black ink, and the bold grain of the paddle's maple wood had turned into white fish-scales. I could read it as a white shark without any trouble; the *National Geographic* magazine had taught me my fish. But, no, Chief said some whales were white, too. I couldn't argue, too dazzled by this staggering demonstration of draftsmanship which had come from the fingers of a real personage with whom I'd shared a recent adventure! It seemed miraculous. It wasn't hard to see how deeply I was impressed. Chief smiled, glancing deprecatingly at his spectacular industry, and mused: "Well, it was all a damn good *exercise* . . ."

From admiring Chief's magisterial production, I found myself disturbed, then irritated; then in no time at all—blisteringly angry. This I managed to smother, but full-fledged fury burned. How dare he call his God-given supremacy mere "exercise"? Having created miraculous results, he dismissed the effort with an insult, and by the same token, I felt he insulted me by denigrating his work as Too Beautiful! His paddles could hang in a museum. He must be teasing. I was only a dumb kid, but I knew art when I saw it. To further smirch sorcery, here was superb skill glorifying mean materials—a wooden tool, no more deserving adornment than tennis rackets or baseball bats.

I might discount this fact with the excuse that he'd chosen raw wood rather than primed canvas in order to spare cash, since I knew he was hardly a rich man. Yet his paddles, in their opulent, unbroken cluster, would never be used to propel a canoe. Maybe they were samples to show to folks who might commission a copy? Yet, obviously, he'd spent so much time and care on each that they couldn't be for sale. Was all of it only for his own pleasure in private labor? Baffling, that weasel-word *exercise*. It rankled like a fever blister.

Then I remembered that earlier I had watched Chris Jurgensen, Chief's girlfriend, dancing alone, clad in a transparent white shift, wholly unobserved save by myself as she moved over a green meadow behind our big barn. She flew over unshorn grass and burdock like a butterfly over bee-humming blossoms. I had never seen a person move with such luxurious, elegant speed. Her toes barely touched earth and she whizzed by in a blur. Suddenly, from nowhere, Chief had been standing behind me and I felt the transfiguration effected now that she had an audience of two. The shine in my eyes may have darkened when I heard him repeat: "Yup; sure is nice exercise." What right had he to be so churlish? What use was critical comment? Could he have moved like that? Would I ever be able to dance like that? Yet, if this was but "exercise," what would complete accomplishment be?

When I was seven, an uncle, fearing latent effeminacy, had taken me to the Rochester YMCA and thrown me into the pool, which was heavily chlorinated. I had sunk to the bottom in a paroxysm of fear. Soon enough I was dragged out, so hating my uncle that adrenaline was restored. Now, to my horror, I was slated to "qualify" in diving in order to be promoted to a higher rank of scout. There would be a corresponding diploma which we were to carry home at the end of summer, proving to our parents the fantastic improvements we had made in physical development. However, I was incomprehensibly slow in penetrating water headfirst. I could swim breaststroke passably. Dive, I could not—never, never, never . . . On the last day and hour, when I should already have earned my mark of merit, I was granted a stay at the springboard long after everyone had gone up to supper. The agreeable junior counselor who superintended water sports was not a hard man, but he had a conscience. So far, he'd marked my hapless starts and stops. I knew I'd never qualify, suspecting he did too. God Himself could not push me past failure. I hit the water twenty times, roughly shattering the surface with gulps and throat-fuls. My hysterical tension and fear of failing produced a relentless blockage. If this torment had not been so boring, it might have seemed funny. In panic I almost hoped, should I plunge again, I would hit bottom as I had in that Rochester pool; whether or not I'd be hauled up didn't much matter to me. However, my instructor was determined to enforce *his* will, if not mine. Also, he was intent on maintaining the professional prestige of his craft. Otherwise, I was to be the one idiot in this summer who did not receive an imitation birch-bark diploma. He'd taught many candidates to master half-gainers and jack-knives, fancy acrobatics with factors linked to muscular control in dancing itself. How stubborn my relentless clumsiness in the face of such surrounding supremacy! Finally, after the sun had sunk, while dusk made it all the more dismal, he said: "OK, Fimp. One more." But it was no-go. I couldn't.

Despite my shame, we walked up to the barn linked in a loose agreement that both had risked their poor, or at least their full, best. Chief Hamilton met us at the kitchen door. There were still warm leftovers. In the deserted dining hall, tables and floor were being swept clear for tomorrow's breakfast. The boy with clean-up duty acknowledged my reappearance with no congratulatory glee. My diving master indicated his half-drowned rat with a weary, deprecatory gesture, impatient and disappointed. There was no need for any explanation. Chief laughed aloud, reassuring his counselor with a pat on his back. On the verge of tears, I was dug in the ribs. "Well, now," he smiled, "it sounds like *quite* an exercise."

Iteration of that word no longer frightened me. How angry I'd been when it was attached to a "serious" subject, like painting or dancing. Now a harsher, less vague supposition all but freed me. Exercise could be repeated twenty times, yet not succeed. But end-results were not the objective; information, states of mind or body were. Exercise strove and strained towards an essential extremity. Arms, legs, swimming or diving could survive metric fluctuations of nerve or muscle, and even end in a balance of failure or victory. In my deep center lurked an area in which I might sink my teeth with less ratiocination or sentimental rhetoric. It was all Work. Already I had my Health. Full of food and warm drink, I could even forgive myself for foolishness. And *Love?* A while later I realized I'd quite forgotten to ask Chief's pardon for my fury and failed to thank a counselor for his care.

Boston and
Exeter, New Hampshire
1918–1922

TOGETHER WITH the splendorification of our house at 506 Commonwealth Avenue, there had arrived a long, black Rolls-Royce touring car with a nude silver sprite on its radiator cap. Inseparable from this machine was the newly hired Thomas O'Brien, master-mechanic, who chauffeured us for fifteen years until he left and was replaced by young Sacco, son of the anarchist executed on the opinion of A. Lawrence Lowell, Harvard's president. Tom O'Brien, along with Fred Rickson, our furnace-man, were my two most efficient early educators.

As far as formal studies went, I obtained a minimum offered by the Boston public-school system, mainly in Brookline's Edward Devotion School. But in mid-9th-grade, I was one night pierced by fiendish abdominal gripes, precipitating my mother into quasi-medieval hysteria. Her panic constated that if I were admitted to Massachusetts General, there I would die. Like Mayor La Guardia, she thought a hospital "no place for a sick man." She convinced an eccentric surgeon whom my father knew slightly to extract my inflamed vermiform appendix on the highly polished mirror-surface of our dining-room table, its usual four leaves extended to six to accommodate my long legs. Melchior Hondecoeter's roosters and rabbits were swathed in bedsheets doused with Lysol. Dr. Leroy Crandon, loyal spouse to "Margery," a notorious trance-medium exposed by the famous and authentic "magician" Harry Houdini, did the trick with a dispatch that seemed like seamless, and to me painless, sorcery.

My appendicitis was thus inextricably linked with the nimbus of a wizard whose annual vaudeville appearances on the Keith-Orpheum circuit were among my earliest theatrical *bouleversements*, outranking Singer's Midgets, Eva Tanguay singing "I Don't Care," and Highland ballads by Harry Lauder. Clad in an ordinary business suit, Harry Houdini permitted himself to be handcuffed, strait-jacketed, plunged head first into a glass chamber. This was then immersed in a metal tub. In a matter of held-breath minutes a curtain lifted, revealing him smiling, high and dry. As encore, to thunderous applause, he swallowed a packet of steel needles which promptly re-emerged from his lips, threaded. Houdini's attacks in the press against Dr. Crandon's sorceress wife could not have helped even a famous surgeon's reputation, while performing surgery in a private home must have done little to blunt further distrust. But to Mother and me, he was canonized by his presentation, in a vial of clear alcohol, of my fat, pink, curled-up worm. A night nurse was engaged to supervise convalescence. Although I was not in the least depressed, she thought it good therapy to make me laugh—indeed I roared so hard at the faintly salacious quips she made when she bathed the wound that Dr. Crandon's stitches came undone. I had to be re-opened and re-sewn.

So I was absent from Edward Devotion for two months. In bed I should have followed ordinary lessons, but I couldn't concentrate. I never took final exams in algebra, geography, grammar, or French. Yet I was allowed to get a diploma with the rest of my class. This seeming kindness at the time made it all but impossible to gain passing marks in further basics due to the lapse in consecutive study. The gap of a few weeks in routine schedules had spoiled me as an average student. Extra instruction was almost no help. I found recently, hidden amongst some old photographs, a letter, written on thick white paper, bordered with a virginal blue line, from one instructor to my mother. In it she claimed she was

sorry to report that the tutorials provided for Lincoln have proved in many respects unsatisfactory. He is an affectionate boy and I am fond of him personally. However, I must tell you that your son is fearfully scatter-brained and prone all too often to wander down imaginative bye-ways of his own devising. As a result, he finds it hard to collect himself and accomplish the task at hand. Perhaps the sterner presence of a male tutor is indicated at this time . . .

Sincerely,
Sophia Foster (B.A.)

Mother was magnificently undaunted and, finally, tricky but tactful tutoring enabled me to be accepted by Phillips Exeter Academy. I suspected my tutor had prior knowledge of my entrance exams. In any case, the consequences were fore-doomed.

My father, as president of the Public Library, could with-draw for my home consumption any book or phonograph record I might have fancied. On a late afternoon in 1921, on the day before Tom O'Brien drove me in his Rolls over to Exeter, New Hampshire, I was summoned to my father's grand office. Such were ominous occasions and usually involved serious criminality, like the theft of cash from my mother's lower drawer, where she kept a stuffed purse. I needed coin that time to buy a surcharged Cape of Good Hope triangular postage stamp for a collection that I was expanding almost entirely on the basis of petty larceny. On this occasion, across from me on Father's square, mahogany, glass-topped desk, lay a pile of small books and pamphlets with their unsubstantial blue paper covers. After I was apprehensively seated, he pushed the heap across the glass towards me. Fumbling one over another, I inspected their titles, taking time in the handling, sensing his agonized silence for a failure to utter any clear reason for perusal. There were half-a-dozen "Little Blue Books" issued by E. Haldeman Julius from Kansas City, Missouri—*What Every Boy Should Know, How Life Begins, Where Do Brothers Come From?*—at a dime each. There was hardly a word imprinted here with which Tom O'Brien or Fred Rickson had not made me fairly familiar. Although I did not betray these informants, my father's painful silence forced a confession. "But Dad—I know *all* about it." He scarcely believed his ears, or my omniscience, but was too relieved to doubt. The printed matter was pushed back at him. Still questioning, mutely wary, he relit his extinguished cigar, extracted from his wallet one $20 bill and gravely handed it to me. I had not fingered such value before and I absorbed its monetary worth as counting for less than the easement of a parent's wonder. The papery cash, its tough, fibrous thinness inlaid with bits of red and green silk (to confound counterfeiters) spared further anxiety. Father gave me a dry kiss on the brow and Tom drove us home to dinner in a partnership of quittance.

I had sometimes privately questioned the gap of twelve years between birthdays of myself and my sister; I noticed that after I left Boston Dad encouraged and even idolized a number of young men whom I also found attractive. But my mother, who was far more generous emotionally than he and quite without any sexual prejudice, recognized that my father was physically cold, a fact she attributed to his having caught something or other before they were married and the cure of which, consisting of mercury injections, was so painful that he had perhaps abandoned further curiosity as bad luck. It would be after another ten years that she, in an abrupt admission when I confessed a strong physical attraction to an older woman, said: "Go ahead; your father never liked it."

Though I endured and survived the appetites of adolescence with minimal anguish, shame, or fear, my knowledge of the difference between girls and boys was still rude and vague. Tremors which might have become critical were also alleviated by my sister, who had become a close confidante. Her own coming-of-age was stormy. One night she wandered into my bathroom when I was in a prominent state. I dropped a towel in surprise. She smiled and lightly touched my cheek, saying that from now on I would be preoccupied with sexuality; not to worry too much.

The day after my talk with Father, Tom O'Brien chauffeured me off to a career at Exeter that was brief and in retrospect highly instructive, even enjoyable. Spottily equipped, wholly unable to conform to ordinary school work, further dislocated by delicious freedom from familiar habit, plus the challenges and excitements of new companions, I took my terms at the academy as something near a loose experiment in hedonism. I had been told that I should "find myself." With this as license, I set out on a primary adventure and, whatever formal attendance lacked, I did not waste time.

The excellent academy and town libraries were richly endowed with packed stacks containing complete runs of popular periodicals. A combination of factors propelled me to spend as much time as I could systematically rifling through their shelves. *Punch, World's Work, Puck,* and the old *Life* acted as a continuous news feature, commencing with black-and-white woodcuts and, by the turn of this century, turning into ubiquitous photography. I managed to spend an inordinate portion of my days in the stacks when I should have been studying or exercising. Tall, bound books of the *Illustrated London News* and *Harper's* flaked off a rusty powder of dried leather on fingers and trousers. It seemed as if the dust of history powdered me. I was a visitor to the Crystal Palace, as inaugurated by Queen Victoria and Prince Albert. I was in Ford's Theater when Lincoln was shot, saw Booth trip on a festooned flag and break his leg. I was in a small boat in Havana harbor when the *Maine* blew up. More remote events in time or geographical location were fascinating but permitted no judgment. Pullman Strike, Balkan wars, the African slave trade never seemed to demand a choosing of sides as to right or wrong. It was comparable, in a way, to the copies of Titian and Velázquez or the electrotypes of Pompeiian bronzes at Mr. Whitney's. Everything which most magnetized me seemed distanced at one-remove and stayed barely real to myself. The enormity of the pageant of which I became pictorially aware had a dramatizing element, not quite rational or credible. But it was without explanation—like a dining table instead of a proper hospital operating room, or the sight of Harry Houdini's mouthful of threaded needles. At first encounter, these kinds of novel but immediate data were far too interesting for my capacity to handle them.

By Christmas vacation 1921, it was plain, at least to me, that as anything approaching a proper student, I had proved hopeless. It could only be weeks before I'd be summoned to the Dean's office for his inevitable verdict, one which deserved no appeal. I tried, in advance, to cushion the blow by direful nightly epistles home detailing my low grades and hopeless progress, but I was further shamed by my parents' patient optimism. They mistook my negativism for inbred modesty and couldn't credit the bald fact that a bright boy, such as their elder son patently must be, was stubborn or stupid. At the same time they were illicitly delighted by a few tiny triumphs.

To *The Exeter Monthly*, I contributed a three-scene drama, the plot and characters of which were swiped from Thomas A. Janvier's *The Aztec Treasure-House*, Chief Hamilton's favorite book, and therefore at the time my candidate for the greatest-novel-ever-written. Action was transferred from Mexico to Tibet, which, I believed, rendered it an "original" work. I also performed a monologue based on biblical incident—the Witch of En-dor; I declaimed Saul. I joined the Lantern Club, a literary groupment to which ex-Exonians returned in order to read from their published pages. There was a minor poet-novelist, Robert Nathan, a youngish follower of Anatole France and A. E. Housman, who had some connection with my first cousin, Margaret Wolfe. He was the first professional literary man who gave me advice. He read my stories and, against all my inclinations, warned me to avoid alliteration in prose, and reiteration in general.

As for games, when there was a census for ball-teams, I was always last chosen, so stayed away as much as possible by becoming an expert malingerer, often amazed when weak apologies or feeble excuses were readily accepted. I think it was universally conceded that so sorry a poop-out wasn't worth a complaint. I must have cast off some blur of eccentricity which licensed tolerance.

Weekends at Exeter were reserved for personal ingenuities, free of study. From pulped newsprint, I made a primitive *papier-mâché*-forged suit of armor, stiffened with silver radiator paint. Its helmet had a crest wrested from a feather duster. This roused admiration from some of the less contemptuous athletes. For one dollar (which seemed about twenty, then), I purchased a cow-horn powder flask from a small antiques shop—my first collectible. It was inscribed with the name Thomas Tippett and the date 1777. I searched a dozen local histories of Exeter and found no mention of any Tippett. But the process gave me a recipe for rummaging through indices. Boys and masters were easy and kind; apart from the sure knowledge that my tenure was brief, I was not nearly as unhappy as I thought I deserved.

Toward the end of May, shortly before summer vacation, I encountered a student whose reputation, via the Lantern Club, preceded our meeting. He was three years older than myself: at that time, this seemed almost the difference of a generation. That we became quick friends was a big step-up for my self-respect. As a bosom buddy, Howard Nott Doughty exerted a strong emotional and intellectual attachment. Decades later, as teacher and critic, he was biographer of his remote kinsman, Francis Parkman, pioneer chronicler of the Far West. From an old Ipswich family, Howard embodied the vital persistence of clans of soldiers, farmers, and craftsmen who packed their powder horns on command from Thomas Tippett or Paul Revere. Intimacies fused like forks of lightning; although there were only a few weeks left of the school term, we were inseparable. We made wide strolls around the town exploring ancient graveyards, keeping notes of comic epitaphs, sketching the more elaborate slates, weeping willows, broken pillars, funeral urns. For him, it was apprenticeship as a professional historian; while for me there was the wild satisfaction of finding an equal heart and mind. Our walks often ended in wrestling matches, in which I fought with as much muscle as I could muster; intimacy of physical contact, for me hardly innocent, pleased both of us.

Howard introduced me to an unsuspected panorama of metrical verse, of which I had had until then no inkling. From the early Romantics—Keats, Shelley, Byron, Wordsworth—through Tennyson and Browning, I became enraptured with all the conventional inherited opinions on genius and disaster. Here was a substructure for my passionate adoption of Swinburne and Oscar Wilde. *Atalanta in Calydon* and *The Ballad of Reading Gaol* all but wiped out everything earlier. Ernest Dowson's "Non sum qualis," Housman's *A Shropshire Lad*, Francis Thompson's "The Hound of Heaven" blazed in naïve ears. Metaphor, metric, rhyme—particularly rhyme—were for me clean of over-anthologized quotation. All was freshly legible; too frequent repetition had not blurred my choices. I was too immature to understand every line, but never again would I enjoy such a dewy freshness of ordered words.

Howard stuffed me with a fat ragbag of memorable quotations, plenty to caption even the most trivial of our daily events. Each seemed to fit with miraculous aptness: "At dawn Tintagel thunders"; "Hollow, hollow, all delight"; "When the hounds of spring are on winter's traces"; "Yet each man kills the thing he loves"; "Iron shard and reeking tube"; "The chestnut casts his flambeaux, and the flowers . . ."

What now seems amazing was his familiarity with contemporary verse. Yeats, Rupert Brooke, and Siegfried Sassoon had lectured widely in the United States. Now Wilfred Owen's astonishing poems with their off-beat assonance were published.

[56]

Here was a victorious violation of inviolable scansion, and I savored his sound like a delicious dessert.

Howard's crowning success at Exeter was a prize-winning essay on Walter Pater, printed in the *Monthly*, with an arresting epigraph, arranged as blank verse, anticipating Yeats's use of it as the send-off for his disappointing *Oxford Book of Modern Verse*:

> She is older than the rocks among which she sits;
> Like the Vampire
> She has been dead many times,
> And learned the secrets of the grave;
> And has been a diver in deep seas,
> And keeps their fallen day about her . . .

Thus, Leonardo's *Mona Lisa*.

When a dread dawn broke, Tom O'Brien drove my mother up from Boston for her appointment in the Dean's office. I had resigned myself for the worst but companionship and instruction with Howard Doughty leached much of my grief, since whatever the future might hold, we must stay friends. When I shyly told him of this wish, he was ready with an exemplary quotation (from Landor's *Pericles and Aspasia*): "There is no breath of passionate love repeated / Of which the echo is not faint at last."

My mother was informed, not in my presence, that while her boy may have shown positive elements of brain or character, it was an unanimous opinion that he might be "happier" in a smaller institution which laid more stress on the "imagination." I have always had a suspicion that, my scholastic aptitudes aside, anti-Semitism had something to do with the Dean's kindly words. For example, I had been housed not in an ordinary dormitory, but in a rather dilapidated private house, a considerable distance from the academy, with three other Jewish boys, or at least I thought they were Jewish. As Cocteau said: "Un juif connaît un autre juif, comme un pédéraste connaît un autre." In the Rolls on the way back, though, I tried vainly to summon some act or gesture for my mother to expiate my guilt over a flat failure.

London and Bayreuth

1922–1924

AS A REWARD for what I had feared could only be considered as outright disgrace, my brother George and I were awarded a first-class cabin on the S.S. *Homeric* to Southampton. We were to spend July, August, and part of September with my sister Mina and her friend, Henrietta Bingham, in Grove House, a pretty Regency villa off Tottenham Court Road.

Having earned a B.A. at Radcliffe with her dissertation on unsigned articles by Henry Adams in his *North American Review*, my sister turned to Northampton to teach Freshman English at Smith. In her first class was a brilliant student, Henrietta, daughter of Judge Robert Worth Bingham, proprietor of Louisville's *Courier-Journal*. He was notorious for the dubious decease of a first wife, with a swift re-marriage to an immense fortune. Judge Bingham would become ambassador to the Court of Saint James's and thus, for the passionate Anglophile in me, a quasi-mythological personage. His striking posture as a "Southern gentleman" of the antebellum epoch with his very attractive son, Barry, who wrote verse, privately printed (which I envied), were contributory factors in an unlikely but picturesque introduction to the real worlds of art and diplomacy. An Olympian team of notables surrounded me. I couldn't connect proper names with their various specialties, but a collective allure, incandescent with talent and prominence, vibrated. Clive Bell, aesthetician and promoter of "Significant Form," was married to Vanessa; there was Roger Fry, painter, curator, and critic; Lytton Strachey, whose matted beard was a badge of curious worth; while Morgan Forster observed, apart—ten years later he would become my mentor and friend. Maynard Keynes, the great economist, was amused by my abject enthusiasm and curiosity. Formality was shed; a firm, if childish, intimacy was allowed; my brother and I were treated as colonial junior cousins.

A tutor was ordained as necessary to make us busy and naturalized, and Alec Penrose, brother of Roland, who in the late Twenties and early Thirties had brought the School of Paris to London, was selected. The Penrose family dwelt in a huge country house, in a rustic suburb not far from central London. Their home could have been built by Norman Shaw, Lethaby, or Lutyens. Its style was odd; it borrowed from several past epochs yet offered an anonymously contemporary impression of fine craftsmanship. Shingles aped the fulsome curves of thatch. Hewn, smooth beams, tiled inglenooks, blonde pear-wood linenfold paneling, waxed oak-planked floors spoke an idiom of native picturesqueness without boast of affectation. Alec Penrose's father had a dazzling library—complete runs of the Kelmscott, Dove, and Vale Presses, Blakes and Beardsleys, *The Yellow Book*, *The Savoy*, and *Country Life*.

The great house nestled in its own tidy woods. When Alec took us on an introductory stroll, I was startled that he shouldered a light rifle. A full-grown, fat rabbit jumped grinning out of brush a few yards ahead. Bang! It dropped. Alec absently picked it up, squeezed urine out of the warm pelt, and strode on. I was stunned by such cold-hearted murder; my shocked eyes leaked. Marking my horror and repugnance, Alec coolly remarked that I was not to wax sentimental over vermin: rabbits were worse pests than vipers. The killer's flat authority upset me, but I was forced to admire assumptions of territorial privilege. It was all part of an empire which seemed to rummage its ancestral past without apology or regret. Here continuous order had established a luxurious background of vital romance, no longer at one-remove for me, as it was in the metrics of Paul Revere's ride or the black-and-white woodcuts in *Harper's* or the *Illustrated London News*.

On and off for the next decade or so, I delighted in summer vacations in Bloomsbury. Easy admittance to a remote, desired domain enabled me to skip what might otherwise have been the slower discovery of identities and possibilities. Was it arcane luck or deserved inevitability encountering and even briefly brushing by characters who rank now as archetypes? As an aging child, I was taken for granted as an honorary adult by my elders and betters. Maynard Keynes, in all the arts a master of private and public patronage, was about to be married to Lydia Lopokova, the delicious soubrette-ballerina of Diaghilev's Ballets Russes, whose annual seasons had been a London fixture since 1911. They were now enjoying a rebirth under the wand of Jean Cocteau with new dances by Léonide Massine. Gossip mostly washed over my head, but I could see Bloomsbury was not rejoicing in Maynard's marriage. I felt negative vibrations, discriminatory sideswipes, even against ballet itself. One late night Grove House filled with guests invited back for snacks and drinks after a performance. My brother and I, roused from bed, were costumed in Mina's red and Henrietta's yellow silk pajamas. Lydia pushed us into an impromptu *pas de trois*. On a similar occasion, Florence Mills, with members of her Harlem troupe from the all-black revue "Dover Street to Dixie," sang and danced. I was urged to ask Lytton if he slept with his beard inside or outside. (Outside, he confided.) And while all this went on, I had no notion of events far from Grove House which would determine my future: at this moment, in Leningrad, Lydia's brother, Feodor Lopokov, was experimenting with novel dance patterns on the body of a fellow student whose Georgian patronymic was Balanchivadze, westernized by Diaghilev as Balanchine.

Maynard Keynes guided me to a show of Cézanne's water-colors at the Leicester Galleries. I couldn't pretend I adored at first sight all that was hung there. Any free-thinking, *avant-garde* preference I might have had was smothered by devotion to Burne-Jones, Beardsley, and academic figurative rendering. Art of this kind was, of course, abhorred by Bloomsbury, along with the Albert Memorial, Gilbert and Sullivan, Peter Pan, Rudyard Kipling, and annual summer shows at the Royal Academy. All were, to me, primers of delight. Cézanne's watercolors seemed clumsy, unfinished, yet broadly descriptive curves and brushed indications of form were obviously intentional, determined; fixed and final rather than haphazard. Keynes noted my wan response. After we had made a circuit of the show, I marked a gallery assistant placing tiny red stickers on a few of the frames. As if justifying his purchases in a manner that might make me reconsider, Keynes gave me a lesson in values apart from aesthetics. After explaining the method of visual abstraction by generalizing shapes, he remarked that there were alternate elements for analysis. Had I noticed that most framed and matted sheets were signed and dated? I had not. This, he said, was as salient a factor as color; it placed art in time, in the sequence of practice. On what other papers had I failed to notice signature and date? He pulled from his wallet a five-pound note, inscribed with the customary dates and names. He explained that art also offered its treasury of worked paper as a negotiable-security. While Aubrey Beardsley's drawings might now be priced less than Cézanne's, this had little to do with any absolute value. Different modes of describing form, flat or full, were only suggestions toward plasticity, the variable spectra of taste. There was a grand flow of paint, old and new, beyond personal like or dislike. Keep your eyes open, clean of received opinion and prejudice. He kept comparisons with commerce, money or dealing, simple. I resisted equivalence between art and stocks-and-bonds, but his cool, dispassionate, ironical manner, which at first seemed dismissive or dispiriting, soon launched a radical reformation in my naïve judgment.

Yet however much enlarged, open, or eclectic appreciation could be advanced, there would be limits I would not extend. Digital mastery and the accurate placement of the human face and form, supremacy in surface and texture, the seizure of exact retinal resemblance, were fixtures in my developing preferences. My ultimate criterion has always been portraiture, not only for its mirror imagery but for psychological anatomy. If a picture could not tell me much about a person, its painter, I thought, was no artist. I could never credit abstraction as anything past an admission of failed skill. Dutifully, I tried to build on Keynes's appreciation of Cézanne's stenography, but my instincts and preferences were of the kind soon to be formulated in Wystan Auden's "Letter to Lord Byron":

> To me Art's substance is the human clay,
> And landscape but a background for a torso;
> All Cézanne's apples I would give away
> For one small Goya or a Daumier.

Then I had a liberating revelation. In the Tate Gallery I came on a brand-new, highly polished, silvery-steel head of Osbert Sitwell by Frank Dobson. It was cast from solid, reflected sunlight, brilliantly burnished, whole, complete, characterizing, yet—oh, well—*abstract!* From here on, I would gaze with abject admiration on pieces by Epstein, Gaudier-Brzeska, and later, and most of all, Brancusi. The providential air of Bloomsbury blessed me with enlightenment. The Sitwell head came from the hands of a sculptor who had as his pupil one who, more or less, would take me in hand.

Stephen Tomlin was son of a Lord Chief Justice. His parent's eminence did not prevent his variant career as sculptor. Tommy's bronze heads of Virginia Woolf and other Blooms-berries stay now in the National Portrait Gallery in London. I came closer to him as he fell precipitately in love with Henrietta Bingham. Her father, like his a judge, commissioned twin stone eagles for the gateposts to his Kentucky homestead. There was their smoldering, off-and-on affair for me to stare at and somehow I'd become helplessly a third party to it. Simply, I fell in love with them both. As for Tommy, I think I amused him. When he bathed, after work in his studio, Henrietta was permitted to scrub his back. I was relegated past shut doors to fit his dress shirt with cuff buttons. His rather more than double-life took him to grand gatherings in his father's world, far beyond the purlieus of Russell Square. Possessed by tangled humors, he was teased by many about an inability to choose between paralyzing enthusiasms, aesthetic and personal. He had an oblique hesitancy sparkling with obtuse frankness, a shyness relieved by abrupt cruelty. This amounted to constant flirtation and provocation in rapid-fire inconstancy, all the acrobatic energy resulting as well in a profound melancholy. Despite his fair-haired grace, he never seemed to suit himself or connect on easy terms with those with whom he said himself to be, for moments, enthralled. I never received from him much more than intermittent recognition of the depthless emotion I gratefully spent. When, some years later, Julia Strachey contrived to marry him, desolate envy obliged me to acknowledge her triumph with the presentation of a single rose. The token was received by Julia in a manner identical to the one used by my nurse's Florida brother. One hardly ever learns.

MY MOTHER nurtured two prevailing passions: a taste for the variety and facture of fine lace, and for the music-dramas of Richard Wagner. Her attention to embroidered fabric sprang more from the diversity of its ingenuity than from any love of the intrinsic beauty of style or pattern. As for Wagner, her devotion was less purely musical than admiration for an achieved vision, a complex apparatus realizing extra-terrestrial magic on a fabulous but worldly scale.

[*64*]

I took slight interest in lace, which seemed needlessly finicky and bodiless, although my mother's obsession was no less committed than my childish devotion to the immaculate design and engraving of fresh-printed postage stamps, of which I was given albums in order to "learn geography." My particular favorite was a recent issue for Bosnia and Herzegovina, which reproduced in a rainbow palette several placid, photographic scenes. The deposits of raised ink, immaculately inlaid on their minuscule surfaces, seemed a peak of digital mastery. Postage stamps, engraved piano music, the obligation to appreciate lace-making—all were signposts, hinting at territories toward which I aspired, and which in time my mother generously revealed to me. There was no analytical understanding except a narrow chance preference, but the scent or aura of a real but remote magic which seemed vaguely attainable became the bedrock of a preoccupation with theater, in its dominantly lyrical mani-festations—ballet and opera.

In the early months of 1924 it was announced that the Bayreuth annual festivals of Wagner's "Ring" and the other repertory would begin again after the interruption of World War I. My parents had resumed European vacations immedi-ately after the peace, and, as I have explained, I had already been to London in 1922. However, except for occasional visits to the Boston Opera House when visiting troupes performed and to Symphony Hall on Friday afternoons, I had no encounter with a focused musico-theatrical experience. Bayreuth, a world wholly, profoundly, dedicated to the realization of the unreal, made a deep and lasting impression, and the seriousness involved in the current festival's operations convinced me that not only was such activity the aim of my life, but that it was also, however remote, a realizable possibility.

When we arrived at Bayreuth late on one fine summer afternoon, my mother presented us at Der Schwarze Adler, the recommended hotel. As far as I knew, neither of us boasted any notable ethnic birthmarks, but perhaps something betrayed us. In any case, we were told that the hotel was full, that our accommodations were not available, and that we might be far "happier"—that epithet again—in the private home of a Frau Steinkraus, a co-religionist. This was not the first time I'd recognized the unhappy stink of ingrained prejudice, but never before had I experienced it in so public or official a dimension. Still, Frau Steinkraus, the widow of a schoolmaster, kept a clean, most comfortable home where we were entirely at our ease. She made us plump ham sandwiches, *Schinkenbrödchen*, which eased the very long intermissions at the Festspielhaus.

Bayreuth had not recovered sufficiently from the war to remount the operas with any progressive productions which could boast an appropriate grandeur. For me, though, this proved most fortunate, for the entire "Ring" was presented with the hardly refurbished scenic investiture of the late 1890s and early 1900s. I particularly admired the innovation of an invisible orchestral conductor leading his band in a curved aperture under the stage. The excessively dry and detailed scene painting, in which every leaf and twig was crisply netted, offered a literally perfect illustration of "forest murmurs"; the dragon Fafner spouted real steam; the three Rhine maidens, supported on miniature pulpits on wheels, swam convincingly; and small boys, strapped to what could have been merry-go-round hobby-horses, streaked as Valkyries across a wondrously inflamed cyclorama.

There were drawbacks. The seating was as hard as football bleachers, and a black-clad priest next to me left no doubt as to his contempt for my fidgety presence. But the *mise-en-scène*, which I quite realized was superannuated and ridiculous, gave a very perfect picture, however ancient, of what Wagner himself had wished for his presentation. Its attempt at attention to conjured specifics and surface detail was almost touchingly sincere, and I recognized the devotion that had prompted it.

The current production of *Die Meistersinger von Nürnberg* was quite another thing. Whatever money there had been available was lavished on scenery of a three-dimensional architectural modernity. The scale of the reproduction of St. Katherine's Chapel and the glorious Bach-like choral singing were photographically convincing, a twentieth-century triumph over what nineteenth-century scenography had not been able to suggest. At the finale of the Mastersingers' contest, the prize-winning, and the last great orchestral salute, the massed audience rose from their seats in an explosion of patriotic ferocity. The Jesuit priest at my side, the cords of his neck seeming to burst through his skin, howled in an access of hysterical rage or joy, and his voice seemed to inflame the rest of the audience into a blurred thunder, which gradually became clarified in the unmistakable slogan of "DEUTSCHLAND, DEUTSCHLAND ÜBER ALLES!" What could my mother and I do but sit there and endure it? It was as if some monstrous radio-newspaper of world-wide coverage were bellowing headlines of a nation's revenge.

Berkshire School

1923–1924

AFTER MY ignominious passage through Phillips Exeter, my father asked President Nielsen of Smith College to recommend other institutions where I might enjoy more "happiness" (and "imagination"). He suggested, among others, the Berkshire School for Boys, set on a broad hillside meadow on the western borders of Massachusetts, under shadows of "The Dome," the highest outcrop in a range of Berkshire hills.

The school was founded and still run by Seaver Burton Buck, a flush-faced Victorian pedagogue who considered himself heir to the ethos of Arnold's Rugby and Thomas Hughes's *Tom Brown's School Days*. This was a history I knew well; I had been horrified and fascinated by the character of Flashman, its sadistic bully-villain. He embodied mania for me, the likes of which I never hoped to meet, but who, with his loose, gangly lurk, had left me with unforgettable hints of hell. I had had little or no firsthand experience of concentrated unadulterated evil; sin, as I could have defined it, resembled bad smells or bad manners. At Berkshire, though, I gained acquaintance with a diabolical malevolence that seemed as powerful as anything in tales by Poe, Stevenson, or Conan Doyle.

Berkshire was a comparatively new, decently unfashionable

school, nowhere near as prestigious as its neighbors Kent, Choate, Loomis, or Salisbury, to say nothing of Groton, Saint Mark's, Saint George's, or Saint Paul's. It aspired to a pallid vein of low-Anglican Christianity and its weekly chapel service would have offended neither Catholic nor Jew. As far as student control or governance went, its faculty was more amiable, tolerant, and casual than scholarly. Any formal educational policy was intended to push very middle-class students into smaller colleges such as Amherst, Bowdoin, or Colgate, rather than risk exams for the Ivy League—the student body was one-third composed of lads like myself who had problematic histories. Seaver Buck cast himself as an experimental Victorian builder, willing to face the unusual or even the troublesome. He recognized an absence of authentic background and tried to invent a sense of tradition with a number of annual rites. "Mountain Day" included trooping up "The Dome" to picnic at its top. "Class Day" was graduation. "Alumni Day" was marked by theatricals which aimed to attract graduates for a weekend return to dormitories where dozens of boys vacated their beds for the benefit of their loyal predecessors. One sensed strained efforts to force-feed a sickly civilization.

A rustic log shack less than halfway up "The Dome" was our escape hatch for nocturnal feasts. Nominally forbidden after-hours, it was accessible, via a rope of knotted bedsheets, from a fifth-floor attic dormitory down to ground, and then up a long slope. Once, a couple of chums and I cooked and ate three pounds of Canadian bacon, crouching stark naked in the hot shack on a frigid February night. All of us were sick enough to seek the infirmary. There were odd gaps like this in the school's discipline; supervision was lazy or followed Mr. Buck's liberal impulses. On some nights, with no advance warning (or reason), a collective insomnia assembled thirty or forty boys in a blacked-out school library, one large room on the ground floor of the main building. It was as if some silent secret signal for protest or mutiny was sparked by collective boredom or excess muscular energy. Loose, careless fun coalesced, seeking a spokesman. Two football heroes, Storm and Stout, were pushed forward as popular voices, candidates for questionable leadership. Storm, a tall, handsome youth with a dazzling mop of bright red hair, would be overtaken by fits of uncontrolled glee. He seized one occasion to make a bumbling oration in which he advised all of us to return to bed and continue playing with ourselves. My first months at Berkshire had no other focus, except obsessive readings of verse. My sister had given me *Come Hither*, Walter de la Mare's splendid anthology, which includes snippets of charms, folklore, and white magic scattered like aromatic clues to a hunted creature's spoor.

Toward the start of my second year, my bedroom shifted from a fourth-floor attic annex to better accommodations. On a long corridor, both sides of which were lined with single rooms each holding bed, bureau, desk, and bookshelves, we were comfortable, enjoying solitary hours if and when we wished. Across from me slept a new student from Omaha, Nebraska. Clayton Turner was a year and a half older than myself; this seemed to make more of a difference than mere months should. He was wiser, had read much more, was physically more mature. He had started to shave whereas my voice had not changed. Like me, he had enjoyed a spurious whack at "education" at another school. He fitted into a nameless band of boys about whom I wondered—had he been admitted through Seaver Buck's compassion, or the school's need for paying pupils?

Clayton Turner was ugly, with casual lack of facial grace; his knobby skull was a warped gourd with jug ears. Preternatural paleness skinned a fleshy nose with flaring nostrils above a lipless mouth over a brutal, prognathous jaw. His body, composed of disjunct members, suggested that each arm and leg was of a different length. He was an aberration, a true *lusus naturae*, which almost pleaded for justification. Instead of being daunted by his fate, though, he seemed to glory in it. Intensely active, nervously energetic in spasms, he could relapse into dumb apathy as if gathering force to boast contempt for the repulsion his looks provoked. Awed by his physical presence, I was mesmerized by his play of mind and utterance. He questioned, explained, or denied—*everything*! Describing data concerning cosmic areas replete with rare lacunae, he juggled good and evil as if Evil was Good while God was Evil. He was always available for short therapeutic interviews, amusing his bait with randy recipes. He blamed most of us for a lack of luck or grace, deftly using his sense of our awareness of his nose and ears as inverse bullying. Most creatures of the age we were then are unformed as individuals, but Clayton, personifying ambiguous doubt of all normal causality, was a mature embryonic monster. Who, indeed, was he? It suddenly snapped. He was a reincarnation of Flashman from *Tom Brown*!

As I had pursued my interests in painting and theater, Clayton immersed himself in magic—black, not white. He was a tributary adept of one major modern sorcerer who actually existed, whom he might have met, and whom we can meet in memoirs by William Butler Yeats and others. Aleister Crowley conceived "The Order of the Golden Dawn," a mystical lodge which replaced Christianity with a "Sanctity of Self." How Clayton came upon this sinister heresy, I never learned. He was certain of its mortal and morbid efficacy, since it was confirmed by "gematria," a cabalistic method of interpreting Hebrew scripture. A, B, C = 1, 2, 3; any name may be awarded its numerical equivalent. Crowley, he assured me, had provided himself with a signature which added up to 666, the name and number of the Great Beast who emerges from oceans in the Book of Revelation. (I never got around to adding up the figures for myself.) In a battered tin box, Clayton hoarded a hairless pig's trotter, snakeskin, dried bat's wing, cactus of unmentionable shape, plus a much-thumbed, greasy postcard. On its face was the photo of a bald, over-fleshed, middle-aged male with an unsettling stare. It could have been the future portrait of Clayton Turner at fifty. On the postcard's obverse were printed five of Crowley's commandments, under the inscription in heavy Gothic type:

𝕯𝖔 𝖂𝖍𝖆𝖙 𝕿𝖍𝖔𝖚 𝖂𝖎𝖑𝖙 𝕭𝖊 𝖙𝖍𝖊 𝖂𝖍𝖔𝖑𝖊 𝖔𝖋 𝖙𝖍𝖊 𝕷𝖆𝖜

1. Man has the Right to live under his own law.
2. Man has the Right to eat what he will.
3. Man has the Right to think what he will.
4. Man has the Right to love what he will.
5. Man has the Right to kill those who would
   thwart these rights.

Each rule was provided with its gloss. Rule 3 obviously applied
to me:

> to speak what he will; to write what he will;
> to draw, paint, etch, sculpt, mould, build
> and dress, as he will.

Further commandments read "Slaves shall freely serve";
"Love is the Law"; "Love under Will." All this should have been
read as pernicious nonsense, but in its frame of private revelation, Clayton Turner's riveting mystery abrogated any doubt.
I craved permission from him to copy out Crowley's card. This
was denied on my first bid and I was led to understand there
was a price to pay for initiation: solemn seriousness and absolute
subservience. I was not too far magicked to accept such conditions. If his secrets had been freely given, he might have had
me. Yet for a creature with his frank, unluckily repellent nose,
ears, and skin to require unbalanced payment made me hesitate
and resist; questioning his authority also gave me time to think.
Sorcerers need servitors: *"Slaves shall freely serve."* Clayton's
bonded serf was a luckless biped who, as I now discovered, had
been months in service. This child, a couple of years younger
than myself, also came from Omaha, Nebraska. Clayton must
have found him at home. Little Joseph Muldoon was notable
for nothing, neither face nor form, except a shivery, skittering
shyness which sprang from terror. Before I gained insight into
the true nature of their alliance, I was given a rough introduction

in borrowings from cabalistic cosmogonies. The extent of universal correspondence had not occurred to me. Metaphysical tabulation, as affirmed by Clayton, did not read as severely outlandish. In brief, every one of us (and perhaps especially, reader, you and I) is governed by planetary control via color, mineral, stone, and creature, and by the interpretations with which certain candidates are favored:

SATURN:	black	lead	onyx	crocodile
JUPITER:	blue	tin	sapphire	eagle
MARS:	red	iron	ruby	horse
SUN:	yellow	gold	topaz	lion
VENUS:	green	copper	emerald	dove
MERCURY:	gray	mercury	agate	swallow
MOON:	white	silver	crystal	dog

I could accept many parallels as easy visual metaphor. If I bridled a bit when urged to murder those who disagreed, I told myself I could postpone decision. I had been provided with a fertile seedbed for suspended doubt and hints of illegible evil. Edgar Allan Poe's loonier horrors, *Dr. Jekyll and Mr. Hyde*, Mark Twain's Mysterious Stranger may not have been convincingly "true" or "real," but they lightly greased a dark tunnel with a sense of superreality. Clayton rifled *Macbeth*; some of the grisly relics in his black box were surely chosen for him by the three weird sisters.

Little Joe Muldoon took my bewitchment by Clayton as further evidence of his master's infernal powers. Revolting and humiliating obligations imposed on him took on more urgency from my own growing fascination. The three of us fed on one another, reciprocal points in a equilateral triangle of threats and promises. Snot, semen, earwax, sweat, pubic hair, all richly laced with diluted iodine, was an infernal potion bound to induce wonder-working nightmares. To enter Clayton's chapter of "The Golden Dawn" for its idiot infant's initiation would have made Aleister Crowley proud. I won't admit I was completely persuaded by all this mumbo-jumbo, but I was romanced, and my desire to be more "interesting" than God intended promoted passive acceptance. At the same time I believed that self-disciplined, external silence rendered me superior in wit and glory to all ordinary ignorance, which I began to imagine was denial and suffocation. A blast was needed to blow all this out of my mind.

Soon, Little Joe Muldoon began to manifest alarming smoke signals. For no reason, he'd collapse in sobs, running wildly off from wherever he chanced to be shivering, as if pursued by horned snakes. I coldly discounted such demonstrations as a ploy to draw attention to himself. This undoubtedly was only partly from what it derived. He was observed by a teacher now and then, but managed to quash eruptions until they further accelerated. When questioned, he had absorbed enough current cant to declare that he was "nervously tired." A couple of days in the school infirmary, removal from Clayton, gentle ministra- tion by a kind attendant nurse, all these were only palliative. Clayton, though, took this pitiful defection as betrayal and treachery, so he set his screws tighter. I felt involved, but was of no mind to admit aberrant fears. Nobody would believe me, even if I confessed—and also, I might be guiltily implicated. Soon after he returned from the infirmary, Little Joe began to think he was in immediate mortal peril. He told me he'd been forbidden to use the bathroom more than once a day, hence hardly drank a glass of water or mouthed a spoonful of food. Clayton threatened to lace his orange juice with spider's gall. Little Joe Muldoon had been corrupted and infected by can- cerous negative energy. This miniature psychomania was con- tested just one inch below the surface of classroom schedules.

One night, after lights out, there was a rap on my door. At the end of our corridor was a bathroom used by the whole floor. The corridor was nominally policed, either by a master whose suite of rooms adjoined the bath, or by senior proctors who never took this duty seriously. Visits to bedrooms other than one's own were discouraged in vain. If caught, both host and visitor were assigned extra hours in study-hall, but risk seemed slight. At the knock, I rose from bed, opened my door to be rudely thrown back onto my pillows by the frail shudders and whimpering frame of Little Joe. Kitten-mewing sobs, he slumped on my bed speechless. I didn't dare turn on the light, but cradled him in my arms, felt his tear-wet breath against my neck. Finally he managed to mutter: "*It's started* . . ." Whatever it was which now commenced crowned all the miasma of sorcery with which I had so avidly wished to connect. "*Oh, God. It's started.*" The chill of evil thrilled into swelling apprehension. God? God now told me I must do battle for His *Right*—and not the Great Beast's. I must, I would, I could and should save Little Joe. I shoved him out into the corridor, soothing him feebly, promising harm could not win. He went away snuffling.

Absolutely nothing followed. It was as if no glint of threat or menace had occurred. As for Joe Muldoon, his piteous, shy glances as we passed in corridor or classroom, bathroom or dining hall, seemed almost apologetic for fictitious perils. Reverberations there surely had been, but they were now inaudible, vague, without a source. Had this entanglement been only self-deception on my part? Or was the kid crazy? Had I been silly or vain enough to deceive myself? Self-interrogation led me nowhere. There was no master or fellow student whom I could delay long enough to narrate so unlikely a situation. Yet Little Joe's hysterical explosion on my bed could not be ignored.

Now spring vacation was over and we were in rehearsal for annual dramatics. The play was *The Galloper*, a three-act melodrama by Richard Harding Davis, treating of a dashing American war correspondent assigned to Greek guerrilla operations against barbarous Turks. Clayton Turner was cast as a Turkish spy, or double agent, whose ultimate unmasking rescued "The Galloper" from a firing squad. I was the maid of a Greek heroine he would save from worse-than-death. Rehearsals were held in our gymnasium, which served as temporary theater, down the hill from the dining hall. Most of the cast had gone up ahead to supper one evening, leaving Clayton and me to straggle behind.

Without warning, he pushed me on my back, thrusting me down hard onto the gravel path. Rough pebbles grazed my cheek. His firm paws held fast, tightening fingernails into my throat. He spat out: "So you *will*, will you!" I lay still for seconds, then managed to breathe: "Get off me, or I'll pee all over you." The strangling stopped and he walked away up the hill. In paroxysms of relief and sexy fright, I passed out. Perhaps he thought I was dead; he must have looked back to see I'd not regained my feet. He raced up to the dining hall and reported that I'd suffered a "heart attack." I came-to fast enough, and, recovering, appeared alive, to eat supper. However, the joke had been too funny for me, and I passed out again at table.

I found myself on a fresh cot in the infirmary, being bid to drink hot broth by a sympathetic nurse. I took a proffered pill, and slept until a nice sickroom breakfast. Little Joe appeared to "thank" me—for what, I wondered. In any case, whatever spell had been woven was now torn and broken. I asked him to bring me a book from my desk, thinking its white magic might set a seal on whatever blackness there had been. Around noon, Seaver Burton Buck appeared. He seemed taken by the volume that lay open on my chest. He ruffled its pages. It was my old childhood breviary, Walter de la Mare's *Come Hither.* He asked me which was my "favorite"? Favorite, among so many? Maybe "Lavender's blue, dilly dilly, lavender's green, / When I am king, dilly dilly, you shall be queen." Or, " 'Is there anybody there?' said the Traveller." Or even—the most help-lessly infantile: "Where have you been, pussy-cat?" (This may have had some unconscious reference to Little Joe.) Mr. Buck's face, close to mine, was seamed in healthy, rose-pink folds. Seen now, in my transcendently clear readjustment to reality, it resembled a bull's healthy scrotum. He did not kiss me as I dreaded, but put both hands grasping my shoulders (rather as Clayton had) and said: "Clayton's gone; don't worry."

Fifteen years later, our small American Ballet Caravan was touring the United States, playing high-school gymnasiums. In Omaha, Nebraska, before a performance I went out to check the gymnasium floor, since these were often so highly polished as to become a hazard for ballerinas' *pointe*-shoes. I was about to register a complaint, when the handyman appeared with mop and bucket, anticipating my need by thought transference. Then I noticed he grinned like a withered gourd with jug ears. It couldn't be. Of course, it was—Clayton! Still resistant and competitive, he contemptuously handed me the mop and pail, turned on his heel and vanished. I strongly doubt if he stayed to witness an excellent program: Paul Bowles's *Yankee Clipper*, Elliott Carter's early *Pocahontas*, and Lew Christensen's Mozartian *Encounter*.

The aftermath of my duel (or duet) with Clayton Turner had its uses. I took time to consider the pathology of our joint mania, based on whimsical error and reciprocal attraction, the desire to dominate and/or to submit. In the realm of theater, of which ballet is a province, hysteria and self-obsession—with their more or less controlled employment as an instrument of expression—may count as a *sine qua non* of memorable or extreme execution. Nijinsky's tragedy, with which I would become involved, and other dislocations sprang from an extension of adventurous discovery warped by neurosis. Even the suicide of promising artists with whom I had worked seldom astonished me after the first shock. I grasped the accelerating frailty of imaginative limits under an abrasion of forced physical and emotional pressures. I tried to estimate to what degree I had contributed to Clayton Turner's obsession, recognizing it was not entirely one-sided, that there was a residue of onus in my eagerness to adopt a preposterously exciting self-indulgence, trying to make myself more extraordinary or mysterious than was God-given. Exploration, even in black magic, willful and witless, opened an avenue toward evil and warned me of the perils of aesthetics, of confusing real life with bad literature, of the quest for emotion for its own sake.

Boston

1924–1925

DESPITE EXPRESS FAILURES in school work and other irregularities, including a non-graduation from Berkshire, as well as a no-go on my first try at Harvard college-entrance examinations, by dint of backups from private tutors and crash courses in my various lapses, I steeled myself to face the examinations again as an ultimate trial of self-respect. Lack of concentration was still a weakness; but my father's patience with my problems strengthened me since I knew I owed him so much. Geometry proved the toughest trick to master, since I had so little talent for abstract notions. This was solved by mindless muscle—I committed to memory all the first five books of Euclid by imposing on their text a grid of false metric, like irregular blank verse. (This ignominious feat of memory ended my active involvement with mathematics, though it did leave me with a stubborn desire to learn more about it. All my subsequent life, I have collected so-called children's books about science, and I think I now know as much about math as any promising twelve-year-old.) After refreshing their sequence by sleepless saturation the night before the examination, I passed the next day and was admitted in 1925 to a freshman class at

Harvard which graduated in 1929. I was almost eighteen, and deemed "old-for-my-age."

The surprise of this unlikely accomplishment, about which my parents had been deliberately unhopeful, caused them to consider me as a brand-new person. Due to my record at Exeter and Berkshire, they may have begun to have second thoughts about my future. Most boys entered college at sixteen; I was already two years older. I'd weathered storms at two prep schools and still aimed to be some type of "artist." Whatever the reason for my father's decision—perhaps even to get to know me better—he decided to delay college for a year, in order to let me "find" myself.

I'd spent hours amongst plaster casts in Boston's Museum School, and even in the Louvre, sketching antique marbles. Smutty charcoals, with no evidence of facility, were undertaken more in hope of stealing magic from famous models than for stern study toward any actual competence. My fingers were all thumbs, nowhere near as nimble as mind or eye. Manipulating a charcoal stump was even harder than banging fruitlessly on piano keys. Maybe a half-forgotten suggestion from John Sargent prompted fate, or Father, to place me as an unpaid apprentice in the stained-glass shop of Charles Connick, located in a big top-floor studio off lower Huntington Avenue.

Due to my sister's preoccupation with Henry Adams, I had fallen in love with the distinction of Adams's character and the elegance of his supercilious self-denigration. His *Education* and *Mont-Saint-Michel and Chartres* became sacred books for us both, so much so that in 1919 my mother, brother, and I had made a pilgrimage to France and been guided through that cathedral's stupendous, glass-blessed maze by none other than Monsieur Etienne Houvet, its famous resident conservator. He had edited eight cardboard portfolios of photographs on pebbly paper, some in dim, false color. These were faint echoes of the breathtaking saturation of sunlight drenching films of tint through the black spiderwebs of leading. The layered light was almost tactile. Afterward, for school themes, I wrote poetry and an extended paper, a kind of Micheletian exordium, describing my raptures over Chartres and vainly trying to capture again the luminous glory of shifting sunbeams through clouds, filtering daylight, sunset, moonlight, and starlight. At the time there were no adequate illustrations in color, and my efforts were a combination of inaccuracy and post-Ruskinian sentimentality. But the impressions of the miracle of light as a vibrating presence were almost more magical to me than oil paint on canvas. In Chartres, and perhaps more in the Sainte-Chapelle in Paris, color glowed thick as honey, not as a cloak for plastic imagery, but as vibrant energy itself, arterial and electric. Also, I had a sneaky suspicion that if I were to try stained glass, correct draftsmanship would be less difficult than it was in portraiture. The naïveté in medieval configuration made its imitation seem likely to be simpler for a student defeated by plaster casts or anatomical verisimilitude.

Charles Connick's studio served the firm of Cram and Ferguson, prolific architects of Gothic churches all over America. These followed the rigorous archeological tenets proposed by Viollet-le-Duc and the monastic revivalists of the early nineteenth century. Connick's craftsmen were similarly bound by methods of traditional French glaziers. Their glass remained stained, not painted. Pristine, clear surfaces of colored sheet-glass took the brush only in thin, black, iron-oxide outline, indicating faces, arms, and legs under linear drapery. Crimson, green, blue, and yellow pot-glass was not over-painted to imitate three-dimensional plastic form as on canvas. Connick considered post-medieval and recent glass had been corrupted by attempts to fuse the techniques of oil paint onto luminescent transparency, which only flubbed the natural lucid dazzle. This severe aesthetic, as practiced by the Connick shop, greatly appealed to me. Here were men operating as they might have done six or seven centuries ago.

Mr. Connick glanced at my sketches, including those copied

(top) My grandmother Kirstein, photographed in 1911 in Rochester, New York, in imitation of Whistler's portrait of his mother; (bottom) Grandmother Kirstein's home in Rochester, ca. 1900

(top) My mother, Rose Stein, at Madame Meares's finishing school in New York, June 1890; (bottom) The large house of Nathan and Mina Stein, my mother's parents, in Rochester, ca. 1900

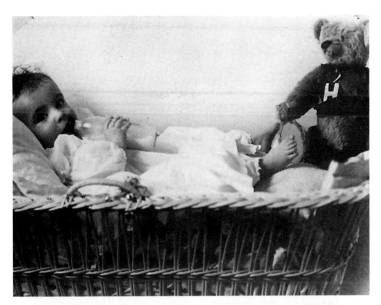

*(top) Rochester, October 1907. Photographed in a crib with bottle and Harvard
teddy bear by my father; (bottom) Father, me in midshipman's uniform by Rowe
of Gosport, and my brother, George. Rochester, 1910*

(above) My cousin Nat Wolfe with his mother, Mrs. Martin Wolfe. Rochester, ca. 1912; (opposite, top) Mother with my sister, Mina, George, and me. Boston, ca. 1914; (bottom) A corner of the living room at 506 Commonwealth Avenue, Boston. Against the wall our landlord Mr. Whitney's glazed library shelves, on top of which are his electrotypes of Roman bronzes

(opposite, top) Dancing like a bough at Camp Timanous, Maine, 1916; (bottom) Camp Timanous fire-ritual; (above) Mina Kirstein, Smith College, ca. 1917

Taken during my brief stint at Phillips Exeter Academy in 1922 (Pirie Mac-Donald)

from Monsieur Houvet's Chartres portfolios. Feeble as they were, they seemed sufficient to legitimize my serious interest and Connick handed me over to Mr. Farnsworth, his shop master, who set me at the desk of Jerry Collins, a junior designer of charm and talent. I had every readiness to learn and the conditions were easy, at least as far as this apprentice was aware. Puttering at my own rate, I hoped I might be useful. Currently, the shop had a contract for the baptistery of a church on East Avenue, Rochester, New York. This seemed a lucky signal to me, so, basing my work on snapshots of sports- and concert-events from the *Boston Post*, I filled roundels with baseball and football figures, culminating in a saxophonist and drummer. Seamed by heavy black charcoal outlines indicating leading, my sketches were estimated as "experimental," even as proof of the studio's progressive attitude toward modernism projected from medieval mannerism. Mr. Farnsworth tolerated, and Jerry Collins welcomed, them, correcting all kinds of slacknesses in my designs. He even encouraged me to cut and spoil glass. With his help I constructed four contemporary figures of the Seasons, two male, two female, in sport dress. These were installed in a "medieval" dining room of Harry Curtiss's farm in Ashfield, Massachusetts, after he married my sister in 1924.

The men's time in the Connick shop was not wholly focused on handicraft for cathedral lights. I could not have guessed, yet at the moment of my arrival there were tremors beginning under the surface habit of daily routine, incipient murmurs of tension. This could not yet be construed as any full-blown strike. It was still defusible as putative work action. Although less than half the men were disputing problems of hours and wages, I began to sense a seething discontent from the older ranks when I went to a washroom or overheard talk at lunch-time, when neither Connick nor Farnsworth was around. Soon the atmosphere grew more sullen and unhappy. Since my professional standing was peculiar, and hence inferior, any question or comment on such undercurrents was to be avoided by me. They were not ignored by Jerry Collins, whose young wife was expecting a second child. She worked as a nurse, and would often be forced to stay home, unpaid.

Then, to my anguished disbelief, I learned that three or four of the older men, who had never noticed me by one word, thought I had been introduced by Connick or Farnsworth as an informer, stooge, or spy; that I was paid to observe and betray whatever plans promised trouble for "Management." Connick used efficient paternalism as a cushion against discontent. Grateful to him for being allowed to play on his ground, I doubted his ill will, and moves toward declaration of a strike were not sufficiently advanced yet to make me choose which side I might be on. Surely, though, I leaned firmly to Jerry Collins and the men. I'd learned from Father that there were at the least "two sides to every question" and I worried over whether I dare approach Connick with my poor plea for compromise. But as between what and which, I had only washroom hints, along with the false rumors that I was a wretched spy.

Jerry Collins needed no proof of my purity. We had become friends and he'd invited me to supper. In his tiny, neat apartment I admired framed drawings of nudes and animals. His pretty, pregnant wife advised me to stay clear of danger. I think, due to Jerry's discretion and my clean, but convincing Army-Navy store work-costume, she assumed that I was paid —as poorly as Jerry himself. It wasn't my fight, if fight there was, but Jerry couldn't afford to be without work. How long did strikes last? Jerry had to admit there was the possibility of one now. I thought of speaking to my father; after all, he had in his employ hundreds of apparently contented, or passive, workers. Yet to propose more grief for him, so soon after a recovery from my late, personal bother at school, only heaped up more worry. I must make up my own mind, and at once I began to dislike Connick and Farnsworth. This feeling I supported by reasoning that, while I was unpaid, my panels inspired by sport and saxophone were shown off to visitors as progressive testimony to the shop's "modernism." Should I not receive consideration as a quasi-professional?

I decided to ask permission for my mother to visit the studio. She had proved an ally in my recent difficulties and I planned for Jerry Collins to escort her through the various stages of window-work, from which she might acquire enough data to provide a basis for further action. But Jerry's role of docent was instantly usurped by Farnsworth, who outdid himself in seductive explanations. I was left with nothing but my mother's abject and all-too-predictable enchantment with a thirteenth century re-born, and my own rankling confusion. Summer was approaching and my term of apprenticeship neared its end. I faced Harvard and could quit here blamelessly and without apology. I was not able of course to guarantee Jerry Collins a solid security in prolonged unemployment and he was touchingly dismissive of such worries when I raised them, saying that he could always shine shoes or sell newspapers. Coming down to it, money was all: I had it and he didn't.

Yet entirely unsuspected by me, I had a confidant of whom I was barely aware because his proximity had been presupposed for so long. Although Tom O'Brien had been our chauffeur for ten years, and his status was less that of a servant than a cozy poor-relation, I rarely shared any mindful or emotional part of life with him. My parents were so used to Tom that he scarcely needed orders: his duties were habitual, anticipated, following without friction. While cooks, maids, and laundresses came and went, Tom was a fixture. For all of us, he made loose edges easy. I seldom saw his wife; he dwelt apart with her in an alien, immigrant-Irish world although his family birthdays or celebrations were always aptly remembered by us.

Now Jerry informed me, as mildly as he was able, that a committee which was not unionized had sent Connick, on paper, their specific demands, which must be read as the first motion toward a strike vote. Why had I not thought of asking Tom O'Brien's advice long before this? Now it dawned on me to arrange a meeting. This took place entirely unsuitably in the

Palm Court of the Copley Plaza Hotel, which was down the street from Connick's shop. An everyday lunchroom would have been less grotesque, yet I persuaded myself that a less opulent surround might suggest that I figured working-class representatives lacked, well, class.

Similarity of status and experience dissolved all residues of small talk and both men were soon discussing the situation with perfect, businesslike candor. Jerry told Tom, in detail, the circumstances of conditions which, so far, I'd been spared. It transpired there was a shady undergrowth of carelessness in handling vexing problems: unfair fines for errors made, time-tables not kept, sick-leave pay denied, and other injustices which saved Management money but cost the men much. Tom asked Jerry if the strike was sure and how long it would last for. How much a month would Jerry and his wife need? Tom enjoyed his role of mentor but his solution was hardly a surprise. I should just go to a man accustomed to manipulate gross charities who must be ready to cope with this uniquely deserving case: my father.

Here was the requital I'd not dared face. A tremendous load vanished, a collapsing cloud breaking over my thick head. I was in the clear much less shamefully than I might ever have dreamed. I would say my goodbyes to Connick and Farnsworth, thank them sincerely for the good times, get the hell out with no malice or offense. However, as if in anticlimax, in the end there was no strike. Its threat may have been countermanded by Cram and Ferguson, the architects who were under contract to complete work on a promised date for dedication. Delays could have brought down litigation, so a settlement of wages and hours, or whatever else, was signed—for the moment. Jerry Collins and his wife seemed saved. While a storm cloud lifted, in its place, half-consciously, there still lay as in ambush my own restive self-accusations. If there had, indeed, been a strike, would Father have acted as I'd been led to believe—or hoped? Of course he would . . . Yet in a genuine crisis, how would I have counted myself? Ambivalence reduced me to lingering guilt for my wan morality which I was unable to push past soothing equivocations. It all lodged on Jerry Collins, whom I now found it impossible to see. I felt there was nothing more to say or share. Threadbare, straggling endings confirmed me as a coward, but the contrast in our respective lives was an inescapable barrier. I had to make a clean sweep of the whole mess; I'd chanced into waters too deep for navigation, so now I steered myself toward smoother sailing: four years at Harvard, which held out plenty of promise. I would prepare myself, this time, not to make more of a fool of myself.

While obtaining her Master's degree at Radcliffe, my sister encountered a number of casual friends, mainly graduate students and teachers. Among these was Maurice Firuski, a recent graduate of Yale, now happily transferred to Cambridge. He was the admired proprietor of the Dunster House Bookshop, lodged in a renovated eighteenth-century tavern on Harvard's club-land Gold Coast, a couple of blocks down from the comic façade of the *Lampoon*. The shop was furnished with tall tables at which one could stand and browse through piles of the latest English, French, and American publications, from the pride of university presses to the oddest opuscules of our next generation's poets and novelists. It specialized in privately printed editions and Firuski himself published small, handsome, richly designed volumes, among them elegant, early, slim works of Conrad Aiken and Archibald MacLeish.

The single clerk in charge of Dunster House was a somber, sardonic young man with a compact frame and mousy moustache. He sprang from local origins, and extreme poverty remote from Brattle Street or Memorial Hall. He had compensated by making himself the best-read individual I'd ever met, familiar with primary texts, old and new. He read, even if he did not speak, French, German, Spanish, and Italian. He'd traveled nowhere, except across the Charles River to Boston's Public Library and the reading room of the Athenaeum. But he stocked every new book from Faber & Gwyer, of which T. S. Eliot was editor, and he considered himself, if not personally then by cerebral sympathy, the buddy of Ezra Pound, Wyndham Lewis, Aldous Huxley, and Ford Madox Ford. His name was Richard Blackmur. Soon he told me that he was starting to study Sanskrit.

Firuski, his easy-going, elegant, modestly glamorous boss, took the profession of bookseller lightly, preferring the role of casual salonist. His Thursday evenings, which soon became a local, nonacademic celebration, took place in his handsome house-library, designed and shelved by Pierre Chaignon de la Rose (born Peter Ross), son of a manufacturer of hygienic ceramics. Maurice Firuski commissioned him to conceive an overdecorated, red-and-black *de luxe* floriate edition of Santayana's closet-drama *Lucifer*. However extravagant an example of patronage, Dick Blackmur quietly esteemed it as slightly old-fashioned, *retardataire* for the advance-guard clientele of Dunster House. The bookshop and Firuski's home seemed like first cousins to Alec Penrose's home or Frankie Birrell's and David Garnett's shop in Mayfair, which I had visited on trips to London. Now I was wise enough to let myself be instructed by Blackmur in the difference between Anatole France and André Gide, d'Annunzio and Leopardi, Henry James and Henry Adams, Joris-Karl Huysmans and Oscar Wilde.

There was a faint odor of Anglican incense around Cambridge apart from Harvard at this time. Pierre de la Rose made designs for carved coats-of-arms commissioned for St. John the Divine in Manhattan. The Anglican order of the Cowley Fathers, known ubiquitously as the "Cauliflowers," had raised their stoic priory on the edge of Charles River Drive, and one day while I was in Firuski's store, a very tall secretary-bird of a poet in a raccoon coat brought in a pink pile of his paperbound poem —"North Atlantic Passage"—for sale. He was on his way to Low Mass with the Cauliflowers. John Brooks Wheelwright in spare time was something of an architect. Of all the notables around Firuski's circle, he was the man I most desired to know. Not yet forty, of a slightly younger generation than Aiken or Eliot, after Harvard he had educated himself in Paris and Florence.

Now he lived in Boston with his sister, in a suite of red-and-black Pompeiian chambers on upper Beacon Street. Not only was he a devout Anglo-Catholic, he was also a passionate, persuasive Trotskyite at a period when Bolshevism was credited with a monolithic theology. To the local gentry, any "communism" at all promised anarchy. But to call Jack "eccentric" would have denied his heavy elements of the proper orthodox Brahmin. He directly descended from Peter Chardon, once the richest magnifico of Massachusetts. His father was a distinguished civic architect, builder of the beautiful West Boston Bridge, whose stone turrets were borrowed from candlesticks by Percier and Fontaine then gracing Jack's Beacon Street Pompeii. Disgusted with the criminal sidelines of Bostonian politics, his father had killed himself, putting an end to the position of architect-arbiter. The city was studded with his self-made monuments: entrances to the subway system, Boston's Opera House, and a pleasure pavilion on a public beach.

Jack Wheelwright was "Wheels," rolling unhurriedly around town at his even, antiquated, but serenely pensive pace. With absolute command in unhurried, patient discourse, he might deliver a lay-sermon at the Church of the Advent, whose steps had been, before Easter, ceremoniously scrubbed by Mrs. Isabella Stewart Gardner. On the next night, Jack, clad in dinner jacket and black-tie, would address a gang of Socialist-Labor Party protesters in Roxbury or Somerville. Afterward, he would ride the subway to a debutante's coming-out ball at the Hotel Somerset where he'd dance with a broad cousinage. His lasting remains are some theological verse, a reflection of his wide erudition while his (very) strange experimental sonneteering contains as many as three individual interior-rhyme schemes— each sonnet was dedicated to the personal friend who inspired it. He wrote a splendid elegy on Hart Crane's suicide and was himself slain in his early forties by a drunken truck-driver. He was my first reviewer, in the *New Republic*, of a bad novel, a thin autobiographical confession called *Flesh Is Heir*; I deserved reproof at my assumption of intimacy with a Boston I barely knew. For me, Jack was a character relayed from *The Princess Casamassima* or, better, *The Last Puritan*. In spite of the influence of Joyce and Gertrude Stein, he proved Brattle Street and Beacon Street could boast of much, including T. S. Eliot, e. e. cummings, and himself. Through Jack, I inhabited a vivid landscape, a fair part of whose meadows extended lushly backward into the century before.

Firuski's salon was hosted by his wife, Isabel, who might have been a model for Henry James's *Portrait of a Lady*. Although Dick Blackmur never felt himself unwelcomed, he was too withdrawn to seat himself beside his customers. Conrad Aiken was shy, a discomfited but bristling bantam. He'd been Tom Eliot's classmate and, if the evening's climate seemed loquacious enough, he might quote scabrous verse about a "King Bolo," which I felt the great author of "The Waste Land" might better have never committed. Dr. Harry Murray, a promising psychologist—perhaps a "psychiatrist," but surely no longer an "alienist"—was interested in me because my sister had been analyzed by Freud's future biographer, Ernest Jones. I discussed with him in clinical tones the diagnoses of my passage with Clayton Turner and Little Joe Muldoon, which he did not find as unusual or as picturesque as I had hoped. There was also Phelps Putnam, a poetic anticipation of Ernest Hemingway's persona, disguised as a reborn Villon. His volume, *Trinc*, tried to cast its hero as a hyper-macho Byron. His ballads were dashing, but liquor rarely pushed his stanzas past the suburbs. S. Foster Damon, Jack Wheelwright's brother-in-law, almost the first, long the best, American recoverer of William Blake and Herman Melville, was soon to become my sophomore "adviser."

Cambridge, as I experienced it the year before I entered Harvard, was a predication of Bloomsbury, two linked provinces in an imperial domain of life-and-letters. I felt like a minnow with the freedom to swim in whomever's wake I wanted. Howard Doughty was now a junior, fully acclimatized, published in the *Advocate* and *Crimson*, and equipped with a gang of entertaining cronies. Howard it was who formally introduced me to Harvard's denizens. He lived in Hollis Hall, along with its twin, Houghton, an unrestored red-brick survival from colonial times. One day he brought me to a man who had rooms in Hollis on its third-floor entry. It was a spacious morning when I penetrated so active an ancient precinct. The stairs up old Hollis smelt damp, musty, like a worn, bound book, and I climbed into the study of Dana Durand, a history major, to be baptized.

Howard Doughty uttered my name as introduction. However, his friend never looked up from the book on which he was intent. Stark naked, seated in an old morris chair with tatty brown-velvet padding, he was reading a big, blue, paper-bound first edition of *Ulysses*. Stephen Dedalus's comic gloss on *Hamlet* is the parody and paradigm of inverse bardolatry which wryly characterized so much received literature, ancient and modern, as domesticated furnishing for the scope of my generation's table. Acquisition and digestion of *Ulysses* certified sophistication for many of us who fancied ourselves as budding novelists or poets. It seemed a totally frank expression of the middle-class ordinary—our daily habit, transmogrified, italicized, glorified. The book's unflinching nakedness was easy to identify with the epoch's expression of our own narcissistic nudity. Durand, keeping his place, closed the big, blue book, stood up, and shook my hand. Forwarded by Howard Doughty, I was ritually admitted to this new world. Dana ignored his own bare muscularity, so that, for my hardly reciprocal response, I hoped he had not caught my blinks. On the floor was a flask of Chianti, mugs, cigarettes. I never smoked, nor drank wine, much as I was tempted to try both as a test, but was too shy at this significant moment to risk burnt lips or a bitter taste. His offer having been refused, Dana Durand sat down and continued reading, only now aloud:

—Mallarmé, don't you know, he said, has written those wonderful prose poems Stephen MacKenna used to read to me in Paris. The one about *Hamlet*. He says: *il se promène, lisant au livre de lui-même*, don't you know, *reading the book of himself*. He describes *Hamlet* given in a

French town, don't you know, a provincial town. They advertised it.
His free hand graciously wrote tiny signs in air.

HAMLET

ou

Le Distrait

Pièce de Shakespeare

He repeated to John Eglinton's newgathered frown:
—*Pièce de Shakespeare*, don't you know. It's so French. The French
point of view. *Hamlet ou* . . .
—The absentminded beggar, Stephen ended.

Durand shut his book, poured a mug, lit a cigarette. Then,
addressing me directly, he asked "Now—*you!* How would *you*
translate 'Angels and ministers of grace defend us!'?" I hadn't
enough French to return an answer to the riddle but Howard
Doughty once more stepped into the breach, replying without
a pause: "*Oh mon Dieu, qu'est-ce que c'est que ça?*"

Harvard, Cambridge, Boston 1926–1927

IT'S HARD TO put any sequential order to the several lives I led when Harvard was my center. In the autumn of 1926 Cambridge lay lapped (for me, at least) in the air of earlier eras. The "Harkness Plan," establishing a colony of independent "houses" which domiciled students in red-brick eighteenth-century colonial pastiches comparable to Oxbridge colleges, would not be instituted until the year after I graduated. The crux of my freshman year marked an epoch's end and I witnessed a culmination of one dynasty at the brink of another's succession. The Harvard Business School had little prestige as yet. The closed code maintaining Gold Coast clubs still had its glamour of ancestral association, although I never had any contact with a member of the Porcellian. And the time seemed redolent of the nineteenth century: men like Dana Durand who had rooms in Hollis or Stoughton could easily have been updated replicas of Henry Adams's companions, Roony Lee, Wendell Holmes, or Robert Gould Shaw.

We were ceremoniously assembled for a welcome by Charles William Eliot, canonized editor of the "Five-Foot Shelf of the World's Best Books." Long retired from Harvard's presidency, he had become a patriarchal icon, his frail grayness trembling on the solemn edge of mortality as he murmured in a doddering monotone. Slumbering through his rambling exhortation, I hooked by accident onto one clearly admonitory phrase. I heard him say: "Free introspection . . ." But, no. He repeated in grave italics: "*Flee* introspection!"

I mused on what tradition prompted such counsel, and reflected that it was quite uncalled for by the bulk of the youth who could have been listening. The classmates to whom I would be most drawn physically had no interest in self-examination or any other arduous mentation. They seemed like expensively-tailored sleepwalkers in a luxurious dream, and no hindrance or tragedy appeared to touch them. I was excited by their assurance of command over the immediate situation; from birth they'd been launched on rigid tracks which led, via the Ivy League and clubs, to offices in State Street and Wall Street or to tenure on prime legal or medical faculties. A handful might teach, write, or paint but introspection would deter few. As a clan, they knew themselves as "The Lads," an inbred dynasty from Hamilton's "rich, well-born and [according to their lights] able." In my time I brushed by their bodies, admiring their good looks, fun, their arrant well-being, their depthless self-satisfaction. Recognizing that their preoccupations could not be more remote from mine, I never felt I was on crusades to convert entrenched Philistia. My several "aesthetic" or "intellectual" pursuits were never disdained, since they were not even noted. I was never harassed by either "The Lads" or by our teachers. On the contrary, a faculty of high distinction provided the solid structure of then-available information which nourished my nascent preferences, developing them into the promise of taste. Apart from invaluable individual instruction, these men were also sponsors and, even more helpfully, collaborators. What was magical about Harvard was its whiff of limitless possibility. Identification with a society of living and thinking New England dynastic actors gave a security and assurance prompting freedom of action which I do not think anywhere else in America then offered. Wide worlds were open; past history implemented a ready present which might be mine to master.

I was eager to drive a fast quadriga. In particular, I still wanted to become a portrait painter. The Fogg Museum's Tuscan tempera panels, as well as the art historians who taught the process for gesso or fresco, prodded my puerile draftsman-ship onward, while turning me on to "modern art." Backed by the functional services of the Fogg, a couple of classmates and I founded the Harvard Society for Contemporary Art, today credited as a forerunner of Manhattan's Museum of Modern Art. John Sargent was gone, yet portraiture survived locally in the amiable hands of Charles Hopkinson, whose solid likenesses hang in the White House and in every Harvard Club across the country, while Augustus John, a popular British practi-tioner, had recently completed (after a dashing image of Tallulah Bankhead) the head and body of a present governor of Massachusetts. Alvin T. Fuller, though, honored art by scissoring out his head, disliking its body, in honorable tradition rejecting an advance-guard.

I also helped edit the *Hound & Horn*, a quarterly devoted to letters and art—it lasted three years in Cambridge, four more in New York. Not exactly incidentally, there were also classes to attend, absorbing and not onerous. There was John Livingstone Lowes's Coleridge: The Road to Xanadu, Irving Babbitt's Rousseau & Romanticism, Leonard Opdycke's Jesuit Architecture. Informally auditing Alfred North Whitehead's Modern Metaphysics, I could not comprehend more than the echoes of his soothing voice, but vaguely felt obligated to try to put my abstract notions in some order. His daughter, de-spite a trying tic (a constant, automatic tearfulness), was the delightful host to young philosophers and inquisitive tyros like myself.

The book from which I drew most discipline and delight while at Harvard was Professor Charles H. Grandgent's trans-lation of the *Divine Comedy*. He wrote in a 1913 introduction to the tome:

This work, the first annotated edition of the Italian text published in America, is intended primarily for the general literary public, although adapted also to academic use. I have aimed to make it so complete that readers will need, for the comprehension of the poem, no other book save their dictionary . . . I have endeavored, by discarding a vast accumulation of interesting but unnecessary erudition, so to curtail the annotation that the reader's attention shall not be constantly distracted from the text.

Grandgent was a paragon of allusive clarity. His lectures, which I attended as a freshman, had fewer absentees than any others I recall. The sonority of spoken Italian overflowed into a visual intensity that offered novel dimensions to Botticelli's damaged panel of Savonarola sermonizing, which Edward Forbes had given the Fogg. I stuck to Dante's text with slavish attention, partly to test my own wan seriousness, but also savoring the resonances which its print projected. I knew a little French, less German. Italian gave voice to an operatic transmission as luminous as stained glass. I interlined the *Inferno* through all thirty-four cantos from:

> Nel mezzo del cammin di nostra vita
> > (*Dante was 35 yrs. old; Florentine polit. sit.*)
> mi ritrovai per una selva oscura,
> > (*to be taken as autobiog. He, coming to*
> > *his senses? or self-knowledge?*)
> che la diritta via era smarrita.
> > (*from evil dread to truth? Consciousness?*)

all the way to:

> salimmo sù, el primo e io secondo,
> > (*mounting upwards, one after another,*
> > *the other?*)
> tanto ch'i' vidi de le cose belle
> che porta 'l ciel, per un pertugio tondo.

(aperture, round hole?)

E quindi uscimmo a riveder le stelle.

(we came forth to see-again; re-behold?
the stars?)

Neither *Purgatory* nor *Paradise* would ever command such solicitude, but what I gained from Grandgent was for me the most, and best, a conservative academy might award.

In an equivalence to the attention I spent on portraiture, "modern art," and editing "arts & letters," there were other, extracurricular engagements. I besieged a picturesque province whose walls and turrets were defended by prototypical paladins. Centered on Boston's Beacon Hill, their reign reached to suburbs studded by houses whose holders were still known as Adams, Cabot, Emerson, Forbes, Hallowell, Holmes, Lowell, Shaw, Sturgis. And there were historiated enclaves north and west of Beacon Hill or Brattle Street—Pride's Crossing, Manchester, Annisquam, Nahant, Milton, Concord, Lexington, and south to Cape Cod and Naushon Island. These bailiwicks were populated by role models at whom I marveled from a distance with little expectation of fraternizing.

I cast myself as an adventurer, though I was one without much of a passport. But *Hound & Horn* and the Harvard Society for Contemporary Art gave tentative admittance to a map of Xanadu, which I interpreted also as an overture to an ongoing epic. Contrariwise, at the moment when joining oneself to modernism (African art, Picasso, Joyce, Stravinsky) was obligatory, my private exemplars were shelved in a secret library. I mirrored myself as Balzac's Lucien de Rubempré, Bulwer-Lytton's Pelham, most definitely Disraeli's Coningsby. I wrote an (unpublished) novel entitled *Choice of Weapons*, which limned the perplexities of a dandified cipher who "couldn't-make-up-his-mind." Should he try to become a diplomat like Harold Nicolson, who'd been kind to me, or a poet like Conrad Aiken or Jack Wheelwright, or a painter like Augustus John? Charles Hopkinson's studio was just down my street.

It was more diverting than reading or writing fiction to slip from a picturesque but as yet unreal present into a remote but still neighborly past. I easily saw myself in the class of 1859, when the heirs of New England abolitionists would, within months, engage their Virginian peers at Antietam or Chancellorsville. Due to my parental provenance, I lacked anything more than a self-signed safe-conduct to probe those parapets. However, Jack Wheelwright on the one hand, and on the other someone I chanced to meet at the start of my sophomore year, cleared all hurdles away.

Waiting my turn at our annual physical exam in a musty basement of the big old gym, I was standing in line half-naked, impatient, bored. Those names ending in K—Kelleher, Kelley, Kent, King, Kinnicut, Kirstein—were followed by L's. Surrendering to common irritation, as if to share some mutual malaise at the tiresome delay, the lost K, I turned around and glanced at the broad bare chest, and then the face, of the first L. A youth of arresting stance, close-cropped fair hair and a big chin, he exuded a wide breadth of ruddy, muscular command. We exchanged tritenesses and lapsed into indeterminate silence. He turned away; then a few moments later I heard him ask if I'd chosen a roommate for the coming year. Neither of us wanted to return to freshman dorms. I'd engaged to be alone, leasing an attic in an old house, 32 Hawthorne Street. It presently lodged Monsieur Léonce LeMaître, an exchange professor from Paris's École des Beaux-Arts, teaching now at the Architectural School. I planned to re-paper a small bedroom and larger living room with the same black-and-silver *art déco* designs with which he'd already covered his dining room. The big boy in line ahead of me seemed unaccountably sympathetic. With a surge of pure, animal attraction I heard myself (with some other person's voice) say: "I've got a place. Would you like to look at it?" He faced me, hard, for seconds, and said: "Sure." I told him I was Lincoln Kirstein, we shook hands, and he replied: "I'm Frank Lowell." Family and friends always called him Frankie. His legal patronymic was Francis Cabot Lowell, and he was a nephew of Abbott Lawrence Lowell, president of Harvard, Guy Lowell, who had built the Boston Museum, Perceval Lowell, who discovered the "canals" on Mars, and Amy Lowell, poetic *Imagiste* and friend to Ezra Pound.

Thus I came to bask in a most delectable season. I no longer lacked a passport; by the middle of that year my name was listed with the mother of every debutante in Boston for coming-out balls at Hotel Somerset or Copley Plaza. One breathless April night I drove back to Hawthorne Street from the Somerset's ballroom to change my waltz-sweaty black tie for a white one (with tails); then I went back again in a tux which had not yet dried out to fill the remainder of a cotillion card.

Next June, Frank Lowell and I split quite amicably. When he decided not to spend junior year with me I blamed myself. I knew he hated my borrowing his razor or toothbrush, my tipsy, absentminded rumbling upstairs long after he'd been in bed. And he was by no means enchanted with the social landscape into which he'd been born. He was a steady, single-minded puritan: no nonsense or waste motion.

However, by the time we parted I'd been bounteously adopted by his father, mother, and two sisters. They bestowed upon me the unadulterated balm which I had failed to purloin from Frank. Fred Lowell, his father, was tall, rigorously made, with a spry, bony diffidence, always silently apologizing for shyness. He was excessively modest about his works, flagrantly outsize watercolors, detailed enlargements of specific flower blossoms. Their fresh, sharp luminosity, respect for particulars of shape and tint, and their transparency of seamless brush stroke seemed to me far superior to the abstractions of Georgia O'Keeffe. But he had no interest in exhibiting, nor much in other painting. He was fantastically prolific, laboring non-stop in a shut studio, to which I was only rarely admitted. When I operated the Harvard Society for Contemporary Art, Mr. Lowell was offered a one-man show, but he would not contribute, even to group exhibitions.

He spoke seldom, but glowed, always in mute contrast to

his wife, an exquisitely aging, *carte de visite* replica of Louisa May Alcott or Emily Dickinson. Her rippling loquacity, jolly homespun tolerance, and sagacious wit were shaded by an aching concern for Frank's younger brother, who, remaining at home, had lost track of who or where he was. As I saw less of Frank, I spent more time with his sisters. Alice was not tall but fair, her hair cropped; she might have been Frank's twin. Marianna was a Minervan brunette. The two sisters had a charming parlor trick: they sang duets, a trace short of professional skill—Elizabethan or Restoration madrigals and catches, Byrd and Gibbons. They inherited their father's wariness of performing in public, but on many private evenings, apparently without rehearsal, they sang together with an intimate, mother-of-pearl cadence.

Their house was a large, hip-roofed castle of comfort, shingled in the Eighties, with a wide inglenook clad with Morris and De Morgan tiles. Upstairs, in a large, airy balcony suite, Grandfather Shaw was at work—a dear, very old, healthily perfect gentleman. He devoted retirement to publication and patient re-editing of an album of ingenious knots, all delineated with the elaborate precision of Leonardo. He did not mind being watched and permitted me to play with lengths of thick silk cord which, twisted, coiled, turned, and finally knotted, could be wrought into knot-archetypes fit for imitation. And there were clipper-ship models under bell-glass, marine mementoes of whalebone or narwhal tusks made by Salem 1812 prisoners of war. Two others, inhabiting an adjoining parallel existence more as companions than servants, were seldom visible. On their Sunday days-off, Paul and Marthe Schmitz left delicious light Swiss suppers of cheese fondues, melon balls, raw spinach, walnuts, and cocoa.

In heedless bewitchment, I dreamed of marrying Alice or Marianna: preferably both. Thereby, I'd become Frankie's brother (skip the "in-law" . . .). I'd learned to ride, after a fashion, at my sister's husband's farm, and, by dint of practice whenever I found a way, I advanced to elementary exercises in classic dressage. In nearby Concord there was a stable with passive or livelier horses for hire. Semi-feudal chores let us wait on odorous, happy beasts: wiping them down after hard rides; currycombing; soaping leather; heaving oats and hay. Alice and Marianna were amazons. We rode daylong safaris over a wide terrain on well-worn trails or paths, across field and pasture, through heavy woods. We dismounted on the edge of Walden Pond to toss stones into a cairn already heaping to Thoreau's memory. In Lexington there was a cottage upon whose small window panes Nathaniel Hawthorne had scratched both his and his wife's names. In its parlor was a long, oak, skeletal laying-out couch, upon which the architect Jack Ames relaxed. Beside him were piled plans for his new Smith College dormitories. He gave us tea, while the horses cropped grass on a front lawn which had not been mown since Hawthorne's day.

In addition to Lowell weekends, there were others with tribal linkage. In Milton, Mr. Cameron Forbes's front lawn was a full-sized, close-mown polo field. His long, narrow dining room had one wall pierced by a breast-high aperture through which his favorite ponies stuck their heads to be sugared by coveys of young girls whom "Uncle Cam" considered prize fillies. He had governed the Philippine Islands after the Spanish-American War; now his rooms were paneled in mahogany, jacaranda, teak, and over a red-granite fireplace shone a map of his former governance in noble metals, with Manila marked by a diamond.

As I risk conjuring all this up, the quatrain of my Harvard years reads as an Edenic golden age. Yet, even while I savored every gilded moment up to its hilt, there lodged in me a vaporous botheration. I came to dread the "life" I'd been living as a fictive veneer upon which I had no true claim and I was eventually driven to mean-spirited, total repudiation of it. After I came to Manhattan in 1931, I never saw Concord or Lexington again and I only encountered the Lowells as a family once more. It was ten years later, at an intermission between the acts of Gian-Carlo Menotti's first operas, *The Medium* and *The Tele-*

phone, which I produced. Mr. Lowell had died during my senior year; Alice was back from Budapest after work with Dr. Sándor Ferenczi, Freud's follower; Marianna was married to Jacques Barzun, esteemed Columbia professor of English Literature; Frank had launched splendid service as a surgeon and medical administrator. We stood in the theater lobby with little to say. How to justify or explain churlish guilt, with my overmastering compulsion to be rid of it all?

I'd been hypnotized by a false position, which I'd not dared define and had then coolly tossed away. My obligation to a competitive past had become so smothering that I could not requite it without seeming to forgo any viable present or future. Thus I wrenched myself loose from a beautiful trap. Twenty years on, I tried to apologize to Marianna Barzun. We met, by no prior plan, at a dinner on Brooklyn Heights. The atmosphere of the surround in which a stricken Roebling had watched the construction of his great bridge evoked for me the world of Grandfather Shaw's braided knots. Trying to evade a gush of shame and sorrow, I quit the dinner table, compounding my ferocious sadness with trivial discourtesy.

"Hound & Horn,"

Cambridge

1927–1931

HOUND & HORN, the literary and "artistic" quarterly funded by my father, which Varian Fry and I started in our sophomore year, has gradually accumulated posthumous kudos, which was scarcely predictable at its demise in 1934. Since then, it has elicited academic dissertations, references in a dozen biographies, and a collection of letters glossing its career. Its origins were various and not lacking in presumption.

Varian Fry, co-founder, had rooms above me in Gore Hall, our freshman dormitory overlooking the Charles River. Its opulent architecture was borrowed from Christopher Wren's red-brick, Corinthian addition to Hampton Court. We ourselves strove manfully to borrow from Britain's literary tradition, which still seemed not past, but electrically present. Varian and I shared a similar conditioning, while differing vastly in details of habit. He was already a fair classical scholar with working knowledge of Greek and Latin, a good pianist, with old-fashioned courtly manners of a sardonic twist. He felt his cerebration superior to that of his classmates. Of this I was less certain, but I found him sympathetic, although I was wary of his covert disdain. That he gave me cause to question my assurance was one of the advantages in our relationship, which also had its cozy, personal side, but it did not prevent us from breaking up eventually, when he decided he'd had enough of my vacillation and lack of firm alliance. While he could boast of hardened maturity, I was a role-playing devotee of Oscar Wilde, whom I honored as a martyr more worthy of recognition by the Church he finally hoped would forgive him than about nine-tenths of the saints whom the popes in their political savvy had seen fit to canonize. And with Wilde's mandate, I was still trying on masks, wondering which one might best fit. I was not exactly "affected," or fancy, but I was very fanciful, and, besides editor, my several disguises included the amateur athlete, the polo player, the fencer, the boxer, the painter, the diplomat, the novelist, and the poet. I wanted to *do* so many things that I had absolutely no notion of what I wanted to *be*.

When I confessed to Varian that I was auditing Professor Whitehead's course in metaphysics, he asserted that modern (and most past) philosophy was nothing but epistemology, a method for grounding of accidental biographical data without relevance to humane behavior and offering no clue to action. I judged him an "intellectual," which I was not. He called me an aesthetic hedonist, implying that he could improve both my conscience and consciousness. I was willing to let him have a go. As for the aroma from "The Lads," he was not seduced as I had been, holding in lodged disdain their mindless games.

The background against which we launched our project we cautiously considered. *The Harvard Advocate*, a passive monthly, had long served undergraduate ambitions. At first, we hoped to gain seats on its editorial board, infiltrating, then controlling. Two of my freshman contributions had been accepted and printed with no opposition. One was a ridiculous parody of Philip Hale's weekly program notes for the Boston Symphony Orchestra under Pierre Monteux. Entitled "The Complete Whifflepink," it purported to be a life of one unresurrectible eighteenth-century Italian composer. The other was an extended poem, "March from the Ruins of Athens," lyricizing Boston's current decadence metrically, in helplessly wastelanded cadence and quotation. However, Varian's tart antagonism and my own strident "modernism" made it plain that we'd never win the *Advocate*.

Before World War I, *The Harvard Monthly* had made its name beyond Cambridge. In it appeared early effusions from Conrad Aiken, Eliot himself, and others of their generation who would become well-known after war had killed the magazine. *The Dial*, supremely well-edited by Marianne Moore, was rumored to be on its last legs. International in scope, with letters from abroad, reproductions of contemporary painting and sculpture, and a roster of the best writers of its time, it offered one possible criterion. But in my final term at the Berkshire School, a teacher had handed me a copy of a clearly printed review from England entitled *The Criterion*. As soon as Fry and I started sketching tables of contents, that magazine immediately became our reference point. Its editor was Thomas Stearns Eliot, Harvard, 1911. Volume I, Number 1 contained an essay "On Dullness" by George Saintsbury, the scenario for a novel by F. M. Dostoevski, an essay on *Tristram and Isolt* by T. Sturge Moore, and some long and wildly eccentric verses by its editor. Neither Varian Fry nor myself knew its roots in *The Golden Bough* and *From Ritual to Romance*, nor the author's dedication to Ezra Pound, "*il miglior fabbro*," expressing gratitude to "my more of a master (than me)," which was added later.

"The Waste Land" read as a tantalizing acrostic, a glowing diadem of riddles, unexplained, and for months inexplicable. Yet it burst on us as a revelation, magically fitting Varian's and my idiosyncratic lexicon, and protecting us from a petrified past and a tangled present, like a well-tailored Savile Row suit. The poem became our breviary. Put to memory, our shavings, showerings, eating, drinking, sleeping, and waking were studded with quotes from its quotations, each one cosmically apt.

Since Marianne Moore's *The Dial* was apparently about to collapse, we had vague hopes of capturing its cachet and its audience. However, I also wanted to rival and surpass *The Advocate*, which specialized in the archeology of Harvard's inheritance. We announced ourselves at first as a "Harvard Miscellany," and I baited an early issue with the football memoirs of an alumnus who had scored famously against Yale.

This sort of compromise infuriated Varian Fry, further convincing him that he was dandling mediocrity on his lap. I entrusted him with "ideas," and chose "prose" as well as "poetry" as my own territory. Also, I assumed control of visual aspects: typography and illustrations. I then admired the painter Rockwell Kent as a draftsman and latter-day William Blake, and dared write him a quasi-begging letter, aping freshman innocence, asking him to design a cover and vignettes to fill up our half-empty pages. I offered him "whatever he'd want" to accommodate our infancy. He obliged handsomely, making decorations for us at what he called "children's prices"—we could send him $100, he said. (I estimate this as $800 today.) We paid. Varian established the tone and style. Our title came from early Pound: " 'Tis the white stag Fame we're hunting; / Bid the world's hounds come to horn."

Varian snatched a tag from Plato as well, enjoining "excellence," which was printed in original Greek. (I could not read it myself, but I insisted on an arrogance of erudition.) Below, he subjoined musical notation, a theme from Brahms's "hunting-horn" trio (Op. 40), which we'd heard at a soirée at Mrs. Kingsley "Queensley" Porter's. There, the *horn* part had been voiced on a viola, making no difference to anyone, except to Varian's ears. *The Harvard Crimson*, an inimical rival from now on, greeted us: "Let Mr. Joyce rejoice; let Mr. Pound resound / With the safe arrival of 'Horn & Hound.' "

Throughout our time of publication, unlettered sports fanciers sent in unsolicited advertisements for geldings, dachshunds, Airedales. Both the *New York Times* and the *Herald Tribune* ran welcoming editorials, charmed by our young-gentlemanly Greek or musical epigraphs, which were interpreted as genteel evidence that we were off on the right road. These editorials had a healthy effect on my father; they were free advertising, although, as yet, what had we to sell?

Due to Varian's sage caution, in the spring of 1927 we decided to spend cash on a "trial issue" about half the size of what we later hoped to publish—this was to be my passport for the summer, which would admit me to the cenacle of Eliot in London and Pound in Paris. Or so I hoped. I had accepted a short poem from an unattractive boy upon whom I misplaced pity. His dismal lines were set in type partly because Varian had not stopped me. Their triteness spoiled the rest of the "trial" (for me) and were eliminated from our eventual Volume I, Number 1, though this gained me a lifelong paranoid enemy who would pop up in the oddest places and times with murder in his heart. This first excision was but the start of the string of precipitate choices I would make in acceptance or rejection, resulting in my developing a low shrewdness in explanatory evasion. This trial issue also contained "The History of the Miraculous Suspension and Levitation of the Immovable Button," a quasi-surrealist allegory by Howard Doughty, which could be read as a pro- or anti-Anglican (or Roman Catholic) fable. It was headed by two incomprehensible quotations. Eliot's unfamiliar quotes infected us all:

The world germ, or seed, was an almond.

More glad than *Wax* of cost
Doth mark at Candlemas
The passion of the Host.

The most considerable contribution was "The Decline of Architecture" by Henry-Russell Hitchcock, who, with Philip Johnson, would herald the "International Style" from the newly founded Museum of Modern Art. There were also "Passages" from *The Journal of Henry Marston*, an imaginary literary critic, by Newton Arvin, who in the next years would write good biographies of Hawthorne and Melville. We reproduced a fine crayon portrait of John Brooks Wheelwright by Maurice Grosser, an able landscape-painter, critic, and for the next half-century companion to Virgil Thomson. Maurice had also painted a clad, black male model echoing Manet's *Olympia*. We reproduced this as a shocker, but it didn't shock. I dared to insert my own "Between the Bells," a damp, lyrical, reminiscent *adieu* to Berkshire School days.

A copy of the trial (or *"Advance,"* as imprinted) issue was dispatched to Mr. Eliot. And indeed, when I was in London in the summer, armed with introductory letters, he was extraordinarily kind, later sending us his "Triumphal March" and magisterial criticism. Varian Fry and I crusaded for his prompt appointment to the Charles Eliot Norton Professorship of Poetry, though he was only honored by this exalted chair nearly a decade later.

Varian should have his version too—this is from an anniversary edition of the *Advocate* printed in 1934:

As I remember it, you and I decided to publish a magazine—a Harvard magazine—because we thought the *Advocate* was very, very bad indeed. It was so schoolboyish, and we were so self-consciously aware of Not Being Schoolboys Any Longer . . . We thought Harvard deserved a magazine like the *Monthly* . . . We believed neither of us could ever make the *Advocate* board; it seemed so much more a club in those days than a magazine. I suspect that in this we were rationalizing an ambition to make a sensation, but at that time the social obstacle seemed very real to us.

And so we thought we'd publish a magazine of our own. Our early ideas, worked over the winter of 1926–27, were very simple. In fact, I am sure that we began thinking of it as a *multigraphed* publication: though the notion was soon abandoned in favor of laid paper, Caslon Old-Style type, and deckle-edged cover-stock . . . But we never, in those cold winter days on the Charles, lost sight of the fact that it was to be a *Harvard* magazine, "A Harvard Miscellany."

Fortunately, our first regular issue improved considerably over the "Advance." Richard Blackmur contributed a heavily serious essay on Eliot accompanied by a first bibliography, complete to that date, by Varian Fry. Dick later wrote earnest critiques of e. e. cummings, Wallace Stevens, and Ezra Pound, as well as many book reviews, all of a mature manner which belied any lack of academic accreditation, a fact which seldom bothered anyone else but continued to plague him, until he turned into a severe scholiast in his own right. Roger Sessions, then on his way to becoming a dean of American music, gave us a note on Igor Stravinsky's Latin oratorio, *Oedipus Rex*, which had recently received its local premiere under Koussevitzky.

Our second volume, Fall 1928, opened with "Fugue," a beautiful story by Seán O'Faoláin, among the best followers of Joyce. He was teaching at Boston College, a first-rate Jesuit school, and where he was also editing a book of Celtic lyrics. He credited us as launching him beyond Cork University, though in the next years one watched with dismay while Harvard's English faculty let slip through its kid gloves O'Faoláin, Conrad Aiken, Newton Arvin, Theodore Spencer, and S. Foster Damon, the pioneer American Blake scholar and essayist for *Hound & Horn* on Melville and *Ulysses*. Ted Spencer was also denied tenure at Harvard, but after a stint at Cambridge, England, he returned and helped me to define the noun "morality," which until then I had thought meant only "puritanical."

In the spring of 1929, Dick Blackmur and Bernard Bandler III, joined Fry and myself as full-time editors. Blackmur was still employed at the Dunster House Bookshop, in close contact with English and French publications, though still, agonizingly, without the fluency in Sanskrit that he craved. As I wandered off, occupied with organizing Harvard's Society for Contemporary Art or to faery islets on Naushon or in Manhattan, Dick held our fort. Bandler had recently graduated and was now working toward a Ph.D. in philosophy. His mind was so febrile, fluent, capacious, that after a first interrogatory conversation, testing each other's temperatures, I felt mentally exhausted. When I dared to fish for his unstated yet profound aim, he was not hesitant: "I wish to be a modern Aristotle." (Many years later, I received a similar answer from a mind much more genially diverse: Wystan Auden told me he'd like to be a minor atlantic Goethe—though when he put this into verse in his elegy for Louis MacNeice, he was careful to add the words "if possible.") To *Hound & Horn*, Bandler contributed dense essays on W. C. Brownell, Charles du Bos, Irving Babbitt. He might have acted as priest or rabbi, but in the end became a psychiatrist. Then he resigned from *Hound & Horn*, fully occupied with study and teaching. Varian Fry took a dislike to his high-octane cerebration, then himself resigned around 1931.

Jim Agee had been a couple of years behind me at Phillips Exeter. I wrote later that it was there we met; we did not, but based an enduring friendship on identical memories and tastes there emboldened. Now he was living in Smith Hall. In 1929 we printed "Anne Garner," his earliest substantial poem, and I reviewed his first collected verse, *Permit Me Voyage*, for the *New Republic*. He was the most gifted undergraduate in my time, as far as poetry went. A few years later, when I was trying to commission libretti for ballets which might be used by Balanchine, Jim offered a "Bombs in the Ice-Box" scenario. Influenced by early Auden, it was not very funny.

Anyway, I would not miss Bandler's titanic lucubrations, since I was now joined by two men whose tastes confirmed my own hardening preferences: A. Hyatt Mayor and Francis Fergusson were together at the American Laboratory Theater, which operated in New York as an exile's offshoot of Moscow's Art Theater. Neither of them academics, both were infused with sophisticated, professional attitudes about qualities of the imagination. Both also wrote easily, with charm and a lightly held appetite for innovation. Hyatt Mayor was already a confirmed classical scholar with experience exploring Greece and Italy, and his essay on "Translation" is a fine short survey. He became a longtime, much-admired curator of graphic art at the Metropolitan Museum, his solid monument a definitive *Prints & People: A Social History of Printed Pictures* (1971).

Writers attached to Eliot's *Criterion* began to accept us as younger siblings, while we dredged far and wide in college faculties here and abroad. After two years, each issue contained at least 168 pages, advertising increased, we began to lose slightly less money, and we printed eight halftone reproductions in each number. We discovered Walker Evans as well, and soon documentary photographs began to supplant book illustration in my pictorial gloss on history, formerly stocked by Maxfield Parrish, Arthur Rackham, and Edmond Dulac. I introduced Walker to Jack Wheelwright and we three toured Boston and its suburbs documenting an heroic age of Federal and Victorian buildings, many now on the verge of collapse. Walker became our perambulating chauffeur and was my first trusted tutor in a postgraduate curriculum when we moved to Manhattan.

As for any intentions toward my ambition as a portrait painter, Walker Evans administered one more *coup de grâce*. I had struggled with my own "phiz" as a stationary model, but because my unattainable ideals were Dürer, Holbein, Corneille de Lyon, Ingres, and Degas, I couldn't advance far. Walker's camera clicked and—*presto!*—I became a *cap-à-pied* look-alike for Jimmy Cagney or T. E. Lawrence. I searched the 57th Street galleries for emerging portrait painters but never found any comparable to Man Ray, Berenice Abbott, or George Platt Lynes.

Hound & Horn cost worry, hard labor, money, but there was still enough left over for Harvard's Society for Contemporary Art. There was also a continent to explore, peopled by those who would have absolutely no connection with either fledgling organization. My reputation for energy amused some neighbors, making it easier to arrive at contact, and, as well, to make new acquaintances who, sooner or later, were drawn into the ambience of *Hound & Horn*, perhaps surprising themselves and certainly delighting me.

In a fine Federal house on Chestnut Street, Beacon Hill, lived Edward Motley Pickman, with his wife, Hester. He was of the clan of John Lothrop Motley, historian of *The Rise of the Dutch Republic*. Ted Pickman was at work on a recondite study of early Christian theology, yet not a Roman Catholic, as his wife was. I was puzzled over preoccupation with a layered faith by one devoid of mysticism but his particular talents lay in a cool, broad fascination with the form which cyclical ideas took.

Hester Pickman was beautiful, a woman straight from Edith Wharton's last novels. For *Hound & Horn*, she made the purest metrical translations of Rilke that I've read. Her brother, Teddy, a youth of my age, was a product of Nadia Boulanger's circle of American composers transferred to Paris, along with Aaron Copland and Virgil Thomson. Teddy Chanler was already writing art songs, and would follow Philip Hale as music critic for the *Boston Herald*. We would endlessly discuss a future ballet repertory, one libretto of which was based on Carl Van Vechten's *The Tattooed Countess*. No note was ever written, but it served to fill my imaginary opera house before I ever worked in one.

Hester and Teddy's mother was Margaret Chanler, Mrs. "Winty" Chanler, who sprang from an illustrious background and whose memoirs, *A Roman Spring*, are among their era's most evocative. I had read many reminiscences of my admired elder figures; Mrs. Chanler was the first with whom I had actually spoken. Her characteristic grandeur and noble authority were magical, yet silencing. She'd seen so much, known so much, that one listened with no feeling of necessity about trying to interest her in oneself. Doyenne of an ancestral domain in the Geneseo Valley of Upper New York State, she commanded a clan comparable to the Brahmin aristocracy in Boston. A devout Roman Catholic, she left on a lamp stand by my bed the large-paper, privately printed first edition of *Mont-Saint-Michel and Chartres* when I visited Teddy. A *dédicace* was in its author's script: "To my sister in Christ—from Henry Adams."

Mrs. Chanler was the first to speak to me as if she realized that Jesus was a Jew; she made no distinction between the Hebrew teacher and Christ. I was impressed by the transparent quality of her faith, which bore a seasoned strength as if she might have known Him, even in His majesty. Her religion differed from that of Jack Wheelwright, who considered himself an Anglican, and whose religion appeared to me remote, bookish, the result of translation. Something of Mrs. Chanler's credence stuck with me, and was there later, when I needed it.

Sunday mornings, she had Mass celebrated in her big, wide-windowed parlor with its pale floor covered in thin straw matting. Seamless, faintly scented, it was a virginal place, as if untrodden by any male boots. A priest was dispatched from a nearby parish as celebrant; he seemed as far from County Clare as I from Rochester, New York. Lightly, Mrs. Chanler forgave us both; for his accent and my heresy, while Father Healy took me for Teddy's brother, blessing us both, with no denial from his mother.

One of her grooms improved my saddle-seat. He moved me inches forward, deprived me of stirrups, braced my knees tight against my mount and stopped my fumbling with reins. A mild mare tumbled me over fallen logs to harmless failures and a few accidentally clean jumps. Shortly before World War II, my mother gave me another horse, a splendid sixteen-hand gelding named Clovis (after the hero of Saki's *Chronicles of Clovis*). He was stabled at my sister's farm in Ashfield and I enjoyed him briefly before I joined the army in 1943, at which time Clovis joined a Boston police troop.

At Mrs. Chanler's, too, I first brushed against crime. There resided in a large, nearby farm a self-styled stock breeder calling himself Tony Ridolfi. His was no mansion, but rather a glorified stable, its stalls extending into an attached dependency, part cottage and part palace. He gave rumbustious parties, more liquored than fed. This was the era of Volstead's Prohibition Act, and it was no secret that Tony Ridolfi was a bootlegger. Teddy Chanler and I were enthralled by gangs of guests shipped up from New York in dashing motorcades. Tony's main room, bordered by separate stalls for his favorites, was enriched by glistening gilt-plastered cornices which appeared rakishly in-appropriate—in fact, the entire establishment had an uncouth air of arrogant unreality, peppery and provocative. In an unreal eyeful, I watched men (with women) frazzled drunk. There were scenes suitable for cinema. I'd read tabloid reports of

"The Real McCoy," a legendary offshore pirate; we were reliably informed that Tony Ridolfi was a key henchman to this Robin Hood-type gangster. Prior to this, I had only had glimpses of extra-legality, mostly in newspapers; here—with the probable connivance of the state police—laws were shamelessly flouted. The concept that crime was real and highly organized, possessing a heraldic panoply of its own, dangled the prospect of another freehold for exploration.

Jack Wheelwright told me, as if I had not granted sufficient virtue to their essence, that, for him, knowing Ted and Hester Pickman were at-home on Chestnut Street made Boston preferable to London, Paris, Florence, or New York. I agreed, until I transferred to Manhattan. Edward Pickman was a personage of stalwart delight, erudition, and glow, and there wafted about him cool breezes of magnetic likability. A movement proposing him to head Harvard gathered force at President Lowell's retirement. Thereupon, with all the pent-up fury of his self-incinerated fist, John Jay Chapman, a Chanler relation, threatened to circularize Harvard's whole alumni body, informing them that Ted Pickman's wife was born a Roman Catholic, and would deliver their Alma Mater to the Vatican. I don't think Ted minded much; he was not interested in administration; the Middle Ages and music meant more to him than manipulation and delegation. Igor and Vera Stravinsky were married at the Pickmans' Bedford farm, and I particularly remember a ceremony in Boston's Symphony Hall, celebrating half a century of the Orchestra's foundation. Edward Pickman, with his anonymous, muted dignity, led the trustees to a large, carpet-covered table set on-stage. When all were seated, he rose to memorialize the event, with faintly sardonic, entirely apt graciousness.

Loomis, Marrakesh,

Fontainebleau

1927

WHO WAS LOOMIS? He was the first influential personal enigma I encountered. I met him on my first visit to New Haven when I was an infantile fifteen, he a manlike twenty-one—six years my senior, when such discrepancies are significant. I was still at Berkshire; he'd graduated from Yale. Usually, it was athletes I idealized. Prone to hero worship, I revered brawn, not brain. Payson Loomis breathed only mind. He displayed no exterior aura, yet incarnated a cerebral, even a moral, self-sufficiency. I judged that he knew just what he wished from life, since his reticence spelled wisdom, the distillation of some extremity I'd never known. He was accustomed to think as an analytical exercise; what one might call "metaphysics" occupied his waking hours. Coolness and remoteness distanced him from my unmodulated enthusiasms, and from the instinctive, elementary greed of most young men I knew. I made it my business to know Loomis as well as I might.

He was neither supercilious nor epicene; his sorcery for me lay in the concrete ordinary, his use of everyday happenings as research into a typology of normalcy. No mindless incident of daily existence failed to demonstrate some significance in his measured analysis of the fabulous rationale of habit or coincidence. Layers of meaning accrued in the way one brushed one's teeth, had one's hair cut, changed one's socks, washed one's hands. These were all digested by Loomis in persistent, questioning exercise.

The common kitchen garden of what was granted by God required daily maintenance; technique for teeth or nails lurked behind habit. He could invest any choice of a shirt or tie (if indeed it transpired that these existed—a question for another day . . .) with lucid significance. He had long since vowed to "save time" by avoiding all color in clothes save black and white. When I figured that he'd accumulated roughly two-and-three-quarter hours a year by such economy, he smiled gravely and asked me if I'd read Rainer Maria Rilke's *Notebooks of Malte Laurids Brigge*. I had not. Well, Rilke's bland young Dane had kept a time bank; at the end of twelve months he found he had no notion of how to spend his unused minutes. Loomis had read "everything," particularly in comparative religion, which I'd not touched: the Gitas, Gilgamesh, the Apocrypha, the Koran, Confucius, and Madame Blavatsky, whom he particularly defended. I'd heard she was a fraud. For him, she'd brought to the West priceless wisdom—texts from a sequestered Orient. I felt an anchored resistance to our Testaments, Old or New. They were, to me, dead origins for vindictive ordering, useful only for Sunday "chapel"; otherwise cruel, benighted. Loomis cited biblical sources and books which might make me doubt, or shiver.

What did he look like?

To be art-historically precise, his was the skull-structure of a Ptolemaic diorite portrait, carved in Alexandria in the first century after Jesus. This was the portrait of an atavistic ancestor, now placed, as I had seen, in the final supplementary room of the British Museum's re-arranged ground-floor galleries. His skin was thin parchment stretched over steel; fullness in the lips denied deprivation of the sensual. Sandy hair, cut close but not cropped. His flesh had a dull blush, a dusty rosiness, not too "pink," but with an unemphatic bloom of perfect health. It was an immaculate freshness without any priggish puritanism. A single adjective would do: "clean"—yet this was forest freshness, nothing scrubbed or hygienic. All this fused in an extra air of superior normality, a level of being which elevated the ordinary into the exotic.

Loomis's magic for me was the distillation of indefinable openings. I admired and was drawn to him; I don't think I admitted, even to myself, that I loved him. His self-sufficiency, dignity—yes; but his "integrity" was not warming. Being as young as I was when we first met, physicality, enthusiasm, expenditure of mindless muscle were gross magnets. Loomis had overcome all that. Indeed, if he'd ever been prone to anything similar, he was now out on another side. Elementary hedonism was to him a waste. His principle was purpose; his aim, a conscious matter of perfectibility. He didn't lack "a sense of humor" but his fun was objective irony, a firm presupposition that nothing under his purview was as it might first appear, and generally was the opposite. His prompt suspicion of every phenomenon that loosely presented itself was that most men and their makings were inadequate or corrupt, harmful, and absurd. This pitted him against his fellows, some of whom seemed ready to curry disdain, as if to be noticed by him were in itself a compliment. When it became clear that his lack of friendly attention was indeed basic, reaction could turn to astonished resentment.

His endemic doubt, his putting every incident to the question, was not cynical. Who was this accidental "*he*" to judge chance, mischance, justice, injustice, cruelty, violence, greed, vanity—all the cold winds of a world? Accepting its horror and terror never robbed him of curiosity or appetite; he breathed moral extremity.

Where did he come from; how did he get his stern way? His family supposedly owned woodlands in Oregon. I never met any of them. He'd graduated from Yale with honors in Russian and Arabic, a parrot's gift for vocables. His friends, those few I met, were a pale confraternity of White Russian exiles, disinherited heirs of Tsarist officials who had found havens at Harvard, Yale, Dartmouth. I assumed he aimed at diplomacy; he fulfilled my notion of one of the second-secretary cubs at a Near-Eastern mission sketched by Harold Nicolson in *Some People*. Actually, nothing interested him less. Since Loomis reduced all toil, and most labor, to basic self-determining work, whether it was the technique of medicine, law, or banking, he agreed that diplomacy was the craft of lying for one's country against equally deceptive allies or adversaries. Politics, national or international, was a gull's game. He was no patriot. His territory, he told me, was the planetary cosmos. After my attraction to him had somewhat run its course, I found myself agreeing with the verdict of a far more mature mentor, my friend Muriel Draper: Payson was a stoppered vial, containing precious elixir, fermented pomegranate juice or carbonated spring water, but the flow had been arrested, leaving a disquieting residue of frustrated disappointment.

Payson's occupation with Arabic and Russian, however fortuitous it seemed at the start, led to a rational crisis in his life, with an influential cross-current in mine. A couple of years after Yale, Loomis was hired as an amanuensis for the Grand Duchess Marie of Russia, who was then engaged on what would prove to be her very popular memoirs. Here he was not merely recounting a reconstruction of history. He was experiencing closely the courts of Alexander III, Nicholas II and Rasputin, events from 1905 to 1918, all through a participant eyewitness. She may have been only a shrewd operator of determined survival, but she was charming to me when Payson asked me to tea. She did not speak of her past, and she treated Loomis as if he were a secretary or courier. She had a high style of authority; I was impressed. In regard to Russia, my inclinations were Bolshevik; near my sister's farm in Ashfield, Massachusetts, dwelt William Christian Bullitt, ambassador to both France and the Soviet Union. He had married Louise Bryant, widow of Jack Reed, a Harvard graduate, the flashy journalist of *Ten*

Days That Shook the World. My father had been friends with Lincoln Steffens, the famous muck-raker, who was with Reed in Moscow during Lenin's October.

Loomis was abjectly anti-Bolshevik, deeply sympathetic to the Romanov catastrophe. His interpretation of events caused me such confusion that I seriously imagined he'd fallen in love with the Grand Duchess, or, if not, that he was perpetrating a preposterous joke. In Loomis's analysis of an historical disaster which I glossed from the traditions of American Liberal Socialism, Rasputin was not the bestial fiend from Pokrovskoye, nor was he a *rasputnik*, a libertine, but a Siberian shaman, learned in the powerful active beliefs of Ural-Atlantic tribesmen which contained useful methods for the control or cure of disease, nervous or organic. Witness his effect, by telegraphic or telepathic means, over Alexei, the hemophiliac Tsarevitch. For Payson (perhaps through information from the Grand Duchess), Rasputin was a *starets*, a pilgrim, a holy man of God, who renounced our ordinary world and behaved free of the customary habits of customary, automatic existence. Dostoevski in *The Brothers Karamazov* defines the *starets*: "He seizes your essence, your being into his essence, into his being. Choosing your *starets*, you abdicate from your own will, and offer it to him in abject fealty and with total self-denial." And why must so drastic a sacrifice be made? Because, says Dostoevsky, "after a life-term of absolute obedience, one may (and this is of course quite conditional) gain absolute freedom, liberty from the hampering, the smothering, the devilish: *Self*."

What were the roots of Loomis's idiosyncrasy and recalcitrance? Was his information true knowledge or the caprice of a prepotent conscience? How could he tell me so much of what I needed to know, and yet leave me dangling whenever I questioned his sources? How had he come to be so absorbed in the negation of everything? Why did the ultimates of life and death torment him in such pressing proportions? Increasingly, I came to judge my actions in the terms he might have judged them. But how could a few vacations in Morocco with a man called Abd el-Kad'r, contact with dukes of the High Atlas, or with exiled Russians, add up to so formidable a position?

It was only later that I learned his pressure on me, the presence of his person, wholly proved, yet partly withheld, resulted from the instruction from an exterior agency. This was an exercise in the manipulation of power, under whose rule he moved in service, possibly to others as much as to himself. My attraction to him, psychic or intellectual, rendered me an easy mark, for in those of his areas which I found most curious I gained absolutely no information.

One day in 1927 during my New York Easter vacation, in the Oak Room bar of the Plaza Hotel, a suitable tapestry against which to gauge one's civilized existence, Payson handed me a paperbound book. Paperbound books were usually containers of French poetry, like *Les Poésies de A. O. Barnabooth* by Valery Larbaud, which Loomis had given me, and which I relished and dutifully imitated. Larbaud, at the start of this century, was a first laureate of urban commercial luxury—the Waldorf-Astoria, Savoy, Ritz. He was a devotee of cityscapes, big department stores, steamships, and historical paintings dusty on walls of provincial Latin-American city halls. Larbaud's notice of the exotic boredom of the close-at-hand turned these scenes into golden nostalgic vapors.

Some hours after I'd left Loomis at the Plaza and was seated in a parlor car on the way back to Boston, I took a look at his paperback. I discovered, with considerable astonishment, that it was by no means more verse in the manner of Larbaud. It was a pornographic novel entitled *Up and At 'Em* by one U. P. Standing. It narrated the adventures of an American marine all over the Orient, following the Boxer Rebellion of 1900. Today it might read primly; at the time, it delivered the disturbing shock and jolt which efficient works of its genre hope to provide, but which an experience of corresponding actuality rapidly dilutes. I swallowed *Up and At 'Em* in one gulp. It produced the intended effect, after which I felt empty and placid enough to relax and ponder the meaning of Payson's gift.

Before this exchange, Loomis and I never touched remotely on the subject of sex, as either physiology or obscenity. Now this provocation seemed enormous; I felt raped. What was he trying to say? Was he teasing? As for his donation of *Up and At 'Em*, it would be naïve to say, in terms of today's post-Freudian semiotics, that here was suppressed desire to "make love" *to* me. In light of what transpired, it seems that Loomis was trying to "make love" *with* me, but whatever the nature of this operation, the means used were vague. As for sex, Loomis never turned me on. As far as his own predilections went, I know he never had a man. In his fierce cold manner, he was a blind womanizer, and, as if condemned to a need he could not exhaust, his lack of passion was but concomitant with his omnivorous distrust. As for me, I've never been troubled about "the body," except to admire it in others. Emotionally, or rather romantically, I enjoyed guiltless liaisons with both girls and boys. I could be called confused, and to a degree this was true, but I had not yet arrived at a crisis in my development where it seemed mandatory to make a choice. From my earliest boarding schools, I slept with whomever I liked or whoever liked me, with no guilt, resentment, or fear—elements which have constantly haunted me about money. Naturally, sexual preference and appetite is endless food for gossip. For me, aged twenty, adult sexual behavior was an uncharted landscape, paths leading to which always commenced and ended with my father and mother in bed, somehow getting me.

At the close of my sophomore year, the specimen number of the magazine *Hound & Horn* had been launched, more or less successfully. I took cautious pride in it as one initial accomplishment and showed it to Loomis when we met again in late May, shortly before I was to leave for my trip to Europe, where I hoped to interest Eliot and Pound in the magazine. Loomis was hardly enthusiastic. For him, our quarterly was but the predictable result of Harvard's genteel deformations. Why should we have troubled so much over tasteful printing, nice paper, charming vignettes by Rockwell Kent? For whom was this dwarf-elegance provided? To what necessity did it correspond? Was there a single piece in our initial issue which might not have been printed somewhere else? As for my own poem about term-end at boarding school, although I had dared to print it after he'd read it in manuscript and judged it the best of what I'd shown him, nothing was said.

His dismissal of my editorial ambitions was blunt; I knew I must not betray disappointment or irritation. He'd become my moral physician; his diagnosis was fair, although I cringed at his opinion of blanket inadequacy. His clinical tone of disparagement was iodine on a cut. His authority, his concrete, objective disinterest, together with his continuing sense of responsibility for my development, made me finally accept his summation. He smiled and, as if to make it more impressively mandatory, spoke with emphasis: "Now that you're so pleased with yourself, I'll expect you in Paris by June 13th. Here's my address. It's Fontainebleau, not Paris, but they're close. Wire me your arrival. I'll find you a room. Plan one free week. And here's how you'll meet Abd el-Kad'r in Marrakesh."

The abruptness of his suggestion, or proposal, whatever it was—challenge or command—left me in a nervous tumult. Courage and will were twisted and locked. It was as if I were in a rocking chair swung between positive and negative determinations. Was this a test, like his gift of the randy American marine, or was it to challenge my own weak and unstable impulses? I took what he said seriously, partly out of confusion, partly because I was flattered that he thought my destiny held interest.

There was also "the material question." How ever was I to get to Paris, or Fontainebleau, or wherever Payson indicated, this side of Morocco? My father had given me an allowance; this hardly included an expensive couple of months of travel away from my chosen path. I had explained a need to speak with Pound and Eliot—Father had already paid for *Hound &*

Horn as my passport and he agreed that now I ought to use it. So here I was, running off to Marrakesh and Paris, three months before the first official issue of *Hound & Horn* was to appear, leaving my colleagues to get the damn thing past the printers.

These considerations were overcome by the insistence of Loomis's titillation. No one else I'd met had taken a more profound interest in my psyche; I felt trust and obligation. I chose to think that my faith in Loomis, which extended into that shady area which, so far, he had not cared to explain, was inevitable and inexorable.

In the final issue of *Hound & Horn* (July–September 1934), we printed an anonymous translation (by Payson Loomis) of a portion of Andrei Biely's great cinematic novel *Saint Petersburg* as well "Twelve Surats of the Holy Quran," signed by Abu-Ali George Khairallah and Payson Walker Loomis. A note prefaced their dozen laconic, severe epitomes:

Over and above the syntactical difficulties always present in the making of a literal and at the same time intelligible translation from any language into any other, unrelated language, there is also in the case of Arabic and English a peculiar difficulty arising from a difference, as between the Arabic- and English-speaking peoples, in the current usage of the current respective vocabularies, as inherited. In the Arabic there is much less of a gap between vernacular and the language of literature. Of the Holy Quran in particular it may be said that it determined the Arabic language as now spoken, and that its language is the language of everyday life, and vice versa. If, then, it be possible to preserve in translation any portion of the force and extreme beauty of the Arabic original, this must be conveyed *insofar as possible* in the language of everyday speech, for the Holy Quran is a popular book, and that is an integral part of its force and beauty.

To me, at this time, the Old Testament and the New were at best pretexts for handsome illustrations by Giotto, Michelangelo, William Blake, or Gustave Doré. Now, the Koran, through Loomis's lectures, in spite of being an unfocused narrative, assumed powerful echoes of marvelous Arabian Nights. Later, in the Fifties, when I was consumed with admiration for the metaphysics, art, architecture, and poetry of Islam, I came again upon these versions and, after memorizing parts of the Koran itself, I felt that Payson (with his friend George Khairallah) had made incomparable renderings. I regret most in the few disappointments I had concerning Loomis, that he abandoned a full translation. He introduced me, via the Maghreb, to a peek at Islam.

Thus it was that, through his instruction and introductions, I was in Marrakesh in early summer 1927, for my first experience of gunfire, my first visit to a brothel with teenage whores, and a first, glancing touch of the "Orient." And through the agency of Loomis's local friend, it was a revelation that almost amounted to a conversion. However, a sense of the ridiculous is a useful demon, so when I went for an initial lesson toward instruction, the mullah, a wise man, tolerant and kindly, defused the romantic longings of an Israelite from Rochester, New York. He advised return to that faith into which I'd been born. But I had no faith in that or any other, and craved solace from ignorance and anxiety. I felt that the testimony built into the magnificence of the fifteenth-century Governor's Palace was enough to prove the majesty of a God who must be merciful and compassionate, who would forgive me, a Jew, for unbelief.

The day before, I had been taken by my Berber guide, whose name, Abd el-Kad'r, was really a Moroccan version of John Smith, to hear a professional storyteller in the great souk. A crowd surrounded a fellow who had as accompaniment a very young boy with a silver flute. In a lovely voice, he intoned words in metrical paragraphs, the sense of which was hidden from me. His audience stood around in rapt attention. The silvery flute-song floated over a smoky cloud of cinnamon and ginger incense from market stalls. I was lost in an Arabian night; when I asked my guide (who spoke excellent French) what it was all about, he replied: "*Il raconte l'histoire de Sinbad le matelot.*"

The mullah, to whom I'd been sent, gave me sage counsel.
Religious aspirations of youth are deceptive; the prestige of
myths as substitutes for sex are scarcely true hunger. Later on
the same day that I had seen the storyteller, Abd el-Kad'r had
taken me to a whorehouse, where I performed without talent.
It was he whom I desired, not the horrid little twelve-year-old
she-kittens who were pushed at me. One of these sank her
blackened, sharply filed teeth into my calf when I pushed her
off. Abd el-Kad'r was sorry I could not enjoy myself. He had
recently another client who refused such pleasure, and (as a
result? he wondered) died of a stroke at the casino that very
night!

The mullah told me: You are a Jew. If there is gold in
your purse, spend it. If, in the end, you come, without fear, to
the essence of Allah, it is well. It is not easy for a Jew, or indeed
a Christian, to accept submission to Order, five times a day, on
your knees, beside fellows whom your own father would have
warned you against. Go in peace; it's likely you'll turn to Christ
before you ever take the Haj. Thus it happened. My own path
toward peace was to push, however perilously, toward the
Eucharist. When at Mass, I, repeating the Lord's Prayer,
sometimes also say Payson's sura "Of the Dawn" (al-Falaq:
CXIII):

> I take refuge in the Lord of Dawn
> From the evil of His creatures
> And from the evil of utter darkness if it fall
> And from the evil of the underminers of the covenants
> And from the evil of the envier if he envy.

So, on the indicated day—July 13, 1927—I met up with
Loomis in Paris. He guided me to a small hotel on the place de
l'Odéon. My room was without a bath; it held a big brass bed,
an oak *garderobe*, an ebony wash-stand with china pitcher, and
a bowl painted with tulips and poppies. The curtains were dusty
red velour; there was coarse lace across the double windows,

an oval gilt mirror, and a framed lithograph of the Odéon theater that stood across the *place*. The room was perfect of its period; I pictured myself as Balzac's Rastignac, come, fresh from the provinces, to conquer a world.

Payson took me for a walk in the Luxembourg Gardens. He spoke of Rémy de Gourmont and Paul Valéry. When I brought up Valery Larbaud, Loomis announced he was through with him—nostalgia, after all, was no subject matter to support the grand-scale. "Charm? Yes, but, after all, is it *charm* we need now?" I sensed this as disloyal and ungrateful: Larbaud had meant so much to both of us. Payson's coolness chilled me with its small treachery. So far, everything had been sunny with us; suddenly I had a bleak slant of doubt, and not only in the qualitative values of my current opinions (taken mostly from him). Might I also, in my turn, be repudiated? Maybe he was not the loyal moralist I had come to depend on. *Be on guard.* We progressed through the gardens, now mottled by huge clouds breasting toward dusk, in silence. The circus of children playing, their nannies in casual attendance and people populating the trim paths, were sufficient to distract me. Then Loomis demanded: "Why are you here?"

His tone was not hostile; his brevity, disarming. I knew it was not enough to counter with "Because you asked me." My arrival, pat upon a date he'd set, called for a modicum of self-explanation. I could use neither Pound in Paris nor Eliot in London, twin monumental pretexts, as vindication. These were too slight to weigh against the gravity of possibility which had somehow landed me here, chained as it were to Loomis. An inexplicable element, undefined, as yet undefinable, was in play. So I was able to answer with a personal question, fending off his, in a style which I defensively stole from his own mystery. I was after *his* secret: "What in the world are *you* finding to do here?"

He answered as if he was relieved, and had been waiting for a chance to respond to my question. What was he doing here? He was studying. Ah, of course: languages, since he already had French, Russian, with some Arabic. No, not languages. Then, of what was he a student? Dancing. Dancing? Born with an enormous predilection for "The Dance," I had had an unappeased curiosity since early childhood for "The Ballet." I was surprised that Loomis, whom I'd not suspected had any interest in theater, was thus occupying himself. Wasn't he much too old to become a dancer? He had no wish to become a professional. He stated he was involved in dancing rather than "The Dance." Subjects that moved him were to be read *without* quotation marks. "The Essence?" Yes: an essence.

I had long welcomed his grace of presence. Now, his anonymous elegance was framed in the verdure of the Luxembourg Gardens, a mannerly background of Gallic "good taste." Flower beds, hedges, cropped trees, and neatly bordered paths proclaimed civil propriety, an ingrained attention to public habit. The Luxembourg corresponded to a level of accustomed necessity, no equal to which I could recall in America. To be sure, there were Public Gardens in Boston with tatty swan boats. Central Park was a genial, faceless wilderness. Here, though, gardeners were public servants, honest workmen, like good cabinet makers. Here one walked through a winelike richness of open air. A rush of consciousness led me to breach my customary formal hindrance. I asked, straight out, who was teaching him "dancing."

There was no answer; maybe he'd not heard my question. I felt rashness reproved. With him, there were limits not to be passed, yet these applied to my attitude toward him, more than to any antagonism he'd taken. Now he asked if I had money enough for the next week. Money was no problem. I couldn't buy any pictures I might fancy, but survival was not in question. Then what *were* my summer plans? I hoped to reach Eliot in London by September. I'd like to wander through Spain. I'd just bought Willumsen's big two-volume monograph on El Greco. I was planning my senior year's dissertation on El Greco and there was his "lost" *Mary Magdalene* from the English College at Valladolid. It would be fun to try to find it.

"Sounds exciting!" Loomis mocked. "However, I think first you better come to Fontainebleau." Fontainebleau? "Yes, it's not far." Fontainebleau—"You mean the palace?" Having taken Leonard Opdycke's survey of French Renaissance architecture, I knew the palace fairly well. Five years before, my mother had led my younger brother and me on an intensive exploration of the châteaux of Touraine. Fontainebleau, one of the most sumptuous royal residences, is a sequence of fine courtyards surrounded by splendid buildings. These include the famous yard of the Cheval Blanc, or, more poignantly, *Les Adieux*, where in 1814 Napoleon bade farewell to his Old Guard. There was the Cour Ovale, the Cour Henri IV, a smaller Cour des Princes. The Salle des Fêtes, in the palace proper, is the grandest sixteenth-century interior in France.

Payson took such guidebook erudition for granted and curtly cut me short. He said firmly: "Not the palace. The Prieuré." Such was my introduction to a grand country mansion once known as Le Prieuré des Basses Loges. Perhaps Françoise d'Aubigné, Marquise de Maintenon, second wife of Louis XIV, nicknamed a comfortable rural retreat the Priory, just as Catherine the Great called her vast palace the Hermitage. La Maintenon was a teacher; in 1686, she founded the École de St. Cyr, an academy for worthy girls which the Sun King endowed with funds from the Royal Abbey of St. Denis. Her term at Le Prieuré is forgotten, but historically it prefaced Gurdjieff's teaching, and before Madame de Maintenon held state there, a religious foundation had existed from medieval times. Here were first produced Racine's great dramas *Esther* and *Athalie*, written for its pupils. Le Nôtre designed grounds set out as formal gardens facing the château's front, with its more than two hundred acres bordering the forest at the back.

Recently, this property had settled on the widow of Maître Labori, who had it from the family of Captain Dreyfus in payment for Labori's masterful defense in the trials of the great *affaire*. Currently, it housed the Institute for the Harmonious Development of Man, directed by a personage known as Georgei

Ivanovitch Gurdjieff, who had owned it since October 1922, roughly five years before my visit.

This Gurdjieff it was who'd been teaching Payson to dance. Often, when one asked Gurdjieff who he was, or what he did, he'd answer: "I am a teacher of dancing." Similarly, when journalists asked Diaghilev what he did, he'd answer: "I arrange the lights." The King of Spain, a protector of the Ballets Russes, once required of the impresario his exact function, and the reply was: "Like you, Sire, I am indispensable." Diaghilev, encountering Gurdjieff, when reputation gathered around his "dances," suggested these be presented as a "novelty" animating one of his Ballets Russes seasons. Gurdjieff declined. In 1915, Diaghilev tried to persuade Stravinsky to compose a ballet for Léonide Massine, his stripling choreographer, entitled *La Liturgie*, exploiting the gorgeous ritual of Russia's Orthodox Church. Stravinsky, a communicant, refused, saying the Eucharist is sacrament, not spectacle.

The château of Le Prieuré had endured many transformations from its once-princely condition, but still held its modest air of stateliness in faded grandeur. Three storeys were built long, broad, and low. Two large chimneys with a cluster of multiple flues symmetrically enclosed slate roofs like solid bookends. A ground floor contained a large drawing room, which, when last decorated, under the First Empire, had acquired the stoic smartness of Percier and Fontaine. Attached was a cozy salon and library. On the second floor, Mr. Gurdjieff and his consort, or perhaps wife, Madame Ostrovsky, a noble Russian lady, had apartments. The corridor walls were adorned with lightly brushed murals by Alexander de Salzmann in the manner of the elder Tiepolo. Here also was a spacious guest bedroom known as "The Ritz." The attic floor harbored a range of bedrooms; in these old servants' quarters slept the younger male students. On my first night as Gurdjieff's guest, I was installed in "The Ritz." (This respectful treatment merely struck me as odd at the time, though afterward I sometimes suspected there had been a political, pecuniary motive behind it.)

I'd been invited to arrive on a Thursday, after supper. Loomis had taken me to dine at an inn on the outskirts of Avon, the neighboring village. He roughly indicated a weekend's schedule at the Institute, adding a summary sketch of its director, with something of the kind of work there undertaken. By now I was passive, definitely on the receiving end; it was no longer possible to press for information. Events transpired with an inevitable, gradual pace and I was glad to put myself under Loomis's stewardship. What was happening seemed charged before coming to climax; its meaning would doubtlessly be revealed in the fullness of time. (And Time, oddly enough, became an active dimension. I wore a wristwatch, and now conceived a notion that particular moments, clocked for example at 4:56, or 5:43, were trying to tell me something.) Loomis was intimately familiar with the local scene; it became clear he held a secretarial post, occupied with staff administration and translation. Free of any formal timetable, he could pass back and forth to Paris as he pleased.

In "The Ritz" I slept well. Payson woke me, waited while I shaved, led me down to a breakfast of classic coffee and croissant, with fresh butter and clover honey, milk from a cow and water from a spring. Other guests included a couple of prim, gray-haired, gray-clad English ladies, past middle age; a fair-haired German girl, matronly and formidable; and a blond American, solid as a draft horse and in his mid-thirties, whom I was drawn to immediately.

There were a number of other faces and bodies; these made no great impression. Loomis's introductions were formal; there was no curiosity as to my presence. After breakfast he showed me around the gardens. Paths adjoining the château were punctuated by generously heaped big rocks, some of which had holes three or four feet deep beside them. Evidently, a renovation, or redevelopment of landscaping was in train. Near the main house were settlements of smaller buildings, in the same style but built later. In a coarse addition to the mansion there were kitchens, servants' quarters, a large *orangerie* glazed with big panes of glass, and a garden-gazebo, or pavilion, known as Le Paradou, which seemed smaller than its actual size. This housed a big band of children, supervised by a guardian or house-mother—a different one from week to week. Loomis explained that *paradou* was an old French military term for a fortification which stops projectiles. His explanation hinted at much more, but by now I pretended to be as stolid as he in facing mystery, so held my peace.

On this initial tour, Payson guided me to a big building he named "The Study-House." Its vertebral skeleton came from a surplus World War I airplane hangar, obtained for its haulage from the French army. Although it covered a considerable tract, it had an unsettling flimsiness, as if it was made of cardboard that might collapse in a strong wind. Roof beams were supported by a double wall of rough lath stuffed with dry, dead forest leafage. Laths were plastered with chopped hay. A ceiling was laminated by tarred felt, in parts thick like fur. A glazed clerestory used the glass from old cucumber frames. Beneath ran a calligraphic cursive frieze, which might have been Arabic, but which resembled the "false" Kufic script of Renaissance pictures, which literally means nothing, but insinuates important secrets.

Loomis took pride in demonstrating each item of construction which had been begged, borrowed, or stolen from materials once in a former use. "The Study-House" was a monument of economy. Its floor was trodden earth, stamped hard and dry, proofed against dust with thick layers of oriental rugs which also draped the windows and walls. In the middle of one side was Mr. Gurdjieff's "Kosshah," or pavilion of honor, a big tentlike enclosure, heavily hung with striped Central-Asian textiles. A balcony hung above; the area was enclosed by a thin picket fence of white lath. Here the Director might survey whatever transpired in center-space. This hall was impressive; it appeared like an oriental circus tent rather than as dance-hall or ballroom. Some elements in it were hideous. Ugly industrial lamps with glaring, porcelain reflectors hung at crazy angles from high joists. One felt an uncomfortable insecurity, as if on the verge of collapse. It was all flagrantly impermanent, yet the scale was palatial, with fragments of atavistic architectural details. Carpentry and metalwork were rough, but there remained the fact of its stubborn completion. Every inch of wall was crammed with paint or decoration, a harsh patchwork, which irritated me in its lack of firm stoutness or tidiness. It strained toward theater, toward a preposterous impression, far more than toward any pretense at the quasi-religious. It was more exotic than in any way "authentic." But the most undeniable residue was its existential immediacy; the damn thing had somehow got itself built, from spare parts and hare-brained engineering. For whatever use it was intended, bad weather could be kept out; I viewed it empty, enigmatic, as if it mocked all ordinary objections.

Loomis took me past the garden area. At first, I judged the work at hand as the labor of civilians on vacation, puttering to avoid boredom. Parterres were being edged in brick, small bushes were being transplanted, but further observation revealed that the "students," whoever they were, seemed to be playing calisthenic games. Paths abruptly turning to nowhere were redirected to further dead-ends. The piles of sizable rocks or damp earth, with big holes beside them, seemed to be waiting to be filled. We were off on a short walk, past increasingly untidy acreage, toward the ancient forest visible beyond a high, unbreakable brick wall topped by broken bottles. I asked if he did not have pressing labor of his own, in which case I would amuse myself. His work today, he said, was to show me around; it would be inconvenient, even unwise, for me to venture alone. This was no answer, and I was left stewing with questions. His withholding or secrecy maddened me, and I began to feel contempt for the discipline involved in the equivocal logic of his mystery-making.

Abruptly, Loomis turned and started back to Le Prieuré, almost as if he were leaving me behind. As we passed small gangs of student-gardeners, I had an impression that, while a few were digging up small stones, more were just throwing heaps of rocks into holes neatly and deeply dug at their sides. Half-a-dozen men, of whom one was too old for his task, transferred heaps of used brick, which appeared to be rationed, each to a person, from the edge of one path across to another. We walked briskly. The day was bright, but there was an unreal air, as if all this activity was scheduled in reverse, illustrating my recent adventures, an Alice after she'd penetrated her looking glass. Here was the mirror-opposite of muscular labor, its aim the negation of construction. This inversion seemed so strong that I dared to rupture my impatient silence. What in the world, really, are all these people *doing*? "In this world," Payson answered, "all these people are working—on *themselves*."

It was now a few minutes before noon. My wristwatch read 11:12. We had arrived in front of the big house. Loomis said evenly: "Your taxi will be here presently." My taxi? Was I being sent back to Paris, my overnight bag still up in "The Ritz," all unshriven because of my bottomless stupidity? Not at all, Loomis replied. He had now to take dictation for three hours and during that time I would be driven into Fontainebleau, where I could inspect the park and palace. The taxi would return me to the Institute before dark. Then, there would be "The Bath." Bath? Then "The Dancing." Dancing? So I was bundled out of the grounds before murmuring protest or dismay, and, sure enough, a taxi was waiting. On the short drive, I had a chance to test my undergraduate French . . . The driver made it easy; he asked me how I liked *le patron*. "*Le patron?*"

"*Monsieur le patron; le chef, comment dire? Le Boss . . .*"

I could only answer: "*Je ne sais pas du tout . . .*" which was the whole truth. I didn't know what he was talking about. He repeated, as if to himself: "*Le contremaître; oui. Lui. Un très grand monsieur.*"

"*Contremaître?*" The word stuck until, later, I found a proper dictionary: "*Contremaître*, n. m. (fem: *contremaîtresse*): Overseer, foreman, forewoman. (Naut.) First-mate, boatswain's mate."

He dropped me at a café. I was about to pay and over-tip

him, since he'd been so *amical*, but Loomis had already arranged everything. Enjoying a delicious lunch at a nice table with a view of the palace pond and its ducks, I couldn't eat more than half of what was set before me. I was aroused by the unexplained, the unexpected; I felt poised on a brink of grand adventure and recalled Chief Hamilton, his "exercise," and the key word: "*work*."

So now, ten years later, in Fontainebleau, I renewed the urge attendant on another marvelous beginning and steeled myself against the disappointment which must, with the law of averages, inevitably come. I began to endure what psychiatry might term as an initial seizure of manic-depressive psychosis. From the recollections of Chief Hamilton, his unblemished splendor and my bright dewdrop glory of infantile innocence, I was suddenly plunged into an access of depression and began to have negative memories of Chief's sardonic, skeptical teasing. My being here, with or without Loomis, suddenly seemed preposterous. How ever might I be equal to the riddles of an Institute for the "Harmonious Development of Man"? What to do? Something near fright overtook me, and in my awed confusion I wondered for a moment whether Loomis was really a guide, an inquisitor, or a fraud. I was unprepared, inexperienced, and scared, as if facing a prison sentence for a crime which indeed I might have committed, but of a nature which I did not know. I thought of leaving and returning to Paris at once, where I could find friends, also on vacation. However, I'd left my small overnight bag at the château. In it was a new toothbrush, a new, expensive shaving brush and a book of poems with its dedication from Ezra Pound. I debated whether or not to accept their loss; Payson could send them on. I was not to be let off so easily. There was still the palace of François Premier. In one way or another, I hoped art might be an answer and a salvation.

It wasn't. The palace's grand hall, with its galaxy of flamboyant adornment by Rosso Fiorentino and his team of experts, seemed almost like a miniaturized Sistine Chapel, with sibyls and prophets reduced to gilt-and-plaster, nymphs and satyrs framing elaborate cartouches detailing the life of Alexander the Great. There was a smothering surfeit of teased-up, overblown design covering every corrugated surface with a surcharge of carving or color. The highly polished inlaid wood of the floor mirrored the intricate visual mathematics above in the coffered ceiling. The ballroom was long, narrow, extremely empty. Could it ever have been filled? There was much luxury but no grandeur; the overall effect was of nervous, wriggling busyness. The sequence of events meant nothing to me and I looked in my guidebook for help. This was nothing to do with the Macedonian Alexander that I'd been taught about. Instead, it was a Franco-Italian ballet, congeries of twisted effeminate bodies, extremely stylized and rather silly. The supreme virtuosity of its execution, the exorbitant largesse of a late Medicean patron, could not be ignored, but the entanglement of surfaces, the mechanical alteration from an incessant repetition of lozenges, broken curves, and diamond inserts was tiresome. How was my boredom to be equated with so painstaking a "work-of-art"? Was I qualified to be bored by so much ingenuity which had survived for four centuries? What good had art-appreciation courses done, if I was unable to enjoy, or absorb, such a monument? My life was in no way enhanced; my understanding of painting or sculpture, as it then was, was only stuffed, coarsened; my "taste," if that was what I had, gagged.

And now it was time to drive back to Loomis and the château. The taxi driver naturally wanted to know how I'd enjoyed the palace. What to say? I had a moment's impulse to spill out my indignation but this would only have involved further trials of translation. The ride back was not long enough for any words approaching truth, so I dismissed it all with: "*très joli.*"

When we arrived back at the Prieuré, I found its façade even more forbidding than I'd feared. There was a protective wall, extending in both directions out past the borders of the entrance. At this portal, which was apparently a back door, hung a bell with a sign reading SONNEZ FORT. I banged the bell. At a small window appeared a head. It was a man's face, of the most piercing, hideous malevolence, personifying a scowl, savage and hostile. That did it. Thanking God for this sign, I turned to take the cab to the station, and back to Paris. But the car had gone. The door opened; Loomis was there. "You are just in time," he said, sounding like the eulogy of an accident.

He steered me to "The Study House," indicating a spot where I might seat myself. This was on a pair of tufted saddlebags for horse or camel. I occasionally fancied myself an equestrian, as I have said, and I had done undergraduate research in horse furniture. I had toured the armories of Madrid and Vienna, and recognized my present enthronement as Central Asian—Bukhara or Kāshān. Confirming this attribution was music which began to sound: its pervasive sonority was "oriental." So, I assumed, must be the performance that was about to take place.

Two dozen people, an equal corps of men and women, clad in vaguely "oriental" pajamas, belted around their middles, were following patterns of movement with mortal seriousness. As for their audience, this consisted of Loomis and myself, with a few restless young children who in no way disturbed the proceedings. I was by now accustomed to theatricals. Yet what I beheld here had nothing in common with any movement I might have expected. Its general visual atmosphere was not precisely "oriental"; there was nothing pantomimic, exotic, or sensual. I began to realize it was governed by counts, that, instead of moving freely, the men and women were mutely counting. As soon as a first strangeness wore off, it also seemed unduly monotonous. Yet details of the intricate interplay made me begin to understand that the exercise was not for an audience, but for the performers themselves, who were obeying an ordering. This comprehended, after about ten minutes, the performance became far less tiresome. Puzzling it was, and curiously interesting to observe. I obviously had no choice but to sit on the saddlebags and try to understand, or at least endure it. At the end of half an hour I began to want to urinate, so, for the rest of the time I was seated, my focus was partly occupied by that simple, if growing, need. But I could hold my water, and interest in the dancers and their movements took over; I began to be almost glad I had gotten myself into this predicament. Now, in spite of myself, I began to see that the "dancing" exercises or patterns were becoming far more complex, and that, although still rather static, the sequence of hand signs and shifting steps was accentuated by a steady rhythm. Abruptly, penetrating music from a small hand-held harmonium accelerated. In one thunderous surge, the entire body of men and women went berserk, and racing, with a startling jump as from a catapult, the whole mass of bodies came hurtling straight at me. I was spared immediate annihilation only when a voice from the central pavilion yelled "STOP!" The amalgam of bodies froze.

It was no orderly arrest; the command "STOP!" had not been rehearsed. Some dancers stumbled and fell over; others were locked in accidental positions—asymmetrical, uncomfortable, awkward, ugly. After a few moments everyone resumed the ordinary habit of their motion. Straightening their pajama tops, they quietly sauntered out of the hall. I felt shaken by a demonstration which, however impersonal, was boastfully outrageous. What on earth was going on here? This was no very skilled performance to whose explanatory preparation I'd been treated in advance. However, the violent collective rush toward me, and the sourceless, shouted "STOP!" gave me a theatrical shudder to which no dance or drama that I had seen could compare. It seemed less of a game than a—what? An event? An inexplicable rite? A spectacle?

After the hall was cleared, Loomis led me around, pointing to the earth floor covered, he said, with sixty-seven carpets of various sizes. Banks of seats were tossed with, he explained, sixty-seven cushions, rugs, saddlebags. There were inscriptions in "oriental" script above the clerestory; much of its glass was streaked over with transparent colors. It was a big room—how large I had not realized until it was voided of human movement and lacked the pervasive squeakiness of the invisible hand-held harmonium. Now I felt no need to urinate.

Loomis led me back to the Prieuré; once inside, he none-theless indicated a lavatory. The relief I experienced was almost sexual delight. Loomis said I was, perhaps, tired and could rest a bit before "The Bath." The bath? In any case, he saw me back to "The Ritz." I found the pretty room; my small night bag was on a dresser. I shed my clothes, lay down on the bed, and fell into dreamless sleep.

When Loomis woke me it was dark. On the way to the bath-house, small lamps glowed, outlining the garden paths. The grounds appeared empty. We entered an amorphous structure, without windows. Inside, it was bright. This was a foyer; the floor, brick; rough wooden benches were ranged around the walls, and heaps of shirts and pants were folded, stacked neatly on a bench as if each had its accustomed burden. I was not enthusiastic about the notion of a public bath and remembered again how Uncle Martin Wolfe had thrown me into the heavily chlorinated Rochester Y.M.C.A. pool, and how I had sunk to the bottom in a paroxysm of fright. Soon enough I was hauled out that time, so hating my uncle that adrenaline was restored. Instinctively I had exploded in revenge. I retched, vomited, but suddenly felt in complete control. Death was not so bad. Instead of being grateful for a test manfully met, the somatic body told the developing brain: revenge is sweet. The better I felt, and I quickly recovered, the more conscious I became. First, pretending to faint, I held my breath, hoping he would think I had died. It worked. Uncle Mart was in terror almost as great as mine had been. My mother could not have believed her brother-in-law would have wished to drown me, but blackmail proposed itself. In any case, he was thoroughly disturbed, while for me the episode added to my fear of physical danger, which took years to fade. When I was taught to jump on horseback, and having been thrown off harmlessly and repeatedly, I succeeded in rolling back to some degree this hysterical apprehension.

Yet there still lurked some dim residue from this early trauma. I undressed, and with a rough but clean towel around me, entered the main steam room gingerly and apprehensively. The space was high, wide, and glaringly lit. Sweating pipes were exposed along the walls; there was rust and the room looked improvised with the same dizzy techniques of "The Study House." Yet much as I felt forewarned, the ambience was not unfriendly. It was reminiscent neither of a gymnasium nor of a hospital. I sat down on a stubby pine bench, and jumped up from its blistering heat. Then I viewed a monstrosity.

On a slate slab was stretched the raw body of an obese, dark-pink male, hairy and with his belly down. On either side of him stood two adult nudes. Between them, they supported a naked boy, maybe nine years old, who was jogged up and down on the lying man's spine. I was suddenly aware of Loomis; for some minutes I'd almost forgotten him. His presence restored some semblance of sanity to the tableau of torture before me. He inquired if I minded the heat. The *heat?* What in hell was going on here? He had noticed nothing at all unusual. I was appalled, but silent. Then Loomis suggested that, as long as the heat was supportable, I should go into the attached steam room. Masking shock and horror, although by this time I realized physical suffering was not engaged in the massage, and also to avoid further watching it, I let myself into a small, cloudy closet, where I endured the impact of boiling steam for less than fifteen seconds, and then stormed back out.

On the slate slab, the little boy was dancing a jig on his victim's backbone. There were no groans, no moans. I felt instead that the exercise was highly enjoyable. The grown-ups handling the masseur laughed as they pulled him up and down; the boy was pounding with glee. The gross and passive older body purred like a stroked tiger.

Payson showed me to a shower and handed me soap,

though by now I was too confused to bathe myself. He pointed to another slab. I took his hint and lay down. He lathered me with a harsh loofah-sponge, rough enough to scrub skin from bone. I turned over to let him have my back. He tossed a pail of ice water at me, then quit, leaving me to dry off with a yardage of rough gray cotton.

In the meantime, the body which had been pommeled by the child had raised itself and, facing my direction, proved not to be either as old or as fat as I had thought. But the man was no beauty with his Mongol features, moustaches of dank ferocity, balding, though with hairy epaulets and matted paunch. His face bore a startling resemblance to the malevolent mask behind the sign which read SONNEZ FORT. The face was impassive as he gave some orders in what I took to be Russian to the two men who had acted as aids in his spinal massage.

I found myself seated, with a delicious sense of absolute well-being, on the same pine bench which had scalded me previously. There were now a couple of layers of toweling under me. This change marked a transfer of fear to one of swelling, positive pleasure. On the bench beside me sat the fair-haired, youngish man I'd noticed at breakfast, drinking hot tea from a glass enclosed in a silver holder. He pointed at the small boy, tapped his tea glass, and soon I had my own, too sweet in spite of its quarter of a thick lemon. The man's physical bulk was so agreeable, the tea was so refreshing, our smiles were simultaneous; Loomis introduced us. He was Martin Benson, an American, and later I learned, a farmer. Payson withdrew. Benson asked what I did, why I'd come here. I told him I was a sophomore at Harvard and that Loomis had brought me. His response was such that I thought he'd never heard of Harvard. What was I studying? This was hard to answer honestly, after all my recent reactions.

Loomis now summoned me to another introduction. He led me across the room to where the heavyset Mongol, now clad in thick Turkish toweling, was sipping tea from his glass. I was still unclothed and shy. The man looked at me kindly and asked: "You? All right?" I nodded. He muttered something like "Good. Good," and stared me up and down. This was not simply clinical, but it raked me with the heartlessness of an X-ray. But, rather than being further alarmed, I felt a superior sympathy from him. There was no negation in his inspection and I felt no need to cringe. I had endured a good number of physical exams from serious illnesses in early youth, and hated the ceremony of medical inspection. No one before had granted me a visual survey so cool, dispassionate, or sympathetic. This all took half a minute. He said to Loomis: "You, let him dress."

While I was dressing, Loomis vanished. Next me, Martin Benson was putting on his own clothes. He asked how long I would be at the Prieuré. I didn't know. How long did I *want* to stay? I didn't know. Had I been asked an hour before, I would have said I'd be going as soon as possible. Now, I didn't know. How long might one stay? "Oh, long as you like." How long did I like? Benson grinned and suggested that if I stayed until tomorrow, I might care to work with him? Yes, very much. I felt solid happiness from his invitation; like a struck match, something flared. A surge of well-being, of which I'd had a faint touch before, rushed up from somewhere to overwhelm me. It was one of the last recurrences of those mystical moments which belong to the instinctive, cloudless miracles of childhood, as when I was first shown what notes printed on a page of music meant. Then I almost lost breath with a realization that at my eyes and fingertips was the whole process of making music. It was magic, not method, a gift of speech suddenly given, the end result perceived, with (I thought) no need of intervening effort to make it come true.

This blessing of limitless capacity I felt at Le Prieuré was not entirely identified with Martin Benson, although he magnetized and focused it. It was the summing-up of a whole chain of connected happenings, each charged with an importance which, while I could not fix it, assumed its premonitory meaning. Martin Benson also relieved me from the faintly oppressive shadow of Loomis. For the first time in a long while I felt unlocked from my dependence on him, as if shedding a coat too heavy for the weather. With Loomis, incidents and ideas were layered with an obligatory response: Yes, or No? With Benson, there was no obligation. I was guilelessly, vividly content, grateful to my cosmos for peril past and futures promised. I felt tears in my eyes, though I was not sure if this due to my gratitude to Great Nature, or to salt left over from the steam bath.

I watched Benson lean down to lace up his heavy boots. Their soles were scraped clean; near their tops, around the eyelets' metal rings, there were thin cakings of dried, yellowish mud. When fully dressed, Benson stood as a classic prototype of an American farmer, with the healthy, all-embracing goodness of family feasts on Thanksgiving. And in all Fontainebleau's shocks and surprises, it was Martin Benson for whom I gave most thanks. Out in fresh night air, the steamy dankness of the bath was washed away in summer's purity and swarming, starlit clouds. Loomis appeared again to pilot me to the château, where, in the main-floor salon, guests had gathered for a feast.

So far, I had barely differentiated the inhabitants of Le Prieuré, since I'd been assaulted by so many unfamiliarities. Now in the big, bright salon, there was a considerable adult population. The men and women quietly assembled were in no individual way remarkable, except perhaps in their collective expectation. Loomis made no effort at further introductions. Martin Benson, in a crisp blue work shirt, without a tie, winked reassurance. I was assigned to an Englishman named Metz, who made no particular impression then, but later would. There was Alexander de Salzmann, painter of the Tiepolesque murals in the corridor to "The Ritz." The two older English ladies and the blonde German girl, whom I'd seen at breakfast but none of whose names I'd caught, stood out in a company of thirty persons. Abruptly entered our host. Heavyset, impassively glowering with tiger-like moustachios crisply curled, Gurdjieff was oblivious to those gathered, who now became silent and motionless. Those previously seated stood up. He waved them back to their seats and greeted a few without individual favor. After a decent interval, Loomis again pushed me over toward him: "Mr. Gurdjieff, will you meet my friend . . ." Gurdjieff glanced at me, and remarked absently, "Friend. Yes. Very nice." He turned away; shortly after, everyone followed him into the dining room.

I can't recall now the exact order of that evening's events. Sixty-six years is a long time, and later there would be other evenings much like this first, but most important, one. It assumed elements of an initiation, and the following account can only fail to equal the lasting impression it made on me.

Mr. Gurdjieff sat himself at the middle of one side of his long, broad table covered with heavy white damask and a profusion of china and cutlery, opposite to which Loomis placed me. At first, Gurdjieff took little part in the meal, speaking only to Madame de Salzmann, who was on his right. Conversation was desultory. There was a separate, round table for the dozen children, usually fed by themselves in Le Paradou. The grown-ups, of whom I was youngest, did not, as one might have imagined, serve the table. The informal formality by which we progressed was waited on by three or four local French maids attached to the estate. There was nothing ordinary about the food.

The center of the board was covered over with a three-ring-circus parade of cold and hot hors d'oeuvres, like those that would be served in a first-class Franco-Russian restaurant. While I relished their diversity and texture, I was shy of helping myself. Martin Benson, who sat some way from me, filled a plate, got up, placed it before me. As far as I could tell, apart from freshly-cut *crudités*, there were interspersed bits of boiled tarpaulin, wax flowers, clippings of sponge or rubber, and glazed knots of rope, lightly varnished in blood. My alarm amused Metz, who sat beside me. As I picked gingerly at a patch of corrugated patent leather, he explained benevolently: "Jerked bear's meat." Not wishing to play the coward, I attacked the barbaric provender with relish. The Zakuski were provocatively delicious. Some hotly spiced, others saline, vinegary, or citron—so many, so much, that each could be counted as a meal. There were no tumblers for water, which I wanted. Wine poured, red and white; there were small brandy glasses at every place. Following the hors d'oeuvres, three large platters arrived; then additional, smaller ones. On the first were steamed carcasses, which I guessed must be suckling pigs. But no: they were baby lambs. Mr. Gurdjieff whetted a small sabre and sliced the meat professionally; full plates passed around. There was no mint jelly to go with lamb, as at my mother's. Instead, we were given a soup of thickened fresh mint. I was bothered by the bare sheep's skulls still attached to the rest of the roast. They were split down their centers, with the grey brains glistening, the eyes withered to black raisins. When everyone had been served, but none started to eat, Mr. Gurdjieff surveyed the company, and with a half-mocking benediction of grace, murmured: "Take. Eat."

There were also broad beans, green beans, *mange-touts*, stewed figs, rice, celeriac, braised endive, and yoghurt. Maids filled and refilled the goblets. A squat, brown bottle stood at every other seat. Mr. Gurdjieff was attentive only to Madame de Salzmann, a handsome woman of forty or more years, her hair firmly drawn back like a character's in a Chekhov play. Indeed, the whole scene might have been set under the direction of Stanislavsky for his Moscow Art Theater, including the elder English nannies and Martin Benson, his blue work shirt changed into the belted blouse of a *muzhik*. French was spoken, also Russian and some English. Apart from Benson, Loomis, and myself, there were no Americans. Metz spoke with an accent which had in it what I took as a trace of Cockney. I made good headway with the baby lamb, which was garlicky and bloody. Abruptly, I heard Mr. Gurdjieff say: "You, Little Father. Take."

"Little Father"? He actually was addressing me. I was surprised but more astonished, incredulous as to this particular salutation, when I saw a long, two-pronged serving fork threatening me, like twin rapiers, on the points of which were black raisins. I cautiously reached for it, murmuring thanks. My hesitancy galvanized a silenced room. Was everyone watching? Yes. My host, looking hard at me, said with a trace of urgency: "Now, eat." I swallowed the sheep's eyes, blinked, and survived. Gurdjieff smiled, turned to his companion, and forgot me. I looked around, hoping for approbation from Loomis, Metz, or Benson. The first two were blank; Martin raised a thumb in an encouraging salute. To a degree crushed, but also relieved, I was emboldened by Metz's question: "Nasty?" It wasn't so bad. "Oh, there's lots worse," he said cheerfully. I asked him, daring a bit: "Why did he call me 'Little Father'?"

Metz said: "Ask Loomis; he knows the lingo."

Perhaps, I reasoned, the name referred to the fact that I might have been taken for an amateur seminarian. I was a sedulous ape of Loomis's taste in clothes. My hair was short. I wore a black silk shirt, a black turtle-neck pullover, and black pants. But "Little Father," which later became Mr. Gurdjieff's greeting to me whenever I was to be teased or acknowledged, was simply a common Russian diminutive. "Little" meant nothing about size; I was a tall boy.

The feast concluded with a stupendous dessert, layers of crisp brown pastry saturated in honey and brandy, and sprinkled with nuts and raisins, topped with a whipped cream stiff as hard sauce, made from crème fraîche. Now brandy—Armagnac—began its infiltration. Mr. Gurdjieff, introducing expectant silence, proclaimed in English: "To all ordinary idiots." Everyone obediently raised a glass. Metz drained his; a woman seated nearby did not. Mr. Gurdjieff noticed this; winked at her. She bowed, smiled; took a sip. He winked again. She smiled again, leaving her glass firmly set down, and was not further reproved; this I interpreted as his passive courtesy. Armagnac burned my lips and throat, although its taste was delicious. I filled my mouth and swallowed. There were still dregs left in the bottom of the glass and Metz nudged me. I drained it.

Then a voice, loud, but not insistent, announced: "To all

zigzag idiots." This was loyally drunk and emptied. I don't remember how many toasts were proposed, how far Gurdjieff pursued his roster that night; round and square idiots were starters. As the toasts followed, glasses re-filled. Metz saw I emptied my share, as indicated. I sipped with increasing ease. I'd been drunk often enough in college, though never on brandy. In fact, in my first year at Harvard the boys I liked most were heavy drinkers, and bootleg alcohol had all the thrill and variety of uppers and downers. It was more or less de rigueur to prove that one could hold one's liquor with no unseemly show of looseness. One made up tests for oneself; and one of the worst falls I ever had off a horse was when I lost a bet to my roommate as to how much we could swallow and still operate.

But that had been a voluntary experiment; the amount of Armagnac consumed on this night in Fontainebleau was an exercise that had been commanded from the outside. I began to feel cosmic affection. It was either the fifth or sixth toast when Gurdjieff proclaimed: "To all compassionate idiots," and, looking straight at me, added, "and, incidentally, Monsieur, to you." I found I had drunk up my last drop and was left nothing with which I might respond. I lifted my glass, an empty gesture, and felt approximately adequate. In fact, I realized I felt absolutely marvelous. Toasts continued. From further acquaintance with this rite, I fancy we, or rather I, got as far as the seventh or eighth, maybe even up to a ninth, to "all blazing idiots." Now drunk, I was ready to be sick. Metz saved the day. He stood me up and suggested bed. I tried to navigate, but couldn't. Mr. Gurdjieff smiled at me kindly: "Sleep well, Little Father." Then Benson took over, guided me upstairs, and in "The Ritz" I fell on the bed. He took off shoes and socks, undid my belt. I was gone.

When I awoke, it was after dawn, yet hardly light. There was a thin blanket over me. I had a ferocious headache, a trying sense of failure and ineptness. Since I had so dim a recollection of the particulars of the night before, this sense of failure soon

welled up in guilt at what I might have done or undone. I felt
deserted. Benson, Loomis, and Metz must feel well rid of me.
A weak impulse was to get myself out of there as soon as I
could, but I didn't have enough energy to figure out how. I
had left my wristwatch somewhere, but midsummer daylight
creeping through the windows might have made it any time
between five-thirty and seven. What about breakfast? I'd de-
voured a mass of food, rich and strange, yet now I was hungry.
This focused my energy and, against all odds, I began to feel
a swarming euphoria, the only release for which would have
been hysterical laughter. It became clear, in one Jovian lightning
burst, that everything was absurd—the preposterousness of this
place, my being thrust in it, and the entire unimportance of
the circumstances which, from a colossal adventure, had collapsed into meaningless triviality. And yet . . . perhaps . . .
there was more.

Loomis opened the door, glanced down at me without a
word, passed into the adjoining bathroom. I heard water
running. I couldn't decide whether this was remonstrance or
pity. "Compassion." Those three syllables had stuck. Lying flat,
I watched him pick up my shirt, jacket, shoes, which had
distributed themselves over the floor. Loomis said I'd best bathe
fast because breakfast was ready, and then he went. I shaved,
washed in a daze, and wondered if I could find my way to food.
My shirt was soiled; in spite of my tepid bath (why hadn't
Loomis let it get hot?) I hardly felt spick or span.

In the half-filled salon, there was hot coffee, croissants,
fresh jellies, and fruit. Metz was seated next to the two English
ladies. I sat down by them. It was going to be a lovely day.
Metz was amused: "I bet you didn't sleep a wink." He knew I'd
been dead in bed. I felt badinage was not suitable for my
condition. If there was anything to the idea of logical accident,
or significant coincidence, why had I brought myself here?
There was, of course, the extreme possibility that the whole
adventure was no more than a picturesque fluke. On the other
hand, along with this growing revulsion there was a feeling that

the shock, my questionings, "STOP!", the steam bath, the toasts, and the systematic assaults on habitual response, might say something. Equating this sensation with the rankling problems it evoked, I felt free to ask Metz about idiots.

He laughed: "Oh, we're all idiots. That's his oldest joke. It takes people down. You're an idiot to get drunk; you're an idiot to be here. You're an idiot to be alive. The whole kit-and-caboodle is idiotic." Was this a cure for my naïveté, or a thrust for not figuring it out for myself? He was refusing to tell me secrets that I wouldn't understand if he did. Loomis appeared. While recently I'd discovered Benson and Metz, it was to Payson I owed a first allegiance, although now I felt he'd rather deserted me—or maybe I'd partly repudiated him. Metz withdrew. Loomis led me out into the garden. It was Sunday, not a working day. He was cool and distant as usual. Sooner or later I would be going back to Paris with a bundle of unanswered riddles. Now, everything seemed tied in a lurid, if undefined, mystery, which was also perhaps a reply to some unexpressed desire of mine. I knew there must be mysteries and that they were certainly too insistent to be solved by being refused, wished away, or submerged.

With a pause which seemed the appropriate preface to something which could not be coincidence (had he overheard my last question to Metz, I wondered), Loomis remarked: "As for the idiots, there's no problem." With magisterial coolness, in his slow, deliberate manner, Loomis explained that *idiot* derived from Greek *idios*—a private individual, a common man, a plebeian, a person without information or wisdom, a layman, a householder; hence, one not well-informed about great matters, uneducated, underdeveloped, a simple fellow, a clown, and so, by degrees of importance or unimportance, a self; thus, by scales which lexicons have developed, an idiot might also be defined as a sleepwalker, a psychopath, even a blathering *idiot*.

The day after Saturday night's feast was, for the Prieuré, a time for rest and relaxation. Some of the Russians would take an early train to Paris for service at the Russian Orthodox

Cathedral in rue Daru. I told Loomis that before leaving, I would very much like to thank my host for letting me come to his house; I'd greatly enjoyed myself. Loomis had made a firm appointment that afternoon for me to meet Ezra Pound, with whom I'd been corresponding on *Hound & Horn* business, and who had just printed a long poem by Payson in a small magazine which soon disappeared after its couple of issues.

I was taken into Mr. Gurdjieff's study. He was seated at a very large desk, which was piled with orderly papers. At the side was a small table with its typewriter—Loomis's place during his secretarial functions and his correction of the dictated manuscript which would, in time, be published as *Meetings with Remarkable Men*. Loomis stood to one side, permitting me to face Mr. Gurdjieff directly. The following account is synthetic, suggesting the tone of conversation rather than aspiring to verbatim accuracy.

G. So, Little Father, you go.

K. Mr. Gurdjieff, I want to thank you so very much for allowing me to come to the Prieuré.

G. Very nice. What you want?

K. I just want to thank you.

G. Mister, I ask you what you want.

K. (*nervously*) I just want . . .

LOOMIS. (*quietly*) What do you want to do, or *be* . . .

K. (*confused*) Now I have to get back to Paris . . .

G. Ah—important appointment.

K. Well, yes; it's important to *me*.

G. Important? How?

K. Loomis has arranged for me to meet a very great poet.

G. Oh—poet. Very important.

K. Well, at least, *I* think he is.

G. What kind poet?

K. Perhaps, actually, for the present our greatest living poet.

G. What language?

K. English, of course . . .

G. English, of course. Not Hungarian?

K. Hungarian? I can't read Hungarian . . .

G. Not read Hungarian. Too bad.

K. I mean to say: the greatest living poet in the English language.

G. What kind poem he write?

K. He writes *every* kind.

G. Every kind. He write sex-poems?

K. Sex-poems?

G. No. I mean fuck-poems.

K. No, Mr. Gurdjieff. It is Ezra Pound. He also writes wonderful translations. He has taught me a lot.

G. Ah. Translation. Already good. Maybe great. What language he translated?

K. From the Anglo-Saxon, Chinese. From the Greek. And Egyptian.

G. No Russian?

Loomis. I don't think Mr. Pound speaks Russian.

G. No speak, but read?

Loomis. He must read it in translation . . .

G. But he speak Anglo-Saxon, Chinese, Egyptian. Get him for me. I need good translator. I pay.

K. (*to the rescue*) His are *poetic* translations. He takes original texts and makes them more beautiful . . .

G. Ah—translator also magician. Takes text; makes more beautiful . . .

K. Mr. Gurdjieff, it's very hard to explain this in English.

G. But easy in Anglo-Saxon or Egyptian.

K. (*Realizes G. is unfair, but holds his tongue.*)

Loomis. Mr. Gurdjieff, he is talking about Ezra Pound's talent.

G. Yes, I know Ezra Pound very well—for long time. He likes my soup.

K. (*incredulous*) He likes your soup?

G. Very much he like my soup.

K. What sort of soup?

G. When you grow up I give recipe. Then *you* make soup.

K. (*deeply hurt*) Mr. Gurdjieff, I am sorry if I have offended you. I just wanted to thank you. I don't want to waste your time.

G. Little Father not offend. Not waste my time. You waste your time.

LOOMIS. Mr. Gurdjieff has known Ezra Pound for many years.

K. (*amazed, to Loomis*) You mean, he really *does*?

G. Really does. You know what Ezra Pound call my soup?

K. Not *really* . . .

G. You know painting?

K. (*modestly*) A little bit.

G. You know Rembrandt?

K. Of course.

G. Of course. You know Piero della Francesca?

K. (*back on his heels*) Yes, certainly . . .

G. Ezra Pound say my Persian-melon soup, compared to borscht, has tone of Piero della Francesca. You know borscht?

K. (*firmly*) I *like* borscht.

G. You like borscht. Pound say my melon soup is clean like Piero della Francesca, compare to shit-color Rembrandt. Now, what you want?

K. (*silenced*)

G. Mister. I tell you what you want. You want pay me.

K. Pay—you—for what?

G. Three things. One thing: Turkish bath. Two thing: Martin Benson. Three thing: eyes-of-sheep.

K. Pay? How much do you charge?

G. I not charge. Pay what you think worth.

K. I don't happen to have much money with me . . . I've got to get back to Paris, and it's Sunday and the banks are . . .

G. No need banks. Give me anything in your pocket. Loomis lend your ticket.

K. I've less than a hundred francs.

G. Oh. Less than hundred. Too bad. Better than nothing.

LOOMIS. I have plenty of money.

G. Loomis, lucky; he have money. Loomis wash hand with ticket. Now, *dear* Little Father. You go.

K. (*Dazed; hands over francs. Turns to go.*)

G. Wait.

K.   (*Looks pleadingly at Loomis.*)

G.   Mister. You wait. You come here. You curious. Very interesting. You have bath. You shock. You meet Benson. Nice man. Benson. Honest workman. You get good food. Very shock: food. Even you see, maybe: dance. STOP! All this—worth—something?

K.   I gave you all I have.

G.   Not yet.

K.   I will send you the rest, just tell me how much.

G.   You pay *now*. If you stay here—you don't need pay.

K.   But, Mr. Gurdjieff, I've got to . . .

LOOMIS.   I'll phone Pound; you've missed the train.

K.   But Loomis made my appointment *weeks* ago. I need to, I must see Mr. Pound . . .

G.   You need many thing, Mister. You go now, you never come back here, and Loomis, you too; Loomis never speak to you again.

K.   (*To Loomis in utter confusion. Loomis turns traitor by his silence.*) I don't understand. You don't understand. I must see Mr. Pound . . .

G.   I understand very well. Now: you go.

K.   (*Helpless, wordless, turns to go, reaches door.*)

G.   Wait, Little Father; come here.

K.   (*idiotically*) But I don't know . . .

G.   That's right. You don't know. Here: your ticket to Paris. Five hundred francs. I keep one hundred. Save rest for ticket back to Prieuré. You like that?

K.   Yes, Mr. Gurdjieff. Thank you very much.

G.   Not thank me. Thank Loomis.

K.   (*recovering*) I thank Loomis for many things.

G.   I also thank Loomis; maybe not *many* things.

K.   (*firmly*) I thank Loomis for *many* things.

G.   Very polite. Many thanks. Now you go. On train you think many things. You think bath. You think Benson. You think sheep-eye. Maybe you think ballet. What?

K.   I'll try to.

G.   Already good. You try. You know who you are?

K.   You said I was a compassionate idiot.

G. Already good: also square idiot, round idiot, zigzag idiot. You, something else.

K. (*taking the game as a joke*) Also, sheep to be shorn.

LOOMIS. Come along now, or you'll miss your train.

G. Goodbye, Little Father: *Do svidan iya. Au revoir. Arrivederci. Hasta la vista. Auf Wiedersehen.* Maybe you learn Hungarian.

I feel paralyzing inadequacy trying to write of Mr. Gurdjieff, and will limit this to his effect on me, rather than trying to sketch his thought, which is covered by substantial memoirs and biographies. He exerted more influence on my behavior than anyone, including my parents. What they'd endowed me with, I absorbed as inheritance. Due to my father's shyness, I took from him ethical parameters but little about how to manage heavier problems. With Gurdjieff it was different. I met him at a peak of disorientation when many choices appeared open, while none commanded. By his canny proposals I felt released. Under the influence of a force amounting to a revelation, I surrendered to whatever of his system I could grasp. The shock of his first impact would be tempered by time, but served, never wholly diminished, as a storage battery. Actual physical contact was no more than a brush-past. It was the intense affirmation of his presence which embodied authority far more than any exegesis or printed pages.

As for the legacy of his thought, inscribed or heard, none of his cosmologies or metaphysical hieroglyphs imposed themselves in any depth, due perhaps to impatience, or my immediate satisfaction at Fontainebleau. When I was questioned later concerning his "philosophy" by those ready to judge him a false prophet or charlatan, I offered no rebuttal. The amorphous load of his precepts suited my temperament. What I snatched from their baffling complexity were a few formulae which I found saved time, worry, and waste motion. That these, when spelled out, sounded naïve, only proved the poverty of my interpretation, not his residue for my utility.

Gurdjieff never proselytized. Instead, he kept a practiced negative craft of off-putting self-protection. Modestly or arrogantly, he claimed to have "good leather for those who need new shoes." Here was an end to it. Those magnetized suffered the pains of being "sheep to be shorn." Instruction was not reciprocal; as in any service transaction, those who profited, in whatever way, were expected to pay. That this may have been in coin more dear than cash could arouse consternation. There were "hopeless cases," who counted themselves cheated or betrayed. I never needed therapy, only information, and I felt that he alleviated drastic problems in which sick souls failed to find succor from any other science. For me, he possessed express data, good rules for eliminating friction as one strove for arrival at an ultimate aim. These rules he pinpointed, intensely beamed at one's central personality while at the same time sharing a common or universal reference which made them all the more convincing. His was the combined operation of X-ray and laser-beam, with the smack of a sledgehammer.

With his "good leather," I took him as a miraculous cobbler, but most of all as "a teacher of dancing." The excellent films of a number of his compositions, taken in Paris in the 1980s, might astound those dubious of his choreography. Like Stravinsky with the Mass, he refused Diaghilev's offer to introduce a sampling as seasonal novelties because his ballets were not designed as spectacles in performance. They were intended not for the amusement of an audience, but for the instruction of their performers. Their movements, deceptively simple, derived from remote historical or geographical sources, which, over the ages, had been found suitable for identification with self-control as well as for majestic praise. There were no solo roles; their celebration was choral, impersonal, deliberate. "Beauty" was incidental, although the dances were often beautiful to watch. However, it was not in their limited vocabulary of corporal movement that their motile remnant lay, but rather in their fluent metric, the accentuation of limpid variety, woven on sonorities of richly subtle textures.

I had no trouble in formulating "dancing" as praise rather than fun. I credited the entity, which many spelled "God," as Order. This was framed with received notions of Good-&-Evil, Right-&-Wrong. Why or how order prevailed over chaos (if indeed it did), or Good was preferable to Evil, why suffering was pandemic, or why so much turned out unpredictably or incalculably, as it so often did, were problems past decipherable causation. Since these problems constantly presented themselves to be managed as unclumsily as possible, it was reckless apathy not to worry for some answer. How I might handle the intrusion of accident, loss, disappointment, death never stayed in focus for me at that time, since I'd not yet been severely tried or tempted. Nevertheless, the Gurdjieffian metaphysic kept me warm. Each crux lay latent, just below the surface, erupting in wakeful dreams, or stubbornly demanding responses that orthodox religion might otherwise have resolved, had I been so conditioned. Rational curiosity was at once exacerbated and smothered by my promiscuous nervous energy. Mr. Gurdjieff projected an enveloping reciprocity of cause and effect on every shaky level; what he construed was a holistic solution, a geometrically poetic constellation. In this divine, multidimensional pattern, it was conceivable that "God," or a prime principle, required our suffering as Its own.

My recension of what I'd been free to believe was released from years of blocked questioning. Serious riddles were postponed while I investigated the tools or rules which I'd now been awarded. Gurdjieff's formula—that most men are sleepwalkers, that most lives pass in mute, self-blinded somnambulism, that there is a factor which compels us to be pleased to exist passively without comprehension—seemed relentlessly reasonable. I hardly needed *Alice in Wonderland* to accept an endemic reversal of physical logic. I was too irritated by habitual restraints of which I couldn't be rid—impatient failures of concentration, judgment from preconception, a fog of sexual confusion possibly derived from infantile illness, fevers of physical attraction, loose and useless—not to hope to rouse myself to a more awakened condition.

Mr. Gurdjieff proposed endless, measureless responsibility to an evolving mechanism which, with constant directed effort, might gratefully respond. This was less an ideal aiming at "perfection" than a process of God-assigned potential, without end save in its own action—and this was as much salvation as one could expect. To desire to develop one's potential to a degree relatively rare among one's kind held risks. It removed a difficult ambition to a special, perhaps an elevated, plane, often tainted by superiority or pride. Had one license to aim so high? My father often warned me against becoming "swell-headed" simply from impulses of energetic or nervous curiosity. Strength in formulating questions was neither a virtue nor achievement. One could accept the onus of difference without a supercilious bias, however. One might forgive oneself for scheming to escape a common failing. Rich, privileged, what passed for "well-educated," I was already fixed in an elite, and had to manage my egotistical preoccupations with as little guilt as possible. I consoled myself that while he whom I now acknowledged as the consummate judge had guessed my root idiocy, he had also granted that a "compassionate idiot" merited attention.

A franchise to pursue life in "liberty" toward "happiness," Mr. Gurdjieff estimated as no "Declaration of Independence," but rather as meaningless seduction. Freedom from uncon-sidered accretions of habit was the only real liberty; the salvation of consciousness, a continual awareness of the precise quality of shifting situations by the process of self-questioning, was the sole stern pursuit. "Happiness" is no more a steady state than weather. A self is a treacherous structure, never to be defined as a single unity, but braided of diverse strains responding to crises which alter, torment, or strengthen the forged centrality. Effort toward self-remembering is the key to all of Mr. Gurdjieff's proposals. Toward this, his "exercises" provided by mental, moral, or physical means an evolution of the individual's somatic mechanism.

Persistence of "normal" or "natural" inertia hinders development. To oppose its weakening dilution, constancy in recognizing and enduring suffering is mandatory, which includes extremities of fatigue, boredom, pain, neurosis, likes and dislikes, "the thousand natural shocks that flesh is heir to." Critical discomfort, as shift, failure, growth, is to be courted rather than evaded, since, ultimately, these all are inevitable and exist to be manipulated with open eyes. The superstition that suffering is "imaginary" (as in Christian Science) is a prototypical modern malady, hardly unique to America. Mr. Gurdjieff's rationally irrational games, a few of which I observed at Le Prieuré involving muscular exhaustion, were psychological sporting events, high-jumps or long-distance leaps, endurance tests toward overall reinforcement. But it would be impossible to go through such effort alone. The ordinary citizen or householder needs the knowing, shared aid of those who've passed further along the path. Saints may triumph in the desert by grace alone, but, with life on an ordinary level, a person like myself was most hopeful on a mutual, collective pilgrimage.

On the morning of my first interview with Gurdjieff, I got to the station just as the train to Paris was slowly drawing away from the platform. I was going to miss my important meeting with Ezra Pound and I dashed after the last carriage, desperate, summoning enough strength to race after it until my lungs were at the breaking point. At the back of the three-car train, a conductor abruptly appeared and saw me. He spat onto the sleepers, contemptuous at my weakness. Imagine the idiot thinking he could catch this train. The malice in his glance defeated me; his look had the concentrated impact of a pistol shot. I stopped dead in my tracks. So did the train. He had signaled the engineer; and by what I deemed a miracle—though I later learned it was common practice on the line between Avon and Paris—I was saved, for a while.

I was by this time sweating heavily, and I could easily smell my own rank scent. What would Pound think of this uncouth sophomore? But I reflected that Pound was a benevolent and a wise man, a friend of Mr. Gurdjieff's: a boy's sweat would hardly put him off. Also, I was not going to be late. I arrived at the Gare de l'Est with twenty minutes to spare. It was Sunday; there were plenty of taxis. I got into the first cab I saw, and sat down. There was a brief, restful silence. Then the silence exploded into a savage anxiety. I had forgotten my little address book. Now I recalled taking it out of my pants pocket when I had emptied it the night before. The damned book had been left on the bed in "The Ritz." I realized time was slipping away again; what sort of an idiot did the *cocher* think he'd hooked? I made a rough guess at the street and number of Pound's apartment and yelled "*Plus vite! Plus vite!*" which did not charm the driver, who reacted by trying to kill us both. Fortunately the greater part of Paris was deserted, and we got to the place I had named in plenty of time. But at that number there stood not an apartment building but a pawnshop, a venue I was sure a poet could never have adorned. I dove once again into my memory, groping again for the address. Another stop, in another *arrondissement*—miraculously, at the address of another pawnshop—and again we found no sign of Pound. I will not exercise the reader's patience by describing all the twists and turns of this search-and-destroy crusade around Paris; by now the steadily mounting cost of the cab ride was about seven times what I had in my pocket. When I got back, desperate, to my hotel there was no one around but a concierge who was not trusted enough to have resort to the *caisse*. Eventually, I was saved, but I never met Pound.

Imagine the care, the patience, the chagrin expended on my letter of apology. Loomis was consulted and together we composed an extremely touching missive based on Lincoln's famous letter to Mrs. Bixby, who, he had been told, had lost four sons in the Battle of the Wilderness. I worked hard with Loomis on the various drafts of my letter. The first was longer than necessary, but it was written from the heart. The more I wrote, the more feeble my tone sounded. What would a master of prose and verse think of the dreck that I, an idiot who presumed to think of himself as an editor, was sending him?

Finally I turned the whole affair over to Loomis. I was a coward, and secretly hoped that Loomis could phone Pound and explain this young man's retarded behavior; but that was hardly fair, and I knew that I personally had to pay. The whole damn, knotty disaster bothered me as a bright, energetic young adventurer can be bothered by so grotesque, so gigantic, so idiotic a failure.

It was not I who turned out to be a compassionate idiot. It was Loomis; he took pity on me and offered to write the letter, finally hoping to put me out of my agony. It didn't take him very long.

Dear Mr. Pound:
I am very sorry to have missed you last Sunday. I had been to Le Prieuré. Mr. Gurdjieff kept me so long I missed my train. I hope we can meet soon.

Yours faithfully,

And while I was never to encounter Pound in the flesh, we corresponded weekly for some months, during which the redoubtable Ezra often referred cheerfully and encouragingly to our magazine as "*Bitch & Bugle*" and myself as "Lincoln Cherrystone." The only good thing about *Bitch & Bugle*, Pound said, was that he, and his gaggle of peculiar lame ducklings—Adrian Stokes, Ralph Cheever Dunning, Louis Zukovsky, and later thin epigones like Charles Olson—all got paid for their efforts. Looking back now, that small spoonful of fiscal civility on our part seems to have had much to do with the eventual demise of the magazine.

I remained gravely impressed by concepts I first heard at Fontainebleau. They have stayed with me at instructive intervals ever since. I've met people more profoundly magnetized, who continued to penetrate far further into Gurdjieff's "Work." There also were those who repudiated it altogether. One man whom I knew well, a world-famous landscape gardener, at his start a devoted disciple, surprised me by asserting that Mr. Gurdjieff was merely one of several similar teachers who may have possessed certain information, but whose fantastically baroque pronouncements, by their very style, diminished their effect. His slippery ingenuities, which were as encompassing as the plainer specifics of Christianity, Judaism, Islam, or Buddhism, related less readily to the digestive curiosity of most mortals. As for myself, his didactic behavior toward attentive followers, his recipes for food and drink, his rigorous physical labor—most of all, his dances—I felt to be more rewarding than canonical orthodoxies, which, for me, lacked an explicit method of behavior except for peremptory commands to be or do "good." I also encountered those who in fits of provocation or rage violently freed themselves from Gurdjieff's thrall— perhaps with means provided by himself.

Such was the case of Payson Loomis, my first and closest contact. Finally, after some five years as translator, secretary, and chauffeur, Payson decided he'd had enough. Characteristically, certificating the separation or dismissal, Gurdjieff presented him with a revolver, offering Payson the choice of murdering his master or shooting himself. I've mentioned that Loomis, early on, had been described to me as a stoppered vial—with a self-justifying complacency only redeemed by an assertion of his own limitations. His subsequent career was properly ironic: he ended composing sermons for the Reverend Norman Vincent Peale, a popular Protestant preacher from a fashionable Manhattan pulpit. Peale was minister to an archetypical congregation of those Gurdjieff termed somnambulistic idiots. Here indeed was a tale which Beelzebub might have related to a grandson: the lapsed herald of an esoteric magus turned turtle as the hired hack of a vulgarian prophet.

The Harvard Society
for Contemporary Art
1928–1930

EVEN BEFORE boarding school I'd fussed with crayons or
Higgins's india inks. I drew decorations for class books, squeez-
ing oils from small, plump, sparkling tubes into strips that
looked more appetizing than candy. When I was twelve, Aubrey
Beardsley's black-and-white shockers exploded on and in me.
Around the same time my sister contrived to obtain Frank
Harris's two-volume biography of Oscar Wilde, from which I
gobbled every detail, up to its deliciously horrific dénouement.
It was less litigation with dreadful Bosie's frightful father than
Wilde's death—"even the bed-clothes had to be burned . . ."—
which roused me and which somehow demanded illustration
by Beardsley. From then, until time came to reject him, I
sedulously copied Beardsley's fetal linear grotesqueries—"decadence," as I translated what I had read that he symbolized,
was really sexy naughtiness alchemized into Beauty, or a license
to act out "art" as it excited me most.

Another pursued Beardsley's formulae, one Harry Clarke,
an Irish illustrator. For my thirteenth birthday I was given one
of his original pen-and-ink drawings decorating Poe's *Tales of
Mystery and Imagination*. It was descriptive, neither especially
wicked nor horrifying. A vaguely tubercular female swathed in

enormous black skirts was in monochrome, except for a single infinitesimal blob of reflective metal. Solidified gold leaf burned into the white paper, balancing the massive black of her crinolines. Yet the picture was a key to reckless liberation from what I'd so far absorbed as good taste. A marvel of freed-associations, I would be undeterred by my temporary inadequacy as a draftsman. I was so delighted in brushing color onto virgin surfaces that I did not worry about quality.

My visual appetite was avid. The art to which I had access drowsed in dull, half-tone, colorless plates in my mother's volumes of *Klassiker der Kunst* and in thick monographs on Dürer, Raphael, Rembrandt, Velázquez. These existed as hungry albums, like those supplied to stamp collectors, squares to be filled, impatient for full chromatics. Reproductions were pale echoes, sights at one-remove, yet I'd seen enough "hand-painted" pictures to know that I wanted to be a painter.

A painter—or illustrator? Still life, *nature morte*, dead nature, had certainly been executed by some agile fingers; yet these fermented, not exactly distrust—it was just that my eyes slipped away from the skins of fruit or flowers. It was never so with faces, or clad and unclad people with provocative members, costumed in an historical surround. Biblical scenes, the "Quest for the Holy Grail," stereoscopic incidents of proud pageantry meant most to me. While I was in Connick's stained-glass shop a nudge was given to my canons of taste, a leap into stylization; I now valued the "neo-primitive," not the sinuously sophisticated like Beardsley, Burne-Jones, Harry Clarke. There was, I learned, no single code for depiction.

I had never had any really focused aim to be a "poet." I liked to write light verse and later, in the army, I produced a bunch of rhymes, the result of a pastime filling gaps in duty. For a while, I wanted, very much, to be a dancer, submitting to primal lessons in the five classic academic positions, but soon accepting age as a conclusive hindrance. With painting there was a difference: in my youth I busied myself with uninterrupted effort toward facility, drawing from dozens of familiar objects and making watercolors of jazz bands, factory machinery, automobiles. This was a rudimentary kind of still life, homeopathically boring, which I deemed "good for me." It was still life and boring, as Wystan Auden defined it, yet not a bore. I began to gain a sense of three-dimensional plasticity and managed some recognizable images without deformation. When I drew in charcoal from plaster casts at the Boston Museum School, I earned the reprimands of the institution's instructor in anatomy and drawing, old Philip Hale, for my edgy angularity of "modernized" form (borrowed, as I did not deign to explain, from Wyndham Lewis).

What propelled my desire to become a painter, though, was less an instinctive joy in pushing pigment on canvas than a quest for the mirrored self-image of a mechanic, mastering the ways to capture human gesture, moving my hand against the flow of time. This was more a branch of literature or biography than the static integrity of paint. To be a painter, then—but like whom? Those who meant most to me were exclusively in museums. I'd been in Duncan Grant's studio, watching him paint my sister's face and arms, and dared estimate his portrait of her clumsy, "all thumbs." As far as sculpture went, there was the iced marble of Colbert's bust in the entrance hall of my home at 506 Commonwealth Avenue. Coils of curly wig, petrified lace and medals, an excess of virtuosity—all leached any breath of flesh or blood, and it was the romance of flesh-and-blood that stimulated my tiny talents. However ignorant or prejudiced, I had notions of what type of artist I did *not* want to be: if my fingers failed to match strokes to a seamless, total realization, it wasn't worth worry. There might be other "art"—Impressionist, Post-Impressionist, abstract—but these to me counted as non-magical. My self, if I was to be a painter, must be a super-illustrator, a magical illuminator.

At Harvard, the Fogg Museum was a pentagon with dependent bastions. There was a rich sampling of Tuscan tempera panels: some of them in good condition, having been treated by a pioneer conservation laboratory staffed by chemists as much as historians. There was also an ample library, not only shelved with monographs and bound runs of magazines, but with tons of tin boxes holding glass lantern slides, all labeled with attributions. There were lecture halls where the gospel according to Bernard Berenson was preached to his honorary heirs. And there were still-living veterans of crusades promulgating perfect taste from the fiats of John Ruskin and Charles Eliot Norton—Classical through Gothic, Renaissance, Baroque—each rigid for its epoch, then supplanted, down to an undefined present. In fact the memory of Norton had a great influence on artistic precepts at Harvard during my time, and it was Norton's advocacy of Ruskin which would be the guiding and abiding influence in the development of my visual taste, and in my liberation, such as it is and was, from received ideas about "art." Directly from Ruskin would develop, burgeon, and then rot my interest in most contemporary art.

The Fogg Museum, upon which our Harvard Society for Contemporary Art depended for existence morally and operationally, was dominated by two characters of opposing origins, who managed through the years to sustain a partnership that, in spite of the usual crises, was singularly effective. Paul Joseph Sachs was a graduate of Harvard. An investment banker, a partner in the firm of Goldman-Sachs, he became uncomfortable on Wall Street. In 1911, he'd been invited to the Visiting Committee of the Fogg. Already a determined, wide-ranging collector of prints and drawings, in 1915 he moved his family to Shady Hill, the house where Charles Eliot Norton had sprouted Harvard's supremacy in art history and museum management taste-making. This big old home was a surpassing relic of authority, but Paul Sachs himself was diminutive. His brief height, as well as a hyper-active intelligence, made him awkward; he hated being a Jew. Affable, suspicious, he never cared for me: I had discourteous contempt for his shyness and lack of ease.

Edward Waldo Forbes, on the other hand, was a grandson of Ralph Waldo Emerson. When I was an undergraduate this lent him the mantle of an imperial inheritance. He was frankly old-fashioned and Quakerlike in reticence, a puritan connoisseur, but a dear friend. He lived in a fine old mansion up the Charles at Gerry's Landing, a perfect pairing to Paul Sachs's Shady Hill at the other end of town. He painted watercolors industriously, with pleasure, but with no need to show. He prized Italian tempera pictures, as much for their material condition as for subject matter, and at the Fogg he founded a laboratory for conservation and restoration which did much to temper the museum's former compulsory aesthetic of Ruskinian and Paterian "appreciation." Instead of considering "Beauty" inviolate, Mr. Forbes and his students dared look on Her bare, down to the bones beneath Her skin.

The Fellows of Harvard's Corporation, while they may have been grateful for the prestige accruing to their Fogg, took a sharp look at budgets, and the ambitious aims toward accession and enlargement which both Forbes and Sachs contemplated. However, Sachs, together with Felix Warburg, was able to draw on a network of Jewish support, and Sachs and Forbes between them guaranteed the Fogg's future personally, independent of the corporation. This enabled them to hire or buy as they chose, without the delay of committees.

As for teacher-painters who had mastered the many styles of art, there was Denman Ross, foundering on the dictates of Dynamic Symmetry which he proclaimed with religious devotion. Arthur Pope was convinced that a rainbow-solar spectrum was uneconomic and, worse, wasteful; one only needed black, white, burnt umber, raw sienna. As an exercise, this may have proved sound; on canvas it was nullifying. Kingsley Porter, whose specialty was revived Romanesque, was still a revelation. Chandler Post's twenty volumes on Spanish painting had splendid photographs; his lectures were as flat as the printed text. There was also, as I have mentioned before, Leonard Opdycke's course in northern Jesuit architecture, which it gave me a tourist's pleasure to recall when my army jeep drove me around Lorraine fifteen years later.

But in spite of all these, I languished for a working master, who would, in person, demonstrate manual method to me. Then my daemon, a good angel who has floated six inches above my head since my eyes opened, bestowed exactly what I needed when I most needed it. I was not really surprised: I've always felt I've been chronologically in luck. The man was Martin Mower, though he never would have classed himself as even a "minor master." Knowledge of museum treasures did not daunt him; he was not competitive. He was professional, like dozens of those supporting peak accomplishments through the ages. Hand and eye stretched the extent of his gifts to their fullness. Energy, informed preference, independence from received taste, alert responsibility for stewardship in craft—all made Mr. Mower a tireless invigorator.

Only signals from a student's flair triggered his attention; he didn't bother with those whose interest lagged. It may have been odd that he consented to teach past time for retirement but the faculty tolerated his tenure's extension, seeing him as an ornament. He represented traditional method, rigor, catholicity, and while denying eccentricity, he stood himself for an amiable exception. He lacked polemic; he'd seen too much to be provoked by what he wouldn't count on and his infrequent eruptions caused little rancor since few took him seriously: he was just a dear-old-thing and this was his armor. Professors given to assigning authorship to undocumented panels rather than to actually painting pictures of ardent aesthetes opting toward curatorship may also have been grateful for one who labored on their land. Apart from the lasting gratitude of those (not very many) graduates who became artists, Martin Mower left few traces.

I was fortunate in adoption more as an apprentice than a pupil. In his home studio, rather than gallery or lecture hall, I absorbed what the Fogg offered. Mower's silvery aura was softly accented by dull maroon. His square-cut head, crowned *en brosse* by pepper-and-salt, and his bristling, trim moustache, framed a sane picture of maturation. Shetland-wool jacket, a burgundy scarf secured by a big garnet, suede shoes buckled in squared silver clad him in High-Bohemian attire.

Worldliness was pricked with clinical judgment, more acid than prim; his wit was low-key, devoid of self-display. Every so often, locutions from lapsed lexicons, lively, though, compared with most tired vernaculars, mildly astonished one. He was as precise with his vocables as with paint: "in fine," "in sooth," "betimes," "quip," "ept," "rapt," "girt," "fret," "pert," all pale enough in print, from his tongue took on italic garnish. There were some whose works were "saucy," "couth," "tetchy," "bereft," "awry." He glossed with quaint irony my confused riddles as I strove to come to terms with modern art and its innovations. Answers I'd extracted from other authorities were ambiguous. Mr. Mower asserted, with no pressure at all, that his own preference was the proper procedure—for him, and for men of his temperament. He set an urbane pavilion in my jungle of values.

He had faced so many jaunty pictures and jolly people that, while still inquisitive, he now discarded anything that stained his peace of mind. But by brief, aphoristic phrasing, he bent a careless attack: curt, prickly responses, distilled from a lifetime's looking, would every so often ignite and accelerate my innocent brain. How dared Martin Mower, a leftover, a sideliner, challenge the rust-proof status of Manet or Maillol? It was from him that I first heard Baudelaire's awesome verdict on his friend who'd achieved *Olympia* and *The Execution of Maximilian*: "You are the first in the decrepitude of your art." Did Mower agree? That was left me to decide. Had Maillol, Meštrović, Bourdelle, Despiau simply found formulae which became mandatory for every cycle? What permitted him to complain about Rubens's slabs of raw beef "so gross that he could not come near Van Dyck"? Or that Franz Hals, flashy enough or too flashy, was but a provincial contender against Zurbarán, Velázquez? Much of this persiflage was Socratic goading. However, it was not from Meyer Schapiro, the first critic of modern art who meant sense to me, but from Martin

Mower that I heard a comparison of Cézanne's voluminous generalization of apples to the rugged grandeurs of the Romanesque cathedral.

He dwelt in a delectable house, up an unmarked alley off Brattle Street. His large, sky-lit studio was tiled dull red. When I mopped the floor, its wet shine faded as if breathed upon. The proportions of the room were strict as in a Vermeer or de Hooch. Light was controlled by long linen shutters. Two sturdy oak easels, each with its glass-topped table palette, claimed that it was canny to play more than one game at a time. Dogged, doltish industry was exiled, his milieu bespoke delight; what was painted should please oneself more than one's patron. But these twain were hooked in professional symbiosis. His insistence on "pleasing" sounded wicked, vain, counterprogressive, unethical. Was not rejection (*les salons des refusés*) the proper platform for heroic behavior? Wasn't all the most renowned modern art prompted by Pain or Disdain? Mr. Mower mixed mustard, vinegar, and iodine. His jesting simmered with a whiff of mock sadism. Was he ever wholly *serious*?

Finished or unfinished canvases were stacked slant against his walls. He never stopped my peeking to uncover ovals or tondos scheduled for ceilings or supraportes. Perky infants with pets and toys leaned against small landscapes, of which Mrs. Gardner owned several. These often pictured sites of faery, but the nature in them, like Gainsborough's, was no genuinely leafed forest but a choice of small rocks, bark, sponge, and feathers—transformed. The room was perfumed by potted orange trees, bougainvillea, blue plumbago, and drooping nasturtium donated some dozen years before from Fenway Court's three balconied drifts. There was a total absence of pinned-up photographs or art books; these invited astigmatism. However, there were oiled, wooden block-cones and sliced cylinders. A half-life-size lay figure was collapsed in a corner. A large armillary sphere, inherited from his late wife's astronomer grandfather, was the studio's single decorative object. Lay figure and sphere were for reference, geometrical, anatomical, mythological.

He painted neatly, without a smock. He told me that John Sargent attacked dukes and duchesses in faultless morning dress; Thomas Eakins, a grubby toiler, depicted an eminent surgeon operating, his starched cuffs enameled with crimson gore. Crisply unfaltering, Mr. Mower fulfilled contracts for interior decorations for Floridian and Californian villas and for Fifth Avenue salons. There was no jot of what might have seemed "feminine." Sensibility was an unselfed surveillance and reticence was his feline nimbus, a house cat's placid reverberation, its tongue a tender, caressing whisk.

I asked him to paint my portrait, hoping, discreetly, to steal some sparks of his magic. Price was a shy-making hurdle, for he needed no payment. "Just stand still. For what ilk of icon do you itch?" His question was further instruction, counting on my self-awareness, past his taste or technique. He put me in the position of serving myself; what he would provide might be less his, than my, choice. Apart from spread pigment, the portrait could be my image of me, more flattering than it would have been had he taken over, assuming I had some definition past disguise. He reduced his personal engagement to providing a spectral spine, leaving me to search for fleshly prototypes.

Uppermost in my mind was Sargent's *Graham Robertson*, a pensive, languorous youth, apparently of my own age. Morning-coated, he fondles a slim, black, jade-handled cane. Ruffed in thick, creamy fur, a chow licks his master's sleek, patent-leather slipper. Flashy, translucent green caps the ebony stick, a flick on the jade's carved grip. Sargent teased a glancing touch, mocking the boy's half-apologetic narcissism, standing there suavely accoutred in the appurtenances of privilege. Accent on the jade, brushed on with a single sweep of firm economy, certified an objective mastery: Graham Robertson embodied the presumptive dandy I longed to appear.

Martin Mower did not refuse photography as a tool; only

he never used a print he'd not clicked-off himself. It was less an aid in matching likeness than a way of choosing silhouettes which drew light to carve shape. He seized a stance, full-frontal, which I felt counted most. Histrionic, I believed it was how Reynolds, Raeburn, Sir Thomas Lawrence, or Sargent himself might have seen me. I didn't worry about my face, which was the least of me. I thought of myself as a dancer in mufti, masker or sportsman, rather than an interesting character.

The apprenticeship continued as he followed the methods of Titian or the later Venetians. My six-feet-and-two-and-a-half-inches were sketched in *grisaille*, a thin, gray-green monochromatic underlayer, then over-glazed with clear pinks, reds, light browns. The completed indications, face, boots, whip (it was an equestrian portrait without a mount), seemed wan. I discovered Mower painted what was primary; a well-cut coat, polished footwear probably bored him. He began to scan facial features. At the end of a dozen sessions, he said the canvas had become "too big for its boots." The next day, when I came to pose, our usual easel was bare. On the second there stared, in a temporary frame, my head, slashed from the original canvas, a small fragment of what I'd intended, the face just tickled up into a plausible sketch. Hardly happy, I paid him with a 17th-century carved frame I'd found in Tours; it was far too fine for a perfunctory face but Mr. Mower accepted it with rapture. Later, it served to surround the dainty features of his daughter Evie. For my relic, he ordered a heavy gilt band rubbed down so smooth that red gesso shone through gold.

The hours I'd stood still, trying not to vex myself, and even his surgery on my portrait, had their consolations. Later, when I posed for other painters and sculptors, I abandoned all preconceptions. It was not that Mr. Mower had failed me; he had triumphed by whetting my self-judgment to its core. I learned about the problems of gaining an objective "likeness," of how little or much it attached to the subject's vanity. What was best, it taught me that I would never become a portrait (or any other type of) painter, and would, more usefully, spend my energy on appreciation, or in service to authoritative manipulation by others. My final public paintings were a hopelessly derivative, Léger-like, Machine Age mural, an allegory of gears and pistons replicating themselves, executed on the walls of the Harvard Liberal Club's dining room in 1928. The effect on clients was to make them feel as if they were miniaturized versions of their normal selves, trapped inside a temporarily arrested meat grinder. The mural was soon veiled behind a wholly abstract coat of white paint.

Later, I would sometimes be asked how I'd become involved in founding the Harvard Society for Contemporary Art. It must have been meaningless to most when I spoke of Martin Mower. But it was his grounding, practice, primary devotion to the skin of structure and the stylish surface of objects too often disdained as superficial, which satisfied lasting scrutiny. The Harvard Society was ostensibly founded to forward modern art. For me, this was rooted in what had been found viable in the last five hundred years. Similar siftings in my reading had launched *Hound & Horn*. My ultimate frustration in posing for a portrait had distilled questions and answers which promised me what was required. The Harvard Society was to prove a luxurious playpen or laboratory in which I could make up my heated, but as yet still smoldering, sense about the difference between "originality," "personality," and "quality," and whatever connected these in the present context.

I had three important collaborators in the making and running of the Society. The first was Edward Mortimer Morris Warburg, the youngest son of one of my father's colleagues, though if anything, this would have kept us apart. We behaved as if commanded to be friends but it turned out that, despite our parents' pressure, we took to each other. Eddie Warburg was two years younger than I, and had more money. He was generous and funny, a declared comedian, close to the practiced clown. Like that of a clown, his bearing was tinged with a reverse, not exactly melancholy, but a lurking apology for jokes that would never spark laughter. He was last-born of three older brothers who systematically bullied him, not always in the friendliest tone. Eddie's father, Felix, was a philanthropist, a collector of Italian predella panels and Rembrandt prints, the American pillar of a famous house of German-Jewish bankers. Eddie lived in a Gothic mansion on Fifth Avenue and graduated from Middlesex, a prep school, which, while not exactly on a par with Groton or Saint Paul's, precipitated him too into the milieu of "The Lads." He was acquainted with luxurious art, and while in college purchased a splendid early, blue-period Picasso. His firmest admiration, though, was for championship tennis players. He had a vestigial taint of Semitic apprehension, but was universally accepted for ebullience and ripe, obligatory fun.

The second was Agnes Mongan, a well-educated graduate of Bryn Mawr, the daughter of a Somerville surgeon. At college she had benefited from association with Georgiana Goddard King, whom Berenson blessed as the best American critic of Italian painting. King's knowledge extended to the Orient and Islam; she had visited museums with Leo and Gertrude Stein. Agnes Mongan was as much an outsider as Warburg or myself. Dr. Mongan's comfortable home was lodged in a proletarian abutment of proper Cambridge—worse still, he was Roman Catholic and all the Mongans were devout. Agnes's O'Brien mother was not permitted study in Britain; she had transferred to the Jesuit college at Salamanca. Many who loved Agnes wondered why, though often courted, she never married: we called her Santa Agnese. She was two years older than I in years, but decades my senior in experience. In the Fall of 1928, she took Paul Sachs's "museum course" and Edward Forbes's "egg-and-plaster" (gesso) lectures in technical procedure. She asked Forbes for work; but he would not hire a non-professional. She volunteered, unsuccessfully, to labor without pay. She then heard that the cataloguer of Paul Sachs's collection of prints and drawings had resigned, sought the job, and got it.

Agnes had been a subscriber to *Hound & Horn*. She was

aware of all that was going on in the worlds with which we wanted to bolster our adventure. Warburg and I lunched with her three times a week at Schrafft's in Harvard Square. Eddie's mother was irritated that her husband, who had given so much to Harvard, had not yet received an honorary degree. Agnes whispered to Paul Sachs, who mentioned it to Edward Forbes; in due time, such an honor was—*considered*. She advised us not to beg room for gallery space in the Fogg Museum itself. Both Forbes and Sachs were content with our putative existence as an undergraduate effort toward an extension of art appreciation. But they were hesitant about our "taste" and unhousebroken behavior. It was better for us all to be independent. We had enjoyed many tours around leading private collections which would later prove basic resources for the Museum of Modern Art. I had attended the sale of John Quinn's great collection of paintings, sculpture, and modern manuscripts in 1926. My mother let me buy a small Ivory-Coast mother-and-child that Paul Guillaume had sold Quinn, early on, as well as a dusky Yeatsian-Irish landscape by the poet A.E. (George Russell), and a wooden figurine by Walt Kuhn. Thus, I had started to "collect" in a modest way.

And there was John Walker III, a rich boy from Pittsburgh. Independence asserted itself when he opted for Harvard rather than Princeton, his father's choice. He had contributed good reviews to *Hound & Horn*; but we did not meet at college until I barged into his room and found framed drawings there by Duncan Grant. His tastes in painting were close to mine; in companions, different. Eligible for the best clubs, he played bridge and was allied to "The Lads." Now mobile and active, as a child he'd survived infantile paralysis. This sickly past lent him a trace of pathos wholly lacking in self-pity. In his memoirs, *Self-Portrait with Donors*, Johnny calls me arrogant and mannerless; in this, I do not recognize myself. He was welcome for the well-heeled social support he brought us. After college, I seldom saw him but when he'd become director of the National Gallery,

I called on him. Naturally, I admired what he'd done, and said so. He replied: "Oh, you think I spend too much time with rich people." It was always part of the job.

A dinner meeting at Sachs's Shady Hill on December 12, 1928, led to the formal incorporation of the Harvard Society for Contemporary Art. There was discussion over a sensitive difference about distinguishing "modern" from "contemporary." I felt that "modern," which often endured an effete pronunciation as *"moderne,"* cast a pejorative sound, while "contemporary" meant something more immediate. My colleagues were not prone to argue; and I was not pressed to delimit the art we wished shown. Boston's Art Club and the Museum of Fine Arts each hung a considerable amount of art done in our time. But this was regressive, uninteresting, "academic"; we endowed "contemporary" with a gloss of progressive, *avant-garde* daring.

A roster of our trustees was impressive. John Nicholas Brown, a hereditary grandee from Providence, Rhode Island, had been called the wealthiest baby in America. He was a serious collector, a patron of medieval scholarship, and would be father to Carter Brown, a future director of the National Gallery. Edward Forbes was hardly an enthusiast of contemporary art, but he kept his eyes open. Philip Hofer was an affluent bibliophile and librarian. Arthur Pope, as I have explained, taught painting at the Fogg. Paul Sachs was indispensable, and enlisted his banker brother, Arthur. Felix Warburg was happy that his son Eddie had found a worthy hobby.

Inconspicuously in the background were two young graduate students. Alfred Barr and Jere Abbott were my tutors, junior- and senior-year. They shared an apartment on Brattle Street and were a mine of information about contemporary, modern, and historic art. They had toured the Soviet Union, met Eisenstein, the great film innovator, considered cinema an art along with architecture and industrial design, as well as the new music, theater, and dance. Alfred and Jere were of our generation and reinforced our less-informed enthusiasms with pinpointed, wide-ranging data. This implemented our program, suggesting prospective exhibitions. In return, I think they learned something of the mechanics of obtaining loans and being polite to lenders. Within three years, they would jointly head the new Museum of Modern Art at 57th Street and Fifth Avenue in Manhattan.

Our Harvard Society may have sparked fire from my flint, yet it relied heavily on classmates, the faculty and maintenance staff of the Fogg Museum, and the goodwill of a cluster of artists and dealers, who, because of Harvard sponsorship, helped with loans, insurance, packing, and shipping. From the start, the directors of the Fogg supported us, possibly happy to be relieved of showing work which, in their estimation, was not as yet up to museum quality. We had no insuperable problems with money, public relations, or the willingness of collectors to loan. This was slightly disappointing, since the scandal we longed to evoke as daring pioneers eluded us.

In Harvard Square, beyond the walled precincts of Harvard Yard, stood the Coöperative Society, the emporium where students could buy necessary books, clothes, and furniture at low cost. We rented for our Harvard Society two large rooms with high ceilings and broad wall space. I knew exactly how they must be decorated: on the walls, putty-gray monk's cloth; on the ceilings, silver-paper squares set in alternating courses. A large table in each gallery was of Monel metal, supported on slim, fancy marble pillars salvaged from a junked ice-cream parlor. These held our catalogues, each carefully designed in styles to fit its show.

We opened in late February 1929. The exhibition was, as my preface promised,

an assertion of the importance of American Art. It represents the work of men no longer young who have helped to create a national tradition in emergence, stemming from Europe but nationally independent.

We were congratulated by the *Crimson* for "restraint," as if anything labeled "contemporary" must be reckless. But our representative artists, neither academicians nor allies of a genuine advance guard, were Thomas Hart Benton, Arthur B. Davies, Kenneth Hayes Miller, Rockwell Kent (who designed our handsome logo—two nude youths, one riding a curveting Pegasus, or Bellerophon, the other restraining it), plus the painter-sculptor Maurice Sterne. The most "modern" pictures were John Marin's watercolor of Mount Chocorua (which I felt feeble) and an inflamed lily by Georgia O'Keeffe (which I thought strong). There was sculpture by Gaston Lachaise, Alexander Archipenko, Robert Laurent. Not one of these artists had been shown at Boston's Arts Club, or the Museum of Fine Arts. We indicated that our debut was but a smattering of what was widely available, and we intended to make up for lost time. There was, to our faint dismay, little objection or opposition. However, the *Evening Transcript* did satisfyingly attack Edward Hopper's frank rendering of some curiously ugly tenements:

By what pretense can such buildings have a claim on art, which, theoretically at least, is synonymous with beauty? Why then dignify them by making them the subject of painted canvas?

During our first week some eleven hundred curious people came. We were deemed a success. Despite the *Transcript*'s attack, both the *Herald* and the *Globe* applauded. In the April issue of *Arts*, Alfred Barr pointed out that both New York and Boston lagged behind Harvard's undergraduates. We paid our patriotic, "American" dues and were patronized by pats-on-the-back—this was not what we'd hoped for at all.

Our second show was "The School of Paris: 1910–1928," featuring Braque, de Chirico, Ségonzac, Despiau's *Diana*, and a standing nude by Maillol. We also borrowed work by Raoul Dufy, Juan Gris, Miró, Man Ray, Modigliani, Pascin, Rouault, Soutine, Vlaminck, Brancusi. We couldn't have done much better: thirty-five hundred people came in three weeks and we were honorably launched on a continuous career.

Theatrical and musical memoirs usually fail completely to summon up the thrills of first nights or spectacular performances. Similarly, exhibitions of painting and sculpture, even reinforced by color photography and a good catalogue, preserve only dim reflections after the loans are packed and sent back. What returns vividly to my mind now after all these years? Recollections of a few golden hours. Buckminster Fuller's bullet head during his impassioned demonstration of a pre-fabricated, hexagonal "Dymaxion House," shown in tandem with a dozen excellent portrait busts by Isamu Noguchi. Noguchi had come back from apprenticeship with Brancusi; his portrait of Bucky Fuller, in glistening polished steel, was kin to Frank Dobson's head of Osbert Sitwell. And perhaps chiefly a show that was intrinsically the work of Eddie Warburg—a one-week, one-man event by another comedian. Alexander Calder was the son of an academic sculptor whose *Benjamin Franklin* stands in precarious balance on Philadelphia's enormous, baroque town hall. A talent for balance descended to his heir. He promised seventeen pieces of bent-wire figures and profiled portraits. Warburg had his own automobile, and picked up the sculptor at the railroad station. Where was the work we were to show? In a small suitcase, it reclined, all of it, consisting of three coils of heavy wire, a pair of pliers, and some wooden blocks. Back in Eddie's rooms in Holworthy Hall, Sandy took off shoes and socks, and changed into pajama bottoms. Using a big toe as anchor, he bent, turned, and twisted his seventeen promised pieces, each affixed to its wooden base. There was a quivering *Hostess* with her shaky lorgnette; a cow with four spring udders and a coil on the floor representing "cow pie." A year later, Sandy gave us the public premiere of his *Circus*, now enshrined at the Whitney Museum of American Art. Unforgettably, before the show, with sly, self-deprecating ingenuity he padded through his audience handing out peanuts.

"Hound & Horn,"

New York

1931–1934

I'VE MADE TOO LONG a digression from my memorial chips
for *Hound & Horn* to provide cover for more than a meager
patch of the remaining plaster. Perhaps it could hardly be
otherwise. Truth is always relative; the enormous ratio of
censorship, invention, forgetfulness, fear, or laziness in my
apologia are faint echoes of what Ruskin, for instance, didn't
say about his wife Effie in *Praeterita*, or how Henry Adams
completed his *Education* without mentioning the suicide of his
wife. I think of my Cambridge hours apart from *Hound & Horn*
as a societal apprenticeship before its professional passage to
New York. Before I transferred to the metropolis, my sister,
now a widow, moved from her Ashfield, Massachusetts, farm
to a small house, one of a pair stuck between big apartments,
at the East River end of 57th Street, neighboring Sutton Place
and almost opposite to where Mrs. Willy Vanderbilt lived with
Anne Morgan. They would introduce me to Romola Nijinsky
and push me further toward the ballet.

I left Cambridge in 1931 with the half-defined idea that I
was uneducated in anything but second-hand opinions and that
most of my activity was calculated as a cushion from compre-
hending what was, for the greater part of the world, reality. I

embraced New York as my second university. There were, for
me, two explorable worlds: high-life and low-life. I had already
had some contact with the first; but while it occupied and
amused me, I had a sense of its superficiality and lack of
meaning. All I had experienced at Cambridge were received
concepts and my rather automatic reactions to them in hopes
of further clarification—possibly through an opposition which
I never obtained. I realized the good by which I'd benefited; it
wasn't enough. I also knew I'd been deprived of great slices of
life, and hoped to make up for it by what I might encounter
in New York. I was hunting nonacademic instructors. One was
Muriel Draper.

I had met her in the middle of my junior year at Harvard,
though I forget the circumstances. She had a considerable reputation at the time, signing herself in reverse "Repard Leirum,"
reporting on interior decoration for the newly founded *New
Yorker*. She was a true daughter of the nineteenth century from
Haverhill, Massachusetts; her father, a man called Saunders,
had experimented on telephones with Alexander Graham Bell.
Muriel enjoyed a flamboyant European education; after marriage to Paul Draper, a charming and careless singer of art
songs, she flourished briefly as a grand *saloneuse* in Florence and
London. Her atmosphere was richly musical and her friendships involved the prominent figures of the epoch's literature,
art, and music. She wrote a haunted book of memoirs, but
Music at Midnight only hints at the sparkling verbal miniatures
of Henry James, Sargent, Gertrude Stein, Diaghilev, and Arthur
Rubinstein she created in her talk. Incapable of halting her
husband's gambling, now the mother of two small boys, she
returned to New York during World War I penniless but
undaunted. Early on, a fairly young widow, she maintained a
ragged salon in a bleak loft over a garage on East 40th Street,
where on Thursdays she kept up an ironic parody of her
London and Florentine grandeur, which was a delight of the
town and where one could meet anyone who, at the time,
figured in the High Bohemia of Manhattan.

It is strange that, so far, she has not been the subject of a biography, since she played the role of prime catalyst of the epoch, before, at the end of her life, turning into a passionate, even perhaps a card-carrying, Communist. She taught me most of what I wanted to have known of people, politics, and principles. Soon after I moved to New York in 1931, I managed to live next to her small, wooden house on East 53rd Street, and intimacy with her on the closest basis was only broken by my marriage some ten years later. My parents looked upon her as a menace, since she was twenty years older than myself, poor, and quite without any conventional restraints, while at the same time basking in the inherited renown of utmost propriety. I owed her much of whatever solid intellectual or moral development I may have made, and through her met the twin strata of society about which I was most inquisitive. The life of the arts she presupposed and its talents were her daily communicants. While I was in awe of their reputation, they seemed familiar enough. What I had not counted on was her complete familiarity with what is called low-life. Or rather, in this case, high low-life. Harlem was home ground for Carl Van Vechten, one of her best friends, and a number of black singers and poets were her familiars. Harlem was a friendly suburb then, by no means a dangerous jungle, and her acquaintanceship stretched into an exciting and barely covert world of extra-legal activity glossing the failure of laws against the sale of hard liquor. Speakeasies and nightclubs were not only rendezvous of exotic characters, but bartenders and gin-runners cast a seriously heroic and glamorous glow which, while not diminishing the appeal of the cultural milieu, set it in a realistic and even a sinister context.

Muriel Draper was described then as having the face of "a white negress." She managed to dress on no cash with enormous elegance, and had a style of speech which mixed Jamesian detail with gutter immediacy. I'd never heard a "lady" use four-letter words before, and I found to my surprise that I was not shocked. I listened to her tales of her legendary encounters as if it was a graduate course in behavior, and as a result acquired a largely false familiarity with her ethos. She became the judge and oracle of most of my activity from the time I left Boston and Cambridge until I began to work with the ballet. Her gift was to enable me to use short-circuits as a method, to aim at a state of bi-location—existence in two, or more, places at the same time—to make snap judgments tested by inner checks and self-doubt, and to behave *as if* I was, somehow, in most cases, a free agent.

WHEN I CAME to New York, *Hound & Horn* itself moved to a pair of closets at 10 East 43rd Street. One held a chair and umbrella stand. The other had our files, desk, and a chair for Doris Levine, a student at Columbia who became more editor than secretary; she managed to get the magazine issued four times a year, on time, for its remaining life. In addition, I hired something we'd not had before—a "business manager," mandated to elevate us into "national scope." He, or she, was to hustle advertisers plus group subscriptions from schools, libraries, and whoever might be inveigled. I was quite content with Mrs. I-Forget-Her-Name when she answered a small but (I figured) challenging ad in the *Times*. Smartly dressed, a graduate of Oberlin, she began improving our image immediately by hiring a friendly interior decorator to do-over our closet-vestibule. Black-and-white linoleum tile was laid on its old floor, the umbrella stand was replaced by a Bauhaus tube table. When the bills came due I was astonished, horrified, and very angry. I had not asked for any references and past employment; charm always went too long a way with me. I telephoned my father's secretary, Miss Effie R. Beverly, who, as usual, rescued me. However, this time she bothered my father with news of my debut far from Boston. He became interested and, with his own means of securing information, we learned Mrs. I-Forget-Her-Name had recently graduated not from Oberlin (or did she say Bryn Mawr?) but from three years in

Sing Sing. My father told me that he hoped I would not turn into a "dead-beat"; also, he reminded me that he was not "made of money." If I had to *earn* what he *gave* me, well, Lincoln, you'd better realize life is a serious and expensive business . . .

This disaster was attenuated by my hiring a candidate highly recommended. Convincing references came from, believe it or not, Mrs. Winthrop Chanler's neighbor Tony Ridolfi, the flashy bootlegger from Geneseo. This applicant was an ex-jockey, spoke very fast, and was very funny. He had once worked, among other jobs, for a racing journal and he showed me a swatch of advertisements he'd managed to cop. His name was Tim Clarke; he had a tight little ass, a svelte manner, and was eager to sweat for a dingbat organ named *Hound & Horn*. Romantically charmed once more, I felt that if he could snag advertisements for quadrupeds, this might overlap onto literary bipeds. It did not, and after Tim agreed to take two months' quittance, I did my silly best flogging round bookstores and publishers. While I had inherited no trace of a merchant's acumen, my father was relieved by this gesture and complained no further. I recognized my error in hiring Tim Clarke, but I seldom admitted to anyone that contact with him did not cease when he left our employ. We had a nice sympathy for one another. He taught me how to costume myself in surplus togs from Army-Navy stores; how not to talk Harvardese and how to volunteer companionable drinks without worry or showing off. I was now hot on exploring low-life, and his milieu extended past racetracks to firefighters, the waterfront, and the police. I don't think I fooled any of his chums; but his common sense about my psychological quest for male impersonation and a dogged hunt for a reality past romance pushed me a big step forward. I duly reported experiences with Tim to Ezra Pound, hoping that my glamorized account of Manhattan might induce him to come over and help us. He answered from Rapallo in May 1931: "Your statement about low-life in America. There is good low-life anywhere. The lower it is, the less it is national and the less it reflects any credit or interest on the *particular* place in which it exists."

While I still kept an apartment in Cambridge, *Hound & Horn* began to be edited from all over. Yvor Winters was in California, Allen Tate in Kentucky. The neo-Agrarians in Nashville and neo-Classicists at Leland Stanford became a double-axis. I didn't give a damn about the politico-philosophical tendencies which began to devour the magazine's space, and I felt I was neither equipped to deal, nor interested in dealing, with them. Tate's friend, Donald Davidson, wrote a heady analysis, "Sectionalism in the United States"; when we met in editorial conference, small talk was taken over by earnest discussions of antebellum politics. They suggested that projections of geographic "sectionalism" as a political Utopia be explored through a series on nineteenth-century portraits hung below the Mason-Dixon line: Calhoun, Ruffin, Rhett, Jefferson Davis, Judah P. Benjamin. The roster had the virtue of unfamiliarity, and sympathy for the Confederacy held nugatory chic. But one editor, who idolized Robert Gould Shaw and was named after The Great Liberator, found it too rich for his blood. Tate tried to equate this direction with our proto-Marxist articles by "Max Nomad," but I judged it tantamount to treason.

That politics was a waste of time detracting from introspection I learned anyway when I received an unaccustomed visit to our New York office from Bernard Bandler III, our ex-Aristotelian. He spoke without interruption for an hour and a half, as if on a mission to save us from something worse-than-death. I'd forgotten how persuasive he was: he sounded like my father, who, alarmed at my pinkish flirtations, had forbidden me to "sign *anything*," especially letters of public protest. Bernard advised me that politics were the drugs with which those who felt free to "flee introspection" abused or amused themselves. Anyone who wished to ameliorate or manipulate "the masses" was an idiot, a charlatan, or a psychopath. In 1932, the acronym WPA was still to be conceived, although I would shortly become involved with Harry Hopkins and the Works Progress Administration. In hopes of sobering me up, my father took me to the Chicago Democratic Convention which nominated Franklin Delano Roosevelt, although his own candidate was Al Smith, F.F.M. (Fulton Fish Market). But any consistent notion I had about passionate utterance from a public podium was confused, homogenized, and diluted by individual physical attraction, in particular to a boy called Wirt Baker, a Southern organizer of sharecroppers, of whom I saw a great deal. I have called myself an adventurer, but with me the adventuring was always more with people than with notions, although the people may have been characterized by congeries of ideas entangling them. Baker seemed to me an updated representative of the Confederacy of the same ilk as General J. E. B. Stuart or his tragic young aide, Major John Pelham.

In 1931 Jere Abbott and Alfred Barr were now, three short years after they had been "advising" me at Harvard, co-directors of the Museum of Modern Art in New York. *Hound & Horn* printed Jere's diary of the trip to Moscow, where, with Alfred, he'd met Sergei Mihailovitch Eisenstein, who soon sent us articles on Soviet, and other, cinema. From e. e. cummings, whom I would see often in Paris in 1933, we received portions of his Muscovite journal, *EIMI*, an acerbic keyhole view of Communist hell. I engaged a card-carrying Party member as film critic, Harry Alan Potamkin, an angelic enthusiast who wrote pioneer articles on Pabst, Pudovkin, René Clair, Eisenstein, with a presupposition of their significance in tones usually reserved at that time for canonizing Picasso, Matisse, and Derain (yes, then Derain was considered their equal). Harry's charm, his untamed outrage, raised hackles of my slumbering guilt, which had already been tousled by Wirt Baker's stories about sharecropping. When Harry became ill, Walker Evans volunteered for a blood transfusion. But before Walker reached Saint Luke's, Harry was dead. I asked his wife if I could do anything. "Yes," she said. "Buy me a red silk dress and yourself a bright red tie; wear it for Harry."

Through him I met Ben Shahn, painter and brilliant graphic artist, who drew me marginally closer to skirmishings in the class war. I knew by this time that slavery was not simply a property of Allen Tate's non-revivable South and that dissident behavior had more formidable attributes than bootlegging. Shahn took me on a quick visit to Rikers Island, where, on blank upper walls of the men's cells, he was starting a mural. He avowed that at least a third of the inmates here should be released forthwith, since they were no more guilty in the sight of blind Justice than the same number now packing Wall Street. Walker Evans, who was close to Ben, seldom gave vent to Ben's depthless indignation, which scared the wits out of me. Eddie Warburg commissioned from him a very beautiful orthodox Haggadah scripted in delicate Hebrew, a text affirming Ben's unjust deity. I asked him to do decor for cummings's ballet *Tom,* based on *Uncle Tom's Cabin,* but this, like other dreams, came to nought. However, Shahn was a considerable admiration of mine: I bought for the Museum of Modern Art his painting of a Bronx River Bridge, and when in 1932 I organized a mural show from which decorators of Rockefeller Center were to be chosen, he contributed an inflammatory panel of the President of Harvard gloating over the open coffins of Sacco and Vanzetti.

By 1933 it was time to call curtains on *Hound & Horn,* though it took us many months to do so. The magazine was priced at fifty cents a copy—at least five dollars, I suppose, in today's cash. This was a lot, even for something appearing just four times a year. A copy cost us about forty cents, since we were still fussy about good paper and print. We (that is, my father) lost about eight thousand dollars a volume on it, which would now be around eighty. After seven years we'd gained a circulation of more than four thousand, counting around seven hundred subscribing libraries, public and academic. Had we had a one-time subsidy of twenty-five thousand dollars, we might have gone on indefinitely.

Facing New York as a complex combination of postgraduate

theater and an unexplored playground in which I was assigned at least a walk-on part, I did not realize how confused I was. In spite of having put some preferences in order, my ambivalence about *Hound & Horn* centered on a doubt concerning my last four years of self-indulgence. I wanted to put a finish to Harvard and Boston, but without their base I was unsure of what to do to prepare any future for myself. Emphasis pointed left, right, up, and down. Instinct pushed me toward investigation of "reality"—the criminal classes—of which I was in itchy ignorance. This was a token of a bulk of data of which, so far, habit and conditioning had deprived me. New York was Vanity Fair for such instruction; but first I felt I had to rid myself of that damn magazine. At the same time, I forced myself to behave as if it did have some future, however dubious; to see that contracted, as yet unpublished, articles, for which money had been paid, would be used rather than lost.

It was some satisfaction that *Hound & Horn* terminated in a burst approaching glory. Bernard Bandler had, at auction, bought an unpublished notebook scenario for Henry James's *The Ambassadors*. With this as the *clou* of a memorial valedictory, ours and an almost forgotten novelist's simultaneously, our "Henry James Number" went a long way to sparking his revival. After renunciation of U.S. citizenship in 1916, an award of the Order of Merit, and then, swiftly, death, his former renown had lapsed. We priced the issue (in preparation for over a year) at one dollar, and sold out. Bernard Bandler gave the scenario to Hyatt Mayor as a wedding present.

The issue had an omnivorous table of contents, led off by Edna Kenton, then America's premiere Jamesian. Marianne Moore, Edmund Wilson, H. R. Hays, Robert Cantwell, Glenway Wescott contributed articles which may still be read with some attention today. Eliot wrote us that, after two attempts, he found he had nothing to say. Gertrude Stein promised something, yet never delivered. In *The Cantos*, Ezra Pound had worshipped "The Master":

And the great domed head, *con gli occhi onesti e tardi*
Moves before me, phantom with weighed motion,
Grave incessu, drinking the tone of things,
And the old voice lifts itself
        weaving an endless sentence.

For *Hound & Horn*, he sent a mean-spirited joke:

Melbourne (15 Jan.)
Rudyard Kipling has agreed to write an ode for dedication of the
city's Shrine of Remembrance.
Paris edtn. N.Y. Herald, 16 Jan.

(Perhaps this was because on the one occasion I behaved really
badly with *Hound & Horn*, it was connected with Pound. I'd
committed us to print four articles by Adrian Stokes, who had
been seconded by Ezra Pound. We printed three; the fourth
reduced me to terminal boredom and I canceled it. We paid,
but neither Pound nor his protegé ever forgave me.) Jack
Wheelwright wrote on James and Stanford White, the architect,
and editorial comment recalled a prior tribute by *The Egoist*
(London, January 1918) followed by *The Little Review* (same
year, New York). After so long a silence a lost voice was finding
itself.

    Further improbable plans included single numbers on
Whitman, Melville, Joyce, Pound. Our original impulse had
come from Dick Blackmur's admiration for *La Nouvelle Revue
Française*'s *hommages* to Rimbaud, Mallarmé, Proust. It filled me
with wry pride to read in establishment magazines—*Harper's* or
Scribner's—fiction that I myself had earlier rejected. I had made
acquaintances and companions; some survived our editorial
trials—Hyatt Mayor, Walker Evans, Marianne Moore, Virgil
Thomson, Jimmy Cagney, Russell Hitchcock; while some did
not—Katherine Anne Porter, John Cheever, Ernest Hemingway, Archie MacLeish.

What come back to me from this one brief period in all my decades are some gleaming images and moments. Dick Blackmur's crabbed, squarish, legible script on small, square, white blocks, always without cross-out or emendation. Trips up to Portland, Maine, with Varian Fry to Fred Anthoensen's splendid Southworth Press, to see a next issue through the press; then, next morning, to fondle the immaculate cut and bound copy, finished, achieved, *done.* Lunch with Bonamy Dobrée at "The Ivy," when he told me Mr. Eliot had recently remarked that *Hound & Horn* had more vitality (mostly due to Ezra Pound) than any similar Oxbridge effort.

Dick Blackmur, even lacking Sanskrit and a Ph.D., turned into a tenured Princeton pundit. Varian Fry became a hero, and, as well, nearly a saint. He shepherded troupes of artists from the School of Paris, Jew or Gentile, across the Pyrenees into the anxious Spanish haven, on their way to New York during the terrible years of German occupation. It was only after Varian's death in 1967 that I had any inkling of this service.

When we finally shut, Malcolm Cowley, poet and critic, and a man I liked, wrote a churlish obituary in the *New Republic*, to the effect of: it died; so what? Years later, when I wrote dance criticism for Klaus Mann's review, *Decision*, introduced by W. H. Auden, his brother-in-law, my fermented manner was similarly *de haut en bas.* Wystan asked me—if all this dancing is so bloody awful, why do you write about it? It was a good question. For *Hound & Horn* I know my own book reviews were too long. In lieu of poor pay, I let some authors go on and on, as long as they liked, diminishing readability. But perhaps there were not many other efforts of the epoch with as much gathered intelligence as our magazine. And as my brother George's track coach barked when he ran for Harvard to lose a Yale race: "O.K., sweetheart; it's not so much the races you win, as the friends you make."

Crane and Carlsen,

New York

1931–1932

I NEVER KNEW Hart Crane personally, though I bumped into him a few times when I came down to New York from Cambridge. He never failed to frighten me. His reputation preceded him, a negative fame of lurid pyrotechnics, at once alluring and repulsive. He could have had small use for a supercilious college-kid, ten years younger than himself, with firm poetic and snobbish prejudices. However, there was a tenuous connection between us. Crane had submitted "The Tunnel," seventh and penultimate canto of *The Bridge*, his masterpiece, to *Hound & Horn*. We refused it.

We had accepted much mediocre, far more forgettable verse among a small number of good poems by well-known names. How could ostensibly sensitive young men with notions advanced for their time and with acquaintance with advance-guard French, English, and American poetry, reject Crane's great evocation of the power and grandeur of Manhattan's mystical bridge and mysterious subway? It had not been refused out of hand, but after discussion led by the purist Dick Black-mur, the Latinist Varian Fry, and myself, who'd been entranced by "The Tunnel" 's epigraph:

Crane and Carlsen, New York

To Find the Western path
Right thro' the Gates of Wrath.

Foster Damon, my freshman adviser, had recently published the first important American explication of William Blake's symbols and story. As a result, Blake's beautiful painting of "Glad Day," a blazingly brilliant nude youth seen against the full spectrum of a rainbow, was my current personification of Melville's Jack Chase and Billy Budd, and of Whitman's comrades. In the arguments over the acceptance or rejection of Crane's poem, I felt he had not lived up to the oracular in Blake's distich. But I was a not-unwilling victim of Dick Blackmur's compensatory stringency, my own snobbery being derived from my recently gained arcane knowledge of Blake's true cosmology. It was a typical example of the academic deformity which we hoped to avoid, the competitive vanity based solely on subjective attachment.

Perhaps I might have felt less responsible about the refusal of Crane's verse when I became conscious of it as a mistake, had I known there were other, much more eminent rejecters —Harriet Monroe of *Poetry*, Marianne Moore at *The Dial*, Edmund Wilson at the *New Republic*. In 1930, reviewing the published *The Bridge* in *Poetry*, Yvor Winters—with Allen Tate, Crane's most constant literary correspondent—criticized his entire achievement. In *Hound & Horn*'s summer issue for 1931, Winters reviewed a French study of the influence of *symbolisme* on American verse, analyzing Crane's presumed debt to Rimbaud, which was here discounted since Crane could read French only in translation. The first poem of Crane's I happened to have read was mainly memorable to me for its dedication to Stanislav Portapovich, a dancer in Diaghilev's Ballets Russes who stayed in the United States after the disastrous 1917 season. In this poem, Crane made the word "Chloe," from *Daphnis et Chloë*, a monosyllable that rhymed with "Pierrot." This was enough to demonstrate to me how ill-lettered and pretentious

Crane was. Winters's analysis of Crane's beautiful "For the Marriage of Faustus and Helen" complained that:

the vocabulary of Mr. Crane's work suggests somehow the vocabulary of Rimbaud's prose and of a very little of verse, in its quality of intellectual violence and almost perverse energy.

"Perversity" and "violence" indeed. In spite of my "pro-modern" bias, if there were two elements lodged in my head to justify the rejection of unworthy or uncomfortable material, they would have been violence and perversity. We were "educated," and as editors we were sustaining humane values, traditional though progressive, against mindlessness, anarchy, chaos. We were mandated by Eliot's "Tradition and the Individual Talent" and Pound's injunction to "Make It New." Dick Blackmur, traumatized by his own permanent lack of a *summa cum laude*, used overkill on Crane; while I'd taken received ideas as scripture and wasn't to be budged against commands I'd stolidly absorbed.

On March 28, 1931, I went to a party thrown by the editors of the *New Republic* in a big penthouse on Fifth Avenue. Present were Edmund Wilson, Paul Rosenfeld, C. D. Jackson, Dwight Macdonald, and Walker Evans, among others. The second wife of Estlin Cummings, a termagant, baited me, deservedly, for being gratuitously rude to Crane at another party at Archie MacLeish's a few weeks earlier. Cummings said that Crane's mind was no bigger than a pin's, but it didn't matter; he was a born poet. Walker, the one person present I knew at all well, was about to embark on a South Seas voyage, on a yacht chartered by Oliver Jennings, to make a film. And it was through Walker I'd encounter Crane's friend, Carl Carlsen, who'd signed-on as an able-bodied seaman.

The *New Republic* party sticks in foggy memory, illuminated by a lightning flash. The air was subdued, with the usual self-enclosed groups in a haze of cigarette smoke and alcohol. Abruptly, in a far corner of the large, high room, angry voices and motion. I had not seen the spark of a fracas; but now there were fisticuffs. Two men traded punches. The taller appeared in control; he held the other at arm's length and hit him hard. Somebody called somebody else something. Whatever the springs of the rumpus, music-under swelled into gathering general irritation. "Chuck the son-of-a-bitch out!" A door onto the elevator outside opened as of itself and Crane, slight, with rumpled shock of hair, helped by hands other than his own, was chucked-out. Quiet resumed, drinks were drunk; nobody paid much mind to an interruption which had not had time to come to serious trouble.

Half an hour later there was a blunt banging on the door. Kicks, knocks, yells; it was opened. Crane bounced back into an unastonished assembly, pursued by a small, furious taxi driver. Crane had hailed him for a run to a Sands Street bar under the Brooklyn Bridge. Then, having arrived, Crane found he had no cash. The driver pushed him down into the gutter, but was persuaded to drive him back to the Fifth Avenue party, where friends would take up a collection and pay for three trips. Crane, filthy, sodden, desperate, was remorseful but morose. The cabbie, given a couple of drinks, was mollified. Crane proclaimed what a marvelous character the man was; he would hire him to taxi to Mexico on his recently awarded Guggenheim Fellowship. Shortly after, they left, quietly enough, together.

This incident, which seemed abnormal to me, was no great event to those others foregathered. For those who lived by lyric imagination, whose craft and career was the play of words and metaphor, Crane was not overly distressing except, possibly, to himself as he sobered up. When he returned with the cab driver, I'd been humbled by his patient penitence, muffled apologies, his small boy's pathetic, instinctive good manners. At first I was inclined to be, or tried to be, surprised, indignant, outraged. Actually, I longed to have the guts to get drunk and pick up a character who much resembled James Cagney in *The Public Enemy*, a brilliant new Warner Bros. film. Partly as a result of my friendship with Tim Clarke, I now aimed to delete conditioning of my schools and class. Walker Evans helped me too, teaching me to keep my mouth shut in Brooklyn bars. So, I penetrated the safer borders of jungles without much threat or risk. Denizens of such areas spot strangers on sight: I smelled different but was tolerated for my curiosity. In this ambience, I met Carlsen, and discovered that he'd been an intimate of Hart Crane.

Learning of Carlsen's ambition to write sea stories, Walker had advised him to send something of what he'd written to me, an editor. Three duly arrived, each neatly typed in an individual spring binder. None made much of an impression and, when Walker pressed me for my opinion, I was slow to commit myself. Eventually Carlsen's quite unmemorable pieces gained only an impersonal rejection slip.

Then, one day when I was to lunch with Evans and Jim Agee at the greasy-spoon near *Time* magazine's offices, Walker brought a scruffy bundle of yellow typewritten sheets, the rough draft of a new story by Carlsen. Its raw presentation and obvious travail attracted me; this was quite unlike the ship-shape type-scripts previously sent. It concerned the stoker in the boiler room of a merchant freighter. An important piece of machinery overheated, perhaps lacking lubrication, or a piston rod split or snapped. The stoker immediately substituted his forearm for the broken part. For some minutes flesh and bone were working replacement for steel and oil. The tragedy, while not entirely convincing as written, obviously derived from vivid memory. Its prose was by someone who knew more about metal and machinery than he did about salable short-story formulae. But I was not entirely disdainful of its stiff, primitive energy; the strained rhetoric was influenced by Melville: overwritten, rhapsodic, rhetorical. Yet somehow, pretentious it was not; there was too much detailed observation for contrivance. The story had power, but its prose was without practice. We still couldn't bring ourselves to print something *primitive*.

I wrote the most encouraging rejection note I could manage

and sent a volume of Kipling's short tales, including "The Ship That Found Itself," in which the intransigent components of a newly commissioned steamer, after its agonizing launch-run, grew to have its stubborn individual parts finally work smoothly together. My note, and the present of Kipling, brought Carlsen to our office on East 43rd Street. He did not appear in person. I was thanked by a typed note slipped under the door: Carlsen found the story I'd recommended unreal; its author was no merchant seaman, a tourist not a professional. I was abashed by the firmness of his negation, and extremely piqued.

Who was Carlsen? I never really discovered, much as I longed to know. Walker Evans could or would not further elucidate, saying only: "a chum of Emil and Ivan Opfer's, Gene O'Neill and Crane's." In 1930 (I later learned), Crane wrote Caresse Crosby in Paris that Carl was "a former sailor who has got tired of office work and expects to hit the deck again for a while." Crane drowned before I had much contact with Carl and I was always loath to mention their relationship, which seemed guarded but precious.

After the appearance under the door of Carlsen's stern note, I pressed Walker to take me to see where Carl lived. This was an oversized doll's house, a picturesque, miniature, semi-secret habitat awarded him by the guardian angels of Whitman and Melville. One passed through an all but unmarked gap in a row of early-nineteenth-century houses in the middle of a block somewhere between far West 17th and 18th Streets. Between the two blocks survived three tidy, two-storied, un-painted clapboard buildings with a joined narrow porch and pairs of gabled dormers. Built any time between 1825 and 1850, they were freshly shingled, ancient but without decay. In the middle house dwelt Carlsen. A single downstairs room was bare, spotless, shipshape, tidy. It might have served for a whaler's cabin, anchored at Nantucket, New Bedford, or Sag Harbor. The only twentieth-century intrusion was a small, shiny upright piano with stacks of sheet music on top. A narrow stair with a rope banister led up above to, I supposed, sleeping quarters. Later, in a back courtyard I would find a common lavatory which served the three buildings. There was a hand pump and gas was laid on, but there was a total lack of heat in the bathroom for shaving-water.

Walker Evans formally introduced me as the guy from *Hound & Horn* who had rejected his story. Carl was a stocky, well-set-up man, thirty-five to forty; clean-shaven, leathery, no extra flesh, apparently hard-bitten. He had coarse, untrimmed, bushy eyebrows, fairer than his ash-blond, close-cropped hair. The piano obviously belonged to the stolid, self-contained woman, perhaps ten years older than Carl, who hovered behind him. Her hair was worn in a stiff, orange, seemingly artificial pompadour. She nodded at Walker and myself without encouragement and abruptly mounted the stairs—up and away, as one might say, in a marked manner. This did not appear to bother Carlsen. He wore clean, threadbare, crisply laundered, old regulation U.S. Navy bell-bottoms, with a drop-fly with thirteen buttons (in honor of the original thirteen American Colonies).

Next to the small gas range was a wooden icebox, maple with nicely turned legs, unpainted. In the icebox, cream and lemon; on the stove, water, boiling. Tea was made, and the master of the house took rum from a cupboard and set the full bottle before me. The (to me) exotic purity or clarity of the ambience bemused me. Speech was slow coming. Soon enough Walker made desultory politenesses, while I studied the room. On the mantel above the wood-framed fireplace were three brass candlesticks, each different. Next to them was a portrait of Crane, by Walker, in an old cork mat. Inside a foot-long green bottle was the model of a fully rigged sailing ship. I asked, in my innocence, how it had managed to get inside the bottle, which couldn't have been blown around it. Carlsen patiently explained that the masts and rigging were laid flat at first; the hull was thin enough to slip inside, and a thread had then pulled the masts upright.

From upstairs came grunts of furniture being moved;

something slammed. Carl rose from the tea table to investigate. I tried to signify to Walker in Carlsen's absence how abjectly fascinated I was by this quaint home. Sounds of an abrupt exchange were heard from the top of the stair. Walker winked. Carl came down; there were no apologies: we were dismissed, leaving warm tea in mugs and rum untasted. He smiled without embarrassment, hoped he'd see me again "sometime," slapped Walker on the back, firmly shook my hand, and we were in his courtyard. There had been no word said about his manuscripts.

I was troubled and loath to leave, as if, somehow, I'd done the wrong thing, for I had been enchanted. Here was a human situation, a compact mystery of class behavior, which I might have read about or suspected, but never touched. I was torn as to what further contact I might seek. How could I warp a half-uttered invitation into some story *Hound & Horn* might print? Walker was no help: on the way back I bombarded him with questions, but his thin answers told me more of Crane than Carlsen, whom he claimed to have met only in passing. Evans had a collector's passion for ephemeral American artifacts— matchboxes, baseball and cigarette cards, old valentines, tobacco boxes, trademarked paper bags, and twine. Carlsen and his background were just another slightly wholesome collectible.

My image of Carlsen, presumably fictive, had little enough to do with his essential self. For me, he incarnated legends. The fact that he was approachable, on the beach (and hence estranged from the ocean), yet accessible, made his vague presence all the more exhilarating. Surely "he knew the name Hercules was called among the women and held the secrets of the sea." Perhaps he only existed between voyages, likely to ship out at any moment. How would I ever find him again unless I were able to conceive a stratagem which, so far, I had not the slyness to imagine? Here, again, Walker Evans was no help at all; he had gone as far as he could pushing Carl toward "literature," and he wasn't particularly generous, or amused by my fascination. If I wanted to see the guy again, no big deal.

Drop in on him, just as we had today. After all, there had been as yet no mention of his writing, nor my thwarting of it.

So, breathless, and in some dread, I did risk it. On my second visit, he was alone. Now, my self asserted its typecasting as college-critic. My sincerity was clear, even if my suggestions seemed limp. Perhaps I was the first to take him seriously as more than a mechanic, and thus I advanced solemnly into hesitant friendship.

At the start, his talk and behavior left me flabbergasted. On one of our first meetings alone we lunched at a cafeteria on West 14th Street. As we spoon-and-forked spaghetti, he told me he'd been a merchant seaman for six years, oiling engines, spreading films of grease on which ball bearings moved hot and cold. He explained the moments when it was possible to insert one's hand into a machine, and how, sleeping next to one once, it had wounded him. Then, changing tack, he said he disliked Joseph Conrad's writing: it was the work of "an officer spying belowdecks."

Bit by bit, over the red-and-white checkered tablecloth, his story emerged. As a kid of seventeen, he'd enlisted in the Navy. Drunk in Hoboken once, he'd overstayed his leave and, instead of reporting to the Brooklyn Navy Yard, had gone to Boston to see his mother. He was arrested and handcuffed at her door, then, to his mother's horror, taken to prison on Commonwealth Pier, where they kept him in a room with fifteen or twenty others. The prisoners there could do nothing for forty-eight hours but stand around and curse. He saw one man who he thought at the time might later bully him, but who he now knew had attracted him. He went up to him quietly and slit him with his razor across the fleshy part of a hand. A fight had started, which was shortly silenced, but he was sent off with a lot of criminals to Deer Island, in Boston Harbor. One day a boy tried to swim the straits to the mainland. He wasn't punished when they recaptured him, but the inmates below had been denied their movies for a week. Cell doors were left unlocked one night and the swimmer was forced to run a five-tier gauntlet. The men struck him with steel chains, pots, and anything else they could lay their hands on. The boy howled and howled until he collapsed at the bottom of the stairs and died. Carlsen was on bread and water for the first month; every third day, a stew was given him. As the prisoners all ate together, they would surreptitiously divide everything up, thrusting a handful of stew into their blue jeans to be eaten later on the bunks, so Carlsen didn't get much benefit from his meager ration. Cigarette tobacco was passed around by being spit along the cells to the last one where the prisoner could spread it out in the sun and smoke it later. Carlsen induced himself into a stupor by masturbating nonstop.

He also told me about the drug habit he developed afterward, and how he'd taken cocaine, opium, and morphine just to experience what it was like. His partiality was opium, with its orderly ritual of pipe, lamp, and flame—he smoked for three months, then decided to stop. When he did, he told me, he lay on his bed with all the paraphernalia beside him, so that he would have to resist an added temptation to resume the habit.

Later, we went back together to his neat little room. He put coal into a small iron stove and I saw an open dictionary on a table. He said it was the first time he'd ever regretted not going to school. He wanted to be a writer, knew what he wanted to say, but couldn't find the words. I asked what he wanted to say and he answered: "The feeling of a man shaving when a woman is watching him and she gets a thrill out of it, and so does he, knowing she's watching." And he also wanted to conjure up the scene of a man going down to the engine room in his best dungarees to oil something, yet knowing no one will see him. Carlsen said: "That's sex exhibitionism." He made tea and told me he'd been taking hashish once, had gotten the wrong stuff and had almost gone crazy. Luckily, there was a friend with him when he started laughing and crying madly. The man thought he was drunk, took him out, walked him from the corner of 14th Street over one hundred blocks to 118th Street, though this had seemed to him one single block. As he talked, I remember hoping that I'd not created a social barrier between us, although Walker Evans had warned me that Carl was a dangerous person. Carlsen kept going, though, and wanted to go out to dinner with me, but I had a date, which I wished I could break, but couldn't. Okay, no matter: he'd stay in and make himself spaghetti.

Steps from cautious contacts like that to relative intimacy were propelled by the abrupt arrival of his brother, a second officer with a coastal freighter on regular runs from San Diego through the Panama Canal up to Portland, Maine. Every three or four months Nils Carlsen enjoyed a few days' liberty from Hoboken. Carl took me over to explore his command. When we first climbed aboard, there seemed to be no one around. One custodian tended pilot fires in the furnace room. Here was surely a site for the split piston-rod and a stoker's shattered arm. Carl drew no special attention to any single piece of machinery. I was about to ask the function of every object, but realized this was his private sacred place, not to be profaned by idle, over-eager curiosity. If I, indeed, had felt awe, then I should let this jungle of polished brass bandings, glistening serpentine coils, and tigerine furnaces purr its hot breath uninterrupted. My brief questions were readily answered by his brother. The latent power in the engines' humming seemed to swell, filling Carl's silence, in which his complete comprehension of mineral potency was haloed by a scent of oil, the slumbering, acrid fragrance of coal-fire, an incandescent bluish gloom through thick-glazed furnace doors. A brutal, delicate mechanism was alive, grossly asleep, lovingly tended, waiting to be ignited into full flame. An unfired weapon immaculately maintained, it called for its own fuel of love, and love is what burnished it through Nils Carlsen's professional attention. Nils apologized to me for the inadequacy of active operation: his ship slept, not to be aroused until it met open sea. As we left, Carl astonished me by saying evenly that if we should ever ship out together, then he would let me learn what hot metal meant as a measure of energy in motion.

That initiation in the boiler room had been a revelation, and Carl's sudden, personal interpolation, tossed out so lightly, exploded that vein of incendiary excitement which is the rapacious flare of first love. While I realized only too well I could never bet on any specific date for our joint voyage, the fact he'd uttered so unusual a proposal diffused logic. After all, his brother was bound to this boat, he could probably arrange things easily. Why shouldn't we, some time in what glorious future, ship out together? I would teach Carl how to write, while he taught me how to live.

Why shouldn't we? For two good reasons, among tides of unanswerable others. First, Carl was in retirement from the sea, by will or chance. He was fixing to be a "writer." He took writing seriously: wrote mornings, he said, every day, from eight to eleven. What he wrote, Bertha, the piano teacher, his consort, typed afternoons. I could imagine that while she typed, he wandered around, did chores. She was the real hindrance for me. I never knew whether or not they "slept" together; it would have been impossible to have guessed otherwise, yet in public there was slight contact. Carlsen never talked dirty or made the exciting, outrageous, or forbidden raw jokes which might have been expected and for which I knew men of his class were famous. This further distanced me from a full unveiling of the many riddles he seemed to hold. Bertha cooked; she kept their house in its thin, immaculate rigor. As I ventured to drop in more often and stay longer, she made polite efforts to speak, but sooner or later retired upstairs. She tried to suggest she knew Carl and I had serious business by which his career might be furthered. Perhaps she also knew somehow that his "writing" was more or less a fantasy, but at least it was an alternative to his going back to sea, which certainly she did not want. She kept him on a loose chain; he had his "freedom" and I hoped he was free enough to include me somewhere in it. He seldom spoke of her. I might have made a silly speech of setting myself up against her, but his perfect manners precluded such folly.

However, eventually, I felt close enough to Carl to risk mentioning that I sensed "Bertha doesn't like me." I dared this, risking a presumption to which I had precarious right. All he admitted was: "You don't bother her." This was no resolution, but I knew enough not to press it. At the time when one is breaking out of post-adolescence, fright, insecurity, and apprehension encourage an appetite for adventure to be dared. Everything I had previously experienced or felt about people seemed now on the other side of a glass wall, and my "education" (*pace* well-beloved Henry Adams) was a half-conscious attempt to eliminate self-protection from some "real world." Carlsen now became my real world; his isolation was at once nearer and farther than anyone or anything. Unfleshed imagination flickers, a vast, amorphous void, filled with rainbow possibilities and doubt. Carl exploded it, bringing to my exercise of heart and mind a chance for three-dimensional existence, released from the prison house of habit. While he strove to make art out of his half-life, I tried to make come alive what until now I had only read about in books, which were the models that stopped him cold.

As for actual contact with Hart Crane, poet, roustabout, heir of Poe, Whitman, and Hopkins, this was tenuous. Although my encounters with Crane were negligible, I depended on Crane's immediacy to certify my contact with Carl. I knew Crane would not have recognized my name or face. However, I was close to some of those who did know him well, including Evans and Allen Tate. I was not drawn to his gift; I barely linked the man with his verse. Both seemed outrageous and unmannerly, although I was not yet ready to face blame for fearing its obscurity. After all, there was "Modern Art," and what a success that was becoming! I was forced to feel, despite prejudice, that there was some irreducible courage in him, both in art and life, a defiance, however gross or unseemly, of which I could not help being envious. Carl was slow to speak of his friend; he volunteered little that was revelatory or proprietary. He shied away from mention of "violence" or "perversity." If they had often been drunk or disorderly together, that was their business; Crane was above and beyond praise or calumny. As for Carlsen's own preference or promiscuity, he let me hear nothing; when he dealt out rum, it was the classic brace at the capstan. I assumed his deliberate moderation was the result of some earlier excess, now monitored by the lady piano-teacher. Yet I was eager to bring Carl into "my" world, to exhibit him to my friends Muriel Draper, Carl Van Vechten, and Jim Agee.

On April 28, 1932, I was invited to Muriel's for cocktails. I wrote afterward in my diary:

I learned of Hart Crane's drowning. A sickening feeling, but I never really cared for him or his work, except for "Hurricane" which I thought magnificent.

> Rock sockets, levin-lathered!
> Nor, Lord, may worm outdeep
>
> Thy drum's gambade, its plunge abscond!
> Lord God, while summits crashing
>
> Whip sea-kelp screaming on blond
> Sky-seethe, dense heaven dashing—
>
> Thou ridest to the door, Lord!
> Thou bidest wall nor floor, Lord!

After this, I hesitated asking Carl to show me more writing, since my early response had been so unwelcoming. With the removal of much compulsion to connect us through "literature," he grew less shy; our relations went from friendliness to something like friendship. An impersonation requiring considerable craft is that of feigning enthusiasm about the disappointing labor of someone whom one likes or loves. Carl was not going to be much of a literary man; if his attempts had been high-school student work by a sixteen-year-old, it might have proved promising. Apt phrasing, careful observation, genuine emotion, brief bursts of oddly personal intonation there may have been, but since he had read so little, and the things he had found on his own to read—Marlowe and Melville in particular—were such monstrous models, since his own vital experience had been so very deep and narrow, one could not hope for quality much beyond the primitive.

There was yet a further, profounder impediment. From inherent shyness or instinctive discretion, he excluded from his narrative any close intimacy of comment. Told to be terse, he stripped too much away, as if he were insisting on an essence which robbed things of their richness. He wrote about the sea and its mariners in terms of popular-magazine illustrations, confused by "literary" rhetoric, avoiding any psychological insight, as if such realism might defeat a "beauty" in simplicity. It was all too complicated and I had very little skill or experience as a helpful critic.

Carl, like his idol Crane, was a rhapsode, not an analyst. The exalted rhetoric of Marlowe and Melville derived in large part from traditions of the spoken word, drama or pulpit; it is the heightened emphasis of vocal utterance. Carl's prose, like Crane's poetry, may have been written to be read aloud: I have yet to hear any speaker give voice to Crane's lines as satisfactorily as one mouths them in the mind, with closed lips. Carl's opacity and stumbling splendor were hard to read and could never force their way into print.

The alchemy of the word is a hazardous science. Carlsen, with his small talent and less knowledge of his betters, was doomed as an artist—awe of the enormous potential in the English language betrayed him. His fathomless respect for literature was a means of touching the magic he couldn't make; and it prompted him to cast Crane as Prospero, transforming Brooklyn and Manhattan into enchanted islands. Did Carl have much notion of what Crane was really attempting to say? We once read together from *The Bridge*:

Whose head is swinging from the swollen strap?
Whose body smokes along the bitten rails,
Bursts from a smoldering bundle far behind
In back forks of the chasms of the brain,—
Puffs from a riven stump far out behind
In interborough fissures of the mind . . . ?

Carl stuck on "swollen strap." Why swollen? Now "interborough"; he could see a subway reference, but asked: "Why in hell can't he say what he means?" In the summer of 1926, Crane wrote to Waldo Frank, one of his first critical enthusiasts:

. . . work continues. The Tunnel now. I shall have it done very shortly. It's rather ghastly, almost surgery—and, oddly almost all from the notes and stitches I have written while swinging on the strap at late midnights going home.

In 1932, after the suicide, introducing a first American edition of *The Bridge*, Waldo Frank explained:

"The Tunnel" gives us man in his industrial hell which the machine —his hand and heart—has made; now let the machine be his godlike Hand to uplift him! The plunging subway shall merge with the vaulting bridge. Whitman gives the vision; Poe, however vaguely, the method.

Partly as a devil's advocate, partly in my role as Professor of Modern Poetry, I tried to particularize for Carl what I conceived Crane's method proposed. I had been struck hard by an arresting image from "For the Marriage of Faustus and Helen" (Part III), which mentions "Anchises' navel, dripping of the sea," wherein I saw an ancestral demigod, striding toward a surf-bound Tyrrhenian shore, a figure by Giovanni da Bologna rather than Praxiteles, a classic marine divinity, perhaps the model for a baroque fountain, one of Bernini's gigantic epitomes. Carl asked: "Who the hell's Anchises?" Making it easy, I might have said that Anchises was another name for Neptune, the sea-god Poseidon, brother to Zeus, enemy of Ulysses, author of his misfortunes—or possibly only a trisyllable that Crane came across, which, like other fortuitous findings, fired his prosody. There seem to be two mentions only of Anchises in the *Iliad*; he was also father to Aeneas, lover to Aphrodite born of sea foam, second cousin to Priam, King of Troy. In Book III of the *Aeneid*:

> When old Anchises summoned all to sea:
> The crew, my father and the Fates obey.
>
> (Dryden)

Years later, a young Harvard scholar told me that in the Homeric "Hymn to Aphrodite," Anchises mates with the goddess, who bears his child in secret. Later, he is punished for presuming to couple with divinity: mortals shall suffer who dare touch the immeasurable. Crane, an autodidact, could have meant something concrete by naming Anchises—he had read widely. With Carlsen it was useless to pursue this; it reduced a marvel to the academic. I did my best by suggesting the taut, muscular belly of an ancient athlete brimming with saline, not very wine-dark, liquor, a substance chill and glistening as in a celestial shower-bath.

Nevertheless, in meetings with Carl, Crane was always an invisible third, spectral but manifest. I could understand well enough what he meant to Carl, but what did I mean—to Carl, or to anyone? Still a rich college kid, twenty-four years old, whose surfeit of "education" had misprized Crane's Pindaric ode to the tunnel beneath that bridge:

> O caught like pennies beneath soot and steam,
> Kiss of our agony thou gatherest;
> Condensed, thou takest all—shrill ganglia
> Impassioned with some song we fail to keep.

And yet, like Lazarus, to feel the slope,
The sod and billow breaking,—lifting ground,
—A sound of waters bending astride the sky
Unceasing with some Word that will not die . . . !

Perhaps my fixation on one of Crane's buddies was my attempt to compensate for such stupidity. But the truth was, Carl hardly connected me with either Harvard, *Hound & Horn*, or Crane. By now the magazine had been completely taken over by Dick Blackmur, Allen Tate and his Agrarians, and other intellectuals with political or metaphysical preoccupations. My postgraduate life was centered on Manhattan and Carl was just mildly amused that I was in love with him.

It wasn't easy to find him. He had his "work," which I assumed was dogged, daily moonlighting, sometimes as handyman or janitor; certainly I knew he didn't write all day and all night. Money never seemed a problem for him. Maybe Bertha's piano lessons covered his drinks; he was scrupulous about paying. Yet he was not someone I felt free to drop in on any old time, particularly if Bertha was likely to be there. Possibly I made her more of a problem than she actually was. Most days, having learned to estimate his working habits, I'd go over with the excuse of asking if he'd like to go for a walk. If he didn't feel like it, and if she were in, she'd promptly vanish upstairs. Her presence was pervasive. I learned that she was not only a piano teacher; she was also an officially licensed Christian Science practitioner. She spent time as a constant healer. This further distanced her and increased Carlsen's unfathomable mystery. What in the world could he see in her? How could he believe in all that crap? Or did he?

Some nights Carl might even walk me to my room on Minetta Lane, where I'd make him tea or a drink. I then shared the place with Tom Wood, an ex-cowboy, who, having been trained as a blacksmith, turned into a craftsman of forged iron. He made handsome fire-screens with carefully cut-out silhouettes of animals, stubby andirons, and pleasant shop-signs. Carl and Tom had shared the experience of handling hot metal; there were also unspoken bonds of class and manual labor. Their immediate, cool rapport made me objectively happy, subjectively sad.

One night, a clear September early evening, I went around hoping to catch Carl in, and on the way bet myself he'd be out—insurance against disappointment. City street-sounds were diminished and clarified, the darkening air all the more transparent from thin punctuation of fragmentary voices. The courtyard in front of his house was swept clean; three garbage pails were in a neat triangle, coverless but empty. Carl was alone. I expected Bertha to return shortly and spoil my fun. He was wearing a crisp pair of regulation white navy ducks. Rum was on his table-desk, the typewriter on the piano. It was almost as if he'd been expecting me. Bertha had gone to Chicago to care for a sick sister (through prayer? I now wonder). How long would she be gone, I asked. "Don't know. You want tea, or grog?"

The abrupt luxury of freedom felt then, I can still feel. It's a shrunken residue, although the intensity of the explosion was that once-in-a-lifetime thrust of luck which only erupts in youth; it was a true joy by which others would later be judged and found wanting. For the first time, I had Carl to myself, in his place, his tavern, his forecastle. Now I would discover everything, how he felt, what he thought, who he was. We drank quietly in rather oppressive silence, speaking of nothing in particular. What I wished to say rushed far and fast ahead of what I could actually speak. Inside, curiosity boiled, but he seemed even more self-centered than usual. My first, wild, manic propulsion subsided into apotropaic depression. I asked what he'd been up to. "Writing." Evening was leaking away in each sip of rum and water. I was an intrusion, whatever his placid courtesy; yet I couldn't bring myself to leave. Talk unraveled. Finally, I had to say: "Carl, you're bushed. I'd better go," and pushed back my chair to stand up. So did he. He put a hand on my shoulder: "Stay here, kid, if you like."

We had nightcaps and I stayed. Thus commenced a brief domestic interlude in which I played substitute housekeeper, enjoying the closeness and coolness of a creature whose mythical image was for me no less mysterious than a unicorn's. Carl's quest for quiet, his spareness in motion, his quizzical softness which was also tender firmness, his nicety in consideration, his dispassionate attention or friendliness, could easily be translated into terms of love. In him, not far below the surface, were layers of reserve which denied any profound exchange. He was not concealing himself; his nature, either from poverty, discipline, or good manners, secreted an unchallenged dignity. Possibly there was fear too, but of what? Such withholding or denial was for me an accumulated provocation. He was not teasing; it was just Carlsen. When I discussed all this, too earnestly, with Walker Evans, he said only: "Oh, that Carl. He's just another one of Crane's characters: another sphinx without a secret."

Despite cold water and intermittent doubt, he remained an enthralling riddle, never more so than when he got up early, boiled his kettle of shaving water, washed from a wooden bucket, and set out breakfast. I stayed in bed, partly to let him have his house to himself for a bit; partly to enjoy and observe his singularity. I don't know whether he wandered about bare-assed when Bertha was there. With me, he never dressed until ready to go out into the street. This wasn't narcissism. He never drew attention to himself, nor was he particularly graced in the flesh. Nude, he might have been any age, twenty-five to forty-five, a sleek, hard, almost hairless male; easy, self-confident, deliberate. Nakedness was just this creature's clothing.

But questions intruded. I couldn't accept my situation for whatever it was on his part; I must worry it, "make sense" of it. Where, and who, after all, was I? Soon, Bertha would come back; she might walk in at any moment—tomorrow morning, tonight, now. Each time that I noticed her stubby piano with its sparkling black-and-white keys, its sheet music stacked neatly on top, I sensed a looming adversary. Yet why should her pervasive if fragile absence cloud my present since it in no way bothered Carlsen? How greedy can you get? We both knew she was inevitably expected; ours was no marriage, nor was it a one-night stand. If I strained, trying to make myself useful by offering some "contribution," Carl didn't notice. This was my business. He wouldn't have asked me to stay if he hadn't felt some need. Guilt was nowhere near, as far as I was concerned; only delight.

I'd hoped to have helped him with his "work," his stories, but he never seemed to have finished one to a degree he thought worthy of being criticized. He kept his papers-in-progress in manila binders. Sometimes, when I was in the house alone, I glanced at a page or two, though this seemed disloyalty for which I might be punished. Then, about a week after I'd moved in, something prompted me to start reading one of his folders straight through. There were some ten or a dozen pages, a few typed, others handwritten. Halfway down the last page, the words stopped in the middle of a sentence. This was the same for all of his work. Nothing was finished; that every one stopped short seemed an odd coincidence. I realized that Carl longed to become a "writer," but he couldn't write. Perhaps this was due, latterly, to the refusal of the editors of *Hound & Horn*. I guessed he knew I knew his secret but mutual convenience prevented it from being admitted. He had rare emotional reserve with no sentimental taint; I recognized him as a classic stoic. Perhaps this is why Crane picked him out. In an untidy universe, he was order, minor magic however miniature, a clipper ship in a bottle.

On December 21, 1923, Crane wrote from Woodstock, New York, to his mother in Cleveland a letter replete with patient sympathy for her maddening complaints about her husband, Crane's father, her divorce, her self-martyrizing, her distaste for her son's way of life. He told her:

I, too, have had to fight a great deal just to *be myself* and *know myself* at all, and I think I have been doing and am doing a great deal in

following out certain natural and innate directions in myself . . .
Suffering is a real purification, and the worst thing I have always had
to say against Christian Science is that it wilfully avoided suffering,
without a certain measure of which any true happiness cannot be fully
realized.

Crane, too early on, had ceased being a child. His physique, gifts, affective life were forced into prematurity. Due to
over-aroused psychic activity, the furious problems of domestic
tension between his ill-assorted parents stoked raw feelings of
antagonism and frustrated escape long before the boy had
any capacity to diffuse them. The anguish in his prepotency
withered him. He quickly became an old youth in an unresisting
body and settled for an hysterical persona laminated to his
true center—brilliant, irascible, coruscating, electric, a rocket
launched toward magnetic relief in its own extinction.

Why should unadulterated animal attraction or sweetness
of spirit be allied necessarily with the capacity to paint tremendous pictures or compose extraordinary poetry? What is its
pay-potential on a humane level? Honest work has to be judged
against what range of talent—lyric fantasy or the genius which
kindles makers and failures? Carl Carlsen had strayed into a
dangerous area, like the thermodynamic transformations which
he had come to image as artistic "creativity." He had stumbled,
unequipped and unendowed, into a field of force. His will to
write, to become "a writer," licensed desire and gave it an
illusion of spirit and ability which was only an echoed promise.
This honest workman had been lent a vision of unlimited
possibility. He should have pursued a more profitable existence
in physics, chemistry, or navigation, insuring an alternative
future, but the words, the fearsome sorcery of words, fixed him
in their web and gave him only a recognition of his ultimate
weakness. Crane launched himself on an inevitable trajectory
only to be arrested at its peak. Carlsen never got within sight
of a start.

Outside the amphitheater at Nîmes, 1922, during a trip to Europe with my mother

(above) In the costume of a Greek heroine during rehearsals for Richard Harding Davis's melodrama The Galloper. *Berkshire School, spring 1924; (opposite, top) George Gurdjïeff, 1924; (bottom) One of the preparatory photographs by Martin Mower for the portrait of me that he painted in Cambridge, 1927 (Martin Mower)*

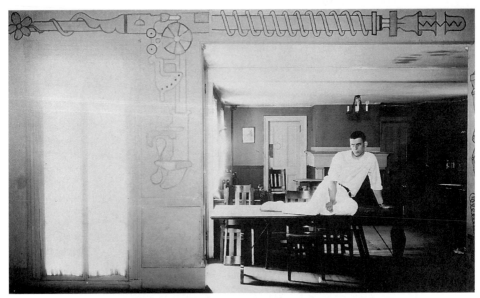

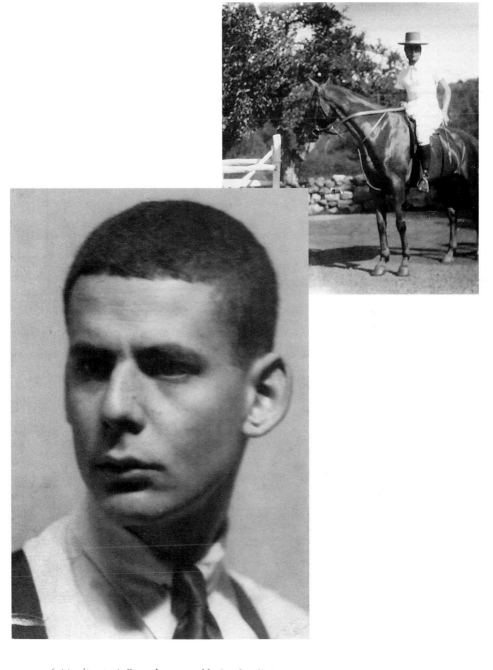

(opposite, top) Seated on a table in the dining room of the Harvard Liberal Club, ca. 1927–28, surrounded by elements of my last mural; (bottom) In Cagney pose—one of the first photographs that Walker Evans took of me in Cambridge, ca. 1928 (© Estate of Walker Evans); (above, top) On one of my sister's horses at her farm in Ashfield, Massachusetts, ca. 1929; (bottom) In New York, ca. 1930

Carl Carlsen, New York, 1932
(George Platt Lynes)

(above, top) Romola Nijinsky with her husband and their daughter, Kyra, ca. 1920; (bottom) George Balanchine, as he appeared in Les Ballets 1933 *program for the Paris season*

Son and father, New York, 1933 (George Platt Lynes)

While I was living in Carl's house, he took good care that I had my own towel, tumbler, and tar soap; he didn't like to share his old-fashioned, straight, bare-blade razor; anyway, I would have cut myself. Everything was shipshape; the days passed, without incident, except we got along well. Sooner or later, I'd have to leave. Either there would be a letter or a telegram from Chicago announcing Bertha's return, or she might surprise us. Carl didn't think that would happen; she had her own kind of consideration, which is why they'd been a pair so long. The delicacy that joined them was not broken by any resentment, although she had no idea that I was temporarily taking her place.

So, her special-delivery letter arrived; Bertha's mission in Chicago was a complete success. Her sister was entirely recovered, although she made no boast of "Scientific" ministrations. She planned to take such and such a train, and could be expected to arrive on such and such a day and hour. There was no big deal about goodbyes; in the few days left we pursued our amiable routine.

The best place to call it a day was in bed. I loved sleeping with Carl; this was no euphemism. We'd learned to sleep like spoons. If either had to get up in the night, it was no problem to reverse positions and sleep the more soundly. Vulnerability transcended? Something like that. Alone together; cozy, quiet. What I felt most was the gravity or power of his light treatment of my fascination with him. He knew I loved him. As for him —he liked me; I was a pet or mascot.

Trying to make a neat end to the episode, I said: "You smell so good. Is it the tar soap?" Any more oppressive farewell would have been unseemly. "Yeah; and that's vinegar water, but not from vinegar. Crane liked that stuff." I told Carl how much I'd enjoyed my vacation. Abruptly, for the first time, there was a hard edge to his voice: "Why didn't you like Hart?" I said I'd hardly known him; he scared me; I wasn't up to him. His disorder, my guilt. My envy. Stupidity. "Funny," said Carl.

"You didn't like him, but you liked me." I heard myself saying: "Oh, Carl; why the hell do you always have to bring Crane into it?"

"Why, you silly son of a bitch," he growled. "If it wasn't for Crane, I wouldn't have given you the sweat off my ass."

Fokine, Madame Nijinsky, New York

1931–1933

ENCOURAGED AS I WAS by my cousin Nat Wolfe's random enthusiasm, ballet early on became something of an unappeased obsession for me. My first brush with the dance as an autonomous, spectacular activity was in 1916, when Diaghilev's Ballets Russes appeared in Boston's Opera House. I was not permitted to attend. This was due to my behavior a season before when, at the tragic finale of *La Bohème*, I became convinced that the soprano who sang Mimì was actually coughing herself to death before my eyes. Hysterical sobs convinced my mother that I was too sensitive to endure further exposure to high emotive display, especially the untoward violence which had been reported of *Scheherazade* and Nijinsky's feline brutality. (Later I learned from Nijinsky's wife that, as a matter of strict fact, he had never danced in Boston. Due to some premonitory mental crisis, his understudy, Alexander Gavrilov, performed *Spectre de la Rose* and *Carnaval* in his place.) In a sense, my mother was right about my fitness to see Nijinsky, since later, my reaction to theater, particularly theatrical-dancing, involved more intense sensations than any attached to most daily existence, even personal attachment. I soon came to believe I was intended for stage-managed experience and would be often confused as to what was falsely real or really true.

If I'd been born with any specific talent, it was appreciation of visual or performing skills. Although I never witnessed Nijinsky onstage with those painted scenic surrounds in which he moved, through a relayed image I was awarded insight into the principles of Post-Impressionism, an enormous progression past the habitual limits of viewing. My grade-school teacher of English wrote children's books in which she shared her advance-guard artistic discoveries with her young pupils. She showed us an illustrated program of the Russian Ballet with its four-color plates of Léon Bakst's designs for *Scheherazade*. At first look, his raw renderings seemed blunt or coarse, achieving an atmosphere quite unlike background scenes common to photographic studios, which in monochromatic, niggling detail approximated to what I felt was a maximum expression of objective reality delineated on a picture-plane. But Miss Baker let us see that Bakst's generalizing brush strokes were intended to carry across to an audience seated at considerable distance from hung backdrops, while his fused spectrum evoked an area which suggested spatial truth. Thereafter, I tended to connect everything unsuspected or innovative with visual novelties belonging to the theater, and in particular the Russian Ballet, as it was then called. And I began to develop preferences beyond what I'd been casually assigned by my background as "good taste." My former criteria had been borrowed from half-tone, black-and-white reproductions in my mother's red-bound volumes of *Klassiker der Kunst*. Now I was forced to admit once more there was more than one mode of placing paint to convince the eye it was seeing tri-dimensional form.

Although denied a glimpse of Nijinsky in his flesh, I saw, in *Vanity Fair*, a reproduction of an etching (by Troy Kinney, I think) which for the moment almost filled this gap. Nijinsky stood in absolute physical and spiritual balance, profiled in silhouette, clad in the black velvet tunic and full white silk sleeves of the male soloist in Fokine's *Les Sylphides*. There was a deeply mysterious, breathless stasis in his stoic silence, something at once commanding, elegant, and very wild. He was the incarnation of Chopin's sonorities as I heard them from my sister's piano practice, and this etching became an icon to which I constantly referred as the sum of masculine possibility. (Oddly enough, this identical image similarly moved two other ballet-omanes whom I later met: Osbert Sitwell and Richard Buckle had clipped the same etching from *Vanity Fair*.)

My initial experience of classical ballet was in the spring of 1918, when the Chicago Opera Company offered "The Dance of the Hours" from *La Gioconda* as an isolated *divertissement* at a matinee to which my mother took me. The strict academic style from Milan's La Scala seemed rigid, clock-like, mechanical, but I loved the full stage crammed with whirling bodies, although dress and decor seemed washed-out compared with what I'd learned to expect from Miss Baker's reproductions of Bakst's designs. Also, there was performed an "American novelty," called *Dance in the Place-Congo*, music by Henry F. Gilbert, which climaxed with a knife fight in a New Orleans slave market, the entire corps de ballet transformed by black or brown makeup.

Memory is unreliable, particularly when it tries to distinguish between what was hoped for, spoken of, or read about, and what was indeed witnessed. I'm therefore not certain if I actually saw *The Birthday of the Infanta*, music by John Alden Carpenter and choreography by Adolph Bolm, an ex-Diaghilev dancer then resident in Chicago. Carpenter's scores for his *Skyscrapers* and *Krazy Kat* were jazz pioneering. Both almost interested Diaghilev, but *Skyscrapers*, borrowing elements from tap dancing, was later produced by the Metropolitan Opera in New York rather than in Monte Carlo or Paris. *The Infanta* followed Oscar Wilde's tale, its visual aspects based on Velázquez's *Las Meninas*. It was vividly reported by H. T. Parker, the eminent music critic of *The Boston Evening Transcript*. Did I see it then, or only read of it in his deftly fulsome description? My recollection is clouded by a snow-storm which I know delayed costumes and scenery shipped from Chicago to Boston, so that its first performance was probably postponed. I had seen its advance publicity; this perhaps merged with my eager expectation.

Whatever it was that lurked as an imaginative need, "ballet" stuck in my elementary judgment as a luminous magnet. This basic bias soon accumulated conviction, sharp preferences rapidly becoming what counted as "my taste." Reputations and fame glowed as a nimbus around the bodies of God-given performers, flaring or withering as I managed to gain first-hand impressions from their galvanic performances. Anna Pavlova, seen by Nat and me on several consecutive nights upon the inadequate platform of Symphony Hall, looked small-scaled, yet intimately perfect. Fokine's *Mecca*, a commercialized, post-Diaghilev dilution, had for background a full flight of steep steps, filling the opera-house proscenium, yet its action was tentative and nervous despite the oppressive grandeur. Isadora Duncan was obese and shy-making. Ruth St. Denis, while personally charming, lacked the swift sharpness of ballerinas on *pointe*, but as alternative to academic ballet her "oriental" pastiches held broadening hints. There were many members of the dance family, but the only one truly blessed in my mind was ballet. Ted Shawn danced nearly naked—what I chiefly recall is his gilded jock-strap, a suggestion of molten bronze. I think it was 1924 when I saw Martha Graham in the "Greenwich Village Follies," framed in the cutout of a huge perfume bottle. However, it would remain the incandescent echo of Nijinsky's image, alongside Bakst's color plates, which determined the flickering vision leading me toward my future.

It was in London, also in 1924, that I first saw a Diaghilev season. *Les Matelots*, with Massine's jazzy sailors who could have been clad from the surplus of an American Army-Navy store, was self-consciously trivial as a work of art, but it indicated a departure from the decorative folklore of the Russian Ballet's initial period, an early statement of post-World-War-I modernity. It satisfied me more as a declaration of policy than as an independent triumph of dancing, but strengthened my faith in the crusading principles of Diaghilev's policy. Here was the breath of quotidian low-life, discreetly devised, framed in the discipline of classic dancing. I identified it with *Imagiste* verse by Amy Lowell and with Jean Cocteau's line drawings, Jacob Epstein's sculpture, and Picasso's painting. The past was abandoned, rhetoric was left behind, and a new and electric sensibility was available and exploited. To be a first witness of such dynamism rarely happens in a lifetime.

My first Stravinsky ballet was *L'Oiseau de Feu*. This was in a diminished recension of its massive original of the decade before, and against its slightly shabby splendor *Les Matelots* glowed all the brighter. However, Kastchei, its evil sorcerer, brandished fantastic crimson stiletto-fingernails with a vicious delicacy far past conventional mimicry. I had no inkling that this wizard was a dancer named Georgei Balanchivadze; it was his first season with Diaghilev. After that, I had no further impression of him until 1929, when a repertory included his *Apollo, Le Fils Prodigue*, and *Le Bal*.

During my Harvard years, there swam in my unconscious filaments of impulse and desire, swarming into an inchoate nucleus, a benign growth, which led me to consider that somehow, sometime, I might forge a link to further concrete possibilities. While a sophomore at Cambridge I took elementary ballet lessons from Edward Duburon, an ex-Chicago dancer who provided a basis of the grammar of classicism. Later, I enlisted in classes from Mikhail Fokine, taught in the drawing room of his Riverside Drive mansion, and struggled alongside the *barre* with Patricia Bowman and Paul Haakon, two reigning soloists of the epoch. Fokine was glad enough to suffer rich idiots like myself. Due to my blind devotion and hopeless incapacity, he also let me stay after class and interview him for a brief biography which was promptly printed in London in 1934, through the agency of Arnold Haskell, Britain leading balletomane. It was not much of a book, but it listed the full range of his ballets, and served as a tangible passport, proving that at least I had more than an amateur's interest. I was greatly impressed by Fokine's talent as a portrait painter. His efficient, full-length canvases of himself and his wife in costume confirmed he could have enjoyed a parallel career. I never really imagined that I, myself, might dance, but the fact that a performer could also become a proficient painter gave me vain, vestigial hope that there was a chance that I too, with my passion for ballet, might also finally turn into a painter.

Such early fevers were no more than a glancing against a remote enormity with which I had no more real contact than if I had been gazing on a mythical map of a future inhabited by damsels and dragons. Yet I would find that, in their human forms, such creatures really existed, while a few danced. In midsummer 1929, I was in Italy researching my senior-year dissertation on El Greco, who as a young student from Crete had probably worked briefly in Venice. I carried introductory letters from Fogg Museum scholars to local collectors, and followed a list of sites connected with his documented career.

On my way off for a day's excursion to Padua with Agnes Mongan, who was also in Venice, we passed the Greek Orthodox basilica of Saint George, where it was easy to imagine El Greco might have worshipped. That morning its façade was heavily draped in gold and black hangings proclaiming a funeral within. I did not risk penetrating what was, after all, a private ceremony, although sounds of celebration and choir music streamed through its portals. Then, at the railroad station, I read in the previous day's Paris *Herald-Tribune* that Serge de Diaghilev had died on the Lido two days before and that his obsequies were scheduled for the morning I had happened to come upon them.

Among painters whom the young Greco may have known in Venice was one Giambattista Zelotti, who adorned a famous Palladian villa on the riverbank of the Brenta. It was convenient to pass by La Malcontenta on our way back from Padua; I had a letter to its owner. This I presented to his butler on the ground floor and we were received by Mr. Alberto Landsberg in the grand vaulted hall of his *piano nobile*. He explained that some even attributed the murals which covered walls and ceiling to Paolo Veronese, though they were now pale, flaked, and fragmentary. Landsberg, while courteous and kind, seemed nervously preoccupied. Conversation soon lapsed. I was relieved when the big room began to fill with a small company of men and women, all clad in black. Among them I recognized Serge Lifar and Anton Dolin, two Diaghilev principals whom, previously, I'd only beheld onstage. Landsberg's guests had been invited to celebrate the passing of their director, and for many, their admired friend. Without troubling Landsberg with perfunctory thanks, we left, bemused by the coincidence of this day's intrusion.

This brush by the source of ballet in my era held, at the moment, small personal significance, yet subsequently it acquired a prophetic symbolism. Picturesque collusion, while attractive in retrospect, I never claimed as a sign of vocation, although taken in sequence with other, similar concatenations, one might be forgiven for imagining there was a superior mechanism stoking one's ambition. Far more significant was my meeting with Romola Nijinsky, the dancer's wife, in New York in 1931.

I fail to recall exactly the run-up to this encounter. Perhaps it was through Malvina Hoffman, a well-known sculptor who had made a series of bas-reliefs of Anna Pavlova and Mordkin from motifs of Fokine's *Daphnis et Chloë*, which I'd been advised to inspect as an illustrative document of a lost choreographic masterpiece. There were few photographs but Fokine, sadly yet proudly, recalled it for me. My first encounter with Madame Nijinsky occurred in the Sutton Place home of Mrs. William K. Vanderbilt, an early, ardent patron of the Russian dancers in America; she was recommended to me when I was gathering data on Fokine. She was generous enough to accept my fascination with her own memories, while in my turn I seemed to interest or amuse her. I gave her Dixon Wecter's history of American High Society in the golden age of Newport and

Tuxedo Park, and in it, she found what she'd quite forgotten
—her brief engagement to Franklin Roosevelt's father. In her
exquisite drawing room, paneled in Chinese-export wallpaper,
I was introduced as a devotee of her husband's fame to Romola
de Pulsky Nijinsky.

Madame Nijinsky was a well-born Hungarian. Her father,
Count (or was it Baron?) de Pulsky, had been chief of the
national museums. Her mother, an actress, was renowned as
"the Austrian Bernhardt"—only a lack of native French speech,
it was said, robbed her of a European reputation. Romola was
well-educated, spoke and wrote four languages, had been
dressed at their expense by the best *couturiers*.

In current terminology, as a 1911 post-adolescent she'd
become a "groupie," helplessly magnetized by the aura of Vaslav
Nijinsky's presence. How or why she was licensed by Diaghilev
to join his troupe was not plain. He always needed money and
attracted younger members of eminent families who enjoyed
backstage privileges and the right to feed hungry dancers.
Romola spoke no word of Russian; Nijinsky's French was
rudimentary. They were on remote terms until the troupe
embarked to tour South America in 1915. Diaghilev chose not
to go; a gypsy had told him he would die on water (and he
did—on the Adriatic). By the time Buenos Aires was sighted,
Romola had contrived to make Vaslav propose. They were soon
married. Diaghilev, in hysterical rage, dismissed him from the
Ballets Russes.

Nijinsky never preferred domination by another male. His
early protector in St. Petersburg, Prince Lvov, was a sympathetic
man-about-town who exchanged the boy for another youth,
then Diaghilev's confidential secretary. There is every evidence
from Nijinsky's diary that he ached to be free of Diaghilev's
possessiveness and that he had a strong desire for conventional
stability. He delighted in the two daughters Romola gave him
and the brief happiness of marriage. Although the breach with
Diaghilev was later patched in New York, enabling a disastrous

American tour, the rupture was deeply wounding to both and neither wholly recovered in its aftermath.

By the time I met Romola she'd endured a legendary life of unlikely adventure. During World War I, she managed to support her ailing husband, two small daughters, and herself through intermittent aid from King Alfonso of Spain, the Aga Khan, Lady Ottoline Morrell, and others. Nijinsky, now with the status of a mindless vegetable, passed from one Swiss psychiatric clinic to another in vain hope of some ultimate cure. Once he was settled, Romola, having done all that was possible, placed her children with her mother in Hungary and felt free to pursue her own peculiar pilgrimage.

Romola was a small, extremely attractive, dark-haired woman with fine features and an immaculate presence. She had the breadth and stance of one who had survived the best and worst. She landed in New York in 1931, accompanied by the body of Frederike Desentije, a young Dutch woman who'd been her companion in the East Indies and had died suddenly in Bali. Before that, there had been Lya da Puti, a popular film star. One of the first of my self-imposed duties after meeting her at Mrs. Vanderbilt's was to squire Romola on weekly visitations to the receiving vault in Woodlawn Cemetery, where fresh bouquets of Parma violets were laid on Frederike's coffin. These flowers were the favorites of the Duc de Reichstadt, Napoleon's unfortunate son, whose princely, androgyne essence Romola had transferred to her dead Dutch friend. Though Frederike was gone, Madame Nijinsky was still attended in this life by an entourage of dubious characters, chief among whom was Mrs. Garrett, an eminent trance-medium, though there was also a shadowy Hungarian lawyer-accountant with a troubling resemblance to Count Dracula, as well as an "international journalist," the pal, it was said, of great press barons including Rothermere, Beaverbrook, and perhaps William Randolph Hearst.

Dominant was "Ma" Garrett, a jolly, past-middle-age piece

of baggage, whose séances were supervised by an ancient Persian mullah and his control, an Ariel-type sprite known as Little Blue-Bell. I attended a few séances, in which tabletops tipped satisfactorily enough, chill blasts of air blew in the windowless chamber, and candlesticks detached themselves upward from a mantelpiece. But the questions asked and the responses evoked were so silly that I soon begged off, and was made to feel like a lapsed Philistine heretic who must pay a ransom to offended spooks. Whether it was precisely to them I paid, was not the point; one way or another, I paid. Romola shared Nijinsky's Nansen passport, the kind that was issued to homeless wanderers through the League of Nations after World War I. However, the U.S. Immigration Service was not satisfied by its current legality and I found myself in constant convulsions of judicial entanglement with trips to Ellis Island or Montreal, where, at the American consulate, permission would finally be wangled for temporary extension of Romola's stay. Mrs. Vanderbilt provided anchorage, but Romola found means to exasperate even her most loyal clientele. There was a forever renewing or declining support system; her psychic energy and her skills for prompt, intransigent persuasion were not inexhaustible. I was not equipped for such emergency operations either. She was continually transferring from one cheap hotel to another less dear. The Transylvanian lawyer-accountant, the international journalist, and, above all, "Ma" Garrett contributed as they were able, but their schedules seldom coincided with her gravest needs, and I was left with more than one fiscal trial on my amateur hands.

We were never anywhere near romantically involved, but I had one hell of a time explaining my attachment to this other "older woman" to my alarmed parents, already made wary by Muriel Draper. I'd been given an allowance which was adequate though not extravagant, but Romola's requirements were superior to it. I was not experienced and Romola was quick to bait my prurient curiosity with intimate details of the private lives of Diaghilev's dancers. She was an adroit psychologist, and dealt out continuous portions of absorbing reminiscences, always, like Scheherazade's, "to be continued in our next."

More important, she was the possessor of a treasure which at the time combined for me the sacral potency of the Rosetta Stone, the Golden Fleece, and splinters from the True Cross. This was a small, brown, hand-written notebook, a manuscript of Nijinsky's idiosyncratic notational system. I did not then recognize that it was mainly an extension of the Stepanov method, taught at the St. Petersburg Academy as an *aide-mémoire* to ballet masters, who depended on it less than they did on their own experience of performance. However, I convinced myself that Nijinsky among his other gifts had, Einstein-like, invented a language of time-space which could be read to revive the entire past or present repertory from dim antiquity into a progressive future. Its anthropomorphic symbols, closely linked to musical notes, would, somehow, make every problem plain. Little of this had anything to do with practical efficacy, but I was so magicked that I felt I was in touch with the lexicon of a lost Atlantis or the language of the Etruscans.

One cold, dismal, late Sunday afternoon, Romola asked me to meet her in the lounge of a hotel from which she was about to be evicted. I was presented with a batch of bills, large and small, while she, God knows how, produced a bottle of champagne and twin goblets. She informed me this was to be our final meeting. The attendant mood resembled a ritual Last Supper. On the morrow, through the guidance of "Ma" Garrett, she would advance toward a higher plane. I was not unduly alarmed; she'd threatened suicide on several previous occasions. But by now I was frightened as to the ultimate fate of Vaslav's sacred choreographic manuscript. I had not intended to let it fall to the tender mercies of the ancient Persian sage or Little Blue-Bell and had obtained a "loan" of the notes and made two photographic copies. But, of course, I neglected to inform Romola of my clandestine operation. Now, raising her champagne *coupe* with a steely smile, she toasted our respective futures: *"Bonne chance!* dear boy . . . You will now return me, together with two copies you've made—Vaslav's notation."

How she'd come by the discovery of my salvage attempt I never knew; perhaps through the ministrations of "Ma" Garrett, or her own delicate intuition and my self-revelatory body language. Romola proceeded to warn me she would write to my father that his son was a common thief who had tried to rob a poor woman of her single source of survival, and so on *ad nauseam.* I cannot begin to suggest the depth of my outrage at her reaction to the conservation of this most precious relic of her miserable existence by my selfless sacrifice. Instead of becoming the heroic savior of the entire ancient tradition of classic dancing, I was now its Judas Iscariot. Also—for I feared her effect on my already suspicious father—naked shame flayed me. Only someone familiar with the extremities of survival could have so accurately estimated the impact of this diabolical manipulation compounded by menace and mystery. She let its poison work and sink in for its full effect. Whereupon, she leaned over, kissed me lightly on both cheeks, and roared with laughter. I was forgiven like a naughty boy. Anger was not entirely submerged in my surge of relief. We drained her champagne. She then took me to an expensive dinner at her favorite Hungarian restaurant, ordering her customary rib steaks, cooked, as she always required, to the consistency of "shoe-leather." I paid. Suicide was relegated to future rehearsals, and I was bound closer.

This marked the commencement of a more or less official partnership in which I served as co-author of her biography of Nijinsky. If there were, as there were bound to be, any lacunae in the narrative, recourse could be had via the omniscience of a Persian magus or Little Blue-Bell. Soon, there would be enough typed pages to show several publishers, some of whom offered advances while not entirely aware there were other candidates in the auction. Such ethical lapses (as they would have been considered then) by this time barely touched my conscience. I imagined myself moved by a higher vocation than prompted most mortals; I felt endowed or, well, *chosen*.

But my hours with Romola educated me in other matters which I was most eager to master. She unlocked for me the closets, corridors, and subcellars of an edifice in which I would spend the rest of my life. For, at one, very frail, remove, without having any immediate contact with it, I became a veteran of Diaghilev's household. I learned at the same time to dispense with burdens of middle-class morality, to adopt chameleon masks adapted for theatrical needs. Aesthetics shared the strategy and tactics of military engagement. The terrain into which Romola guided me bordered on controlled hysteria, without a fair peppering of which stage performances are seldom memorable. But management of the unfettered imagination could make everything logical and available; flexibility, a capacity to analyze and act with quick confidence, no matter how temporary lesions in fate or fortune intervene, are practices only gained by experience. Romola grounded me in sly disciplines for which I was never, perhaps, properly grateful, since, even at the time, I felt I was paying in full. Benefiting from her style, though, and her supremacy over every harassment, I considered myself initiated into a partnership of free-booters. I had penetrated a gypsy brigand's sanctum whose lyric dimensions were wholly apart from anything for which I'd been prepared by my "education." Almost every incident of my history with Romola, whether with the immigration service, hotel bills, journalists, or publishers, would recur in the years to come. Familiarity with their elements made handling them simpler and gave me a premature professionalism, of which I could later take advantage.

So, equipped with the typescript of my booklet on Fokine, a contract for Nijinsky's biography, and a vacation allowance somewhat augmented by the generosity of my mother and father, I arrived in Paris in the midsummer of 1933.

Paris, London,
Balanchine
1933

IN PARIS, with a strong but unfocused aspiration toward
some kind of involvement in the activity of ballet, I managed
to find a room at the Hôtel du Quai Voltaire, a place which
had magical associations, both of historical and practical significance. It was here that Richard Wagner stayed during rehearsals for *Tannhäuser*, at whose first night the lordly members of
the Jockey Club roared down the Venusberg ballet with which
Wagner had dared to open his opera, instead of meekly
relegating it to the correct place in a later act when the aristocrats
were accustomed to come in at their own convenience and
inspect their proprietary ballerinas. But the more immediate
and practical meaning that the hotel had for me was that it was
next to Virgil Thomson's permanent apartment, and upon
Virgil I depended for the keys to the city. He was already an
accepted and knowledgeable citizen—bilingual, and experienced in every milieu and activity. He provided a prompt and
accurate map of the town's atmosphere and personnel, and
within a couple of breakfasts with him and his companion,
Maurice Grosser, he had supplied me with the informal but
invaluable information of gossip and history that launched me
painlessly into a *terra incognita*.

Virgil's tonal precision extended to his effortless analysis of the style and climate of our particular period. In his magisterial but offhand manner, he constated that the dominant *chic* was no longer "American-exile"—Pound, Gertrude Stein, Hemingway—but Marxist-tinged, "German-refugee," a result of the influx of self-exiles from Hitler, whose presence was signified by the mass of German automobile license plates visible in the streets. As for theater, and particularly the domain of dance, Diaghilev was four years dead and there was evidence of an active and competitive succession. The Ballets Russes de Monte Carlo, with support from the hereditary gambling casinos' annual seasons, represented the conservative inheritance, under the artistic direction of Léonide Massine. Boris Kochno, Diaghilev's former private secretary, was the candidate of the progressive and riskier inheritors. Backed by the anonymous purse of Madame Chanel, Kochno and George Balanchine, Diaghilev's final ballet master, had aroused advance-guard expectations. Balanchine would have seemed to be the presumed new chief for Paris's Grand Opéra, whose appointment was in the hands of Madame Misia Sert, though she favored Serge Lifar, the ultimate of Diaghilev's star performers. As for Balanchine, he'd been diverted to the Royal Danish Ballet, and was not in the best of health. Kochno had managed to find a lavish backer in the person of Edward James, a young English *milord*, whose mother had been the close companion of Edward VII. Whether or not the illegitimate scion of royalty, Edward James had inherited a large American railroad fortune and was among the first patrons of the Surrealists, promoting, in particular, Salvador Dalí.

The Ballets Russes de Monte Carlo, with the bulk of Diaghilev repertory revivals, was performing at the big, civic Châtelet theater. Balanchine had contributed two brilliant works for their previous inaugural season, but now he was preparing his *Ballets 1933*, in the comparatively small but more prestigious Théâtre des Champs-Elysées, the site of the original Russian Ballet's inaugural seasons. The two teams, captained by Massine and Balanchine, enjoyed a bristling anticipation comparable to a sports event, and each had its enthusiastic supporters. For me, it was an intoxicating landscape, and it seemed that the theatrical activity of this rather specialized area dominated my entire interest. Ballet had its undeniable presence in the city, not as massive as the growing role of Hitler, but a force still electric, personal, immediate. What was more, I was here, an observer, almost a reporter, a representative witness at the birth of a novel development which I could equate with the early days of Diaghilev's own innovations. While not actually involved yet, I felt I was as close as one might get to the prime spring of things.

Assiduously I researched dance documents in the libraries of the Grand Opéra, the Arsenal, and the new Archives de la Danse in Passy. I met historians and critics, survivors and scholars of a golden age. Their clinical attitude about the present and future, their presupposed professionalism, added to my conviction that there was a valid body of work, past any trivial gossip, supporting the seriousness of theatrical-dancing. I knew I could not myself be a dancer, but there was a possibility as a scholar, perhaps even as some sort of participant. I did not yet dare think of myself as anything so unlikely as an impresario. But . . . maybe, perhaps . . . in time?

I was confused by the relics which all the archival material exposed for me. Nijinsky's penciled notes for his *Faune* and *Sacre* were unintelligible, but they existed rather as Mayan hieroglyphs awaiting decipherment. They also gave the lie to bickering and backstage rumors that, nonetheless, I could not help longing to learn. Virgil Thomson took me to lunch with the excellent portrait painter Romaine Brooks. She had brought along Dolly Wilde, Oscar's niece, who recalled her uncle to an astonishing degree: jowls, full lips, and a hearty, benevolent, all-embracing smile. I asked her why there seemed to be no possibility of friendships in Paris, only fierce competition or envy. She thought this was universally the case, but Paris could seem to possess a more gilded or generous frame for these rivalries. Romaine Brooks added that Paris was a jungle disguised as a garden; here there were only *convenable* alliances, few real *amitiés*. I remembered that Oscar Wilde had said on his release from prison: *"Plus des amis, plusque des amants"*; Dolly was delighted. I surprised myself by the social ease I seemed to feel in so alien an atmosphere, and began to assume some small moral security which would masquerade as authority. In any case it saved time and seemed to work.

We went in a body to the première of *Les Ballets 1933* at the Théâtre des Champs-Elysées. A basic reason for Edward James's sponsorship was to promote a career for his new wife, Tilly Losch, a Viennese dancer of striking personality but no classic academic training. She had made her reputation in Vienna, and was considered a prime example of *hoch modernistische Kunst*. The evening was something of a long-delayed triumph for Christian Bérard, a young painter of great if disorderly gifts, who in spite of his living with Boris Kochno had never attracted Diaghilev. Bérard provided the costumes and decor for *Mozartiana*, Balanchine's first recension of Tchaikovsky homage. A tomato-red silhouette of the child composer at his harpsichord introduced a purely Parisian vision of Tamara Toumanova, one of Balanchine's newly discovered "baby-ballerinas." She had been given a beautiful supported adagio in a nightmare funeral procession borne by four unicorns. The ballet skirts combined the traditional tarlatans with bodices that were pure Chanel, and Dolly Wilde gripped my hand as if somehow to share our mutual enthusiasm, whispering vehemently: "This is where we want to be; nowhere else. Paris is the only place."

Mozartiana, as an overture, ensured the success of the enterprise. While by no means startling, it satisfied the expectations of a greedy, informed audience by its pathos and piquancy. But the scandal and success of the evening, and indeed of the fortnight's season, was Pavel Tchelitchev's *Errante*, set to Schubert's "Wanderer Fantasy" with Balanchine's striking processional choreography and Tilly Losch's manipulation of a fourteen-foot sea-green satin train. For me, *Errante* would remain a milestone. On the afternoon before the première, I had my first experience of a stage rehearsal. Virgil Thomson let me in, and sat me next to Bébé Bérard, who, without interruption during the extended exercise, made extremely comic and critical remarks about the dancers' efforts on stage. I realized that Virgil had thought he'd done me honor by the association with Bérard, whose viper tongue darted its casual venom until I could have killed him. The scene was a cone of white translucent vellum, lit from behind with shifting colors, accompanying the movement of the corps de ballet as it paraded always from right to left, and off. The dancing, or plastic mimicry, was an animation of Tchelitchev's masterful drawings of human bodies in acrobatic space. All through this rehearsal, stage carpenters hammered away, battling the orchestra in a raw, clattering counterpoint. Interruptions to stage action almost angered me, as if a sacred ceremony were being violated; I also found it hard to accept the complacent behavior of Charles Koechlin, the arranger of the Schubert piano piece, and Darius Milhaud, the composer, who talked through the noise and playing as if none of it were worth their notice. After a particularly loud eruption from backstage, Koechlin said to the "modernist" Milhaud: "That's your sort of music, isn't it?" Here was the superior professional intimacy of theater, which I could see was the underlying structure of its final magic, but its technical informality seemed a desecration. The ballet rehearsal appeared drastically disorganized and I couldn't imagine how everyone concerned seemed so calm with a first performance but hours off.

There was another territory of active, provocative mystery which ran parallel to the province of ballet, and to which Virgil Thomson also possessed a key. This was a Parisian circle of blue-stocking *femmes savantes*, more or less marshaled by Mademoiselle Nathalie Barney, who lived in a famously decorated house at 20, rue Jacob. Originally a free-spirited young woman from a good Washington family, she had become a Parisian landmark, and the questionable ensign of her life was Courbet's big oval ceiling panel of two female nudes ardently entwined. She was by now a notorious figure through having been recognized as the *"Amazone"* of Rémy de Gourmont's elegant *lettres*. Dressed in a splendid white *tailleur*, she guided me into her small garden, which was the dainty setting for an eighteenth-century *pavillon d'amitié*, once the property of Adrienne Lecouvreur. Mademoiselle Barney obviously felt herself to be in the same line of Parisian *grandes dames*. Her tiny temple was domed, with stone ionic columns, between which were suspended airborne transparent cambric curtains, embroidered with mottoes from La Rochefoucauld. She held out one in particular for my inspection, and while her gesture might well have been perfunctory, I could not help taking its message as personal: "Self-love is the greatest flatterer of all." This seemed a warning against speedy presumption, and shook the overweening pace of my possibly incautious self-confidence. I felt uncomfortable the rest of the afternoon.

In spite of this chilly augury, I returned several times to Mademoiselle Barney's. One day, with Dolly Wilde, I sat next to a delightful young Oriental in a colonel's uniform. Slowly I began to discern that she was a girl from Vietnam. She'd been fighting the Chinese for six years and we politely shared our admiration for Mei Lan-Fang, the great actor-dancer. Also, there was Professor Mardrus, translator of the complete *Arabian Nights*, who was claiming to have given the libretto of *Scheherazade* to Diaghilev. Mardrus admitted to the colonel his single weakness as a linguist was that, having mastered half a dozen Semitic tongues, he knew no Oriental language. He wore a kind of Arab caftan and horn-rimmed spectacles, and he smoothly fondled the colonel's little, beautifully manicured fingers.

Through the years of editing *Hound & Horn*, I knew a number of American writers currently in Paris, and I was seeing something of Estlin Cummings and his beautiful friend, the fashion model Marian Morehouse. Cummings was rather cool toward my preoccupation with ballet; I had already, however, privately chosen him to write a scenario which might be

Balanchine's first "American" work. This was to be based, so I mused, on *Uncle Tom's Cabin*, and it would become one of my earliest disastrous proposals. When, two years later, he actually wrote it, it would be a verbally picturesque example of Cummings's poetic prose, offering very few pretexts for danced steps, save some explicit mimicry that could have resulted only in a naïve dumb show. Katherine Anne Porter was living in a large apartment at 166, boulevard Montparnasse, on its seventh walk-up floor. The quarters overlooked a serene convent in a green park, which might have been miles away in the country. Sitting by the louvered window, we spoke about an "American" ballet involving witchcraft and the Salem milieu of Nathaniel Hawthorne. She had once written the scenario of a Mexican folk-dance work for Anna Pavlova, and spoke with unbridled excitement of her Mexican days and the horror of Hart Crane's last months. Then, like a schoolmistress, she lectured me on the nature of American literature; why it was that our best male writers refused to face themselves both as men *and* women, with their constant fatal conclusion that American women were failures, since it was in this particular province that Hawthorne, Melville, Whitman, and now Hemingway had themselves so signally failed. Here, obviously, was a proposal for some future essay for *Hound & Horn*, that all-but-forgotten core of my avid energy, which ballet had now virtually annexed.

In between these meetings, I attempted to compensate for my lack of immediate contact with ballet performers by archival research and by familiarity with what existed on the stage. At the Grand Opéra, Serge Lifar, costumed and made up identically to Nijinsky, appeared in his version of Fokine's *Spectre de la Rose*. It was an adequate archeological reconstruction of lost visual aspects, but soulless as far as dancing was concerned; the final, legendary leap through the window was not even attempted. If I had been ignorant of what it represented, it would probably not have interested me at all. As Romola Nijinsky said, jumps or no jumps, it was all unrepeatable. But like an avid bird dog, I was hunting every available trace of Russian-ballet memory, and after the performance actually penetrated to Lifar's dressing room, with the excuse that I had photographs (photostats and very poor ones) of Nijinsky in the obscure role of Tyl Eulenspiegel (1916) to give him.

Later, Balanchine told me that Lifar said I had behaved like a ridiculous groupie in my apparent adoration of his fame. And it was quite true that I acted as if I were in some hypnotized dream in which I was a pilgrim, a student, an apprentice, almost a worthy participant. I existed in an enthralling confusion, full of curiosity but without a plan, and no self-confidence or reason for imagining that such frantic mental activity might lead somewhere.

Should I, I asked myself, follow Virgil Thomson's advice toward something useful and practical: proceed to Holland, where Romola was staying with the family of her former companion, and attempt to finish the Vaslav biography? There was still an active season of dancing in Paris which I felt I could hardly afford to miss. I had achieved, as yet, no real contact with Kochno or Balanchine. How serious was I about what vague future? What was self-indulgent woolgathering, what part of my anxiety was cautious and logical analysis?

At this point, as at several times in my life, I was provided with a providential instructor. Monroe Wheeler, backed at the time by the fortune of a young American woman, was a *de luxe* typographer and editor of avant-garde books old and new. Soon he would become director of public relations for the newly founded Museum of Modern Art in New York, but he was already a seriously respected (though anonymous for the great part) manipulator behind the scenes. His pleasure was the guidance of painters and poets, and his influence, not always recognized, was broad and beneficial. For the next thirty years, I rarely made a drastic move without vetting it with Monroe, and he never failed to correct both my rashness and my fears.

At an extended lunch, *chez* Laurent in the avenue Gabriel, Monroe cross-questioned me like a skeptical trial-judge. He imposed some order on my loose ambitions simply by making me answer specifics about basic problems that I had neither the courage nor the critical acumen to pose to myself. What was it that I wished to be doing one year from now? Two years? Five? What kind of money could I command? What was my relationship to my parents? What did I intend to do with *Hound & Horn*? As for ballet, if that was what seemed to be my fate or path, who was I actually counting on? Boris Kochno was an important figure in Paris, but would he, with his grand-ducal Russian manners, transfer to New York? Was I sure that it was Balanchine, and not Massine, that I judged meant the future for classic ballet? Could I persuade Balanchine there was a path forward without Kochno, or his whole Russian team? Monroe provided no answers but the fact that he took me seriously, that he seemed to feel my preoccupations were worthy of worry, gave me a necessary shot of adrenaline, a jet of self-confidence that ultimately determined much.

At Mademoiselle Barney's, where Dolly Wilde had taken me once more, I collided with Professor Mardrus. I told him I had been reading his beautiful translation of the Koran, which had indeed been a revelation to me. He asked, with disdain, why I had taken such trouble? Few had. I protested my sincere admiration and, softened, he asked my faith. I said "Israelite," and he smiled; oh, well then, the Koran was the last book written by a Jewish prophet. There was nothing in it which a rabbinate might object to or deny.

The atmosphere of Paris was so continuously picturesque or exotic that it was hard to make any useful practical comparisons with the possibilities I might face in America. In Boston, everything possible seemed already to have happened; in New York, little had taken place. Virgil said that in contrast the French were prompt to make their past and present permanent. They erected monuments to national figures at every *carrefour*, and named streets after them as a form of *Dictionary of National Biography*. Statues seemed filed as reminders of cultural necessity or achievement. The importance of music, painting, even dressmaking was, he explained, what made the world go round.

He took me off to see Christian Bérard, who was lying, enormous, unshaven, and rumpled, on a dirty chaise-longue, under a quilt like a horse blanket.

Bérard responded to my admiration for his designs for *Mozartiana*, and was happy that it had been announced *Les Ballets 1933* were to have a fortnight's season in London. I felt emboldened to ask, as much as I dared, about Balanchine's personality; and Bérard was not entirely malicious, as I might have expected. Balanchine was a mystery, Bérard maintained, he seemed to have no exterior, visible identity. Masterful in manipulating his craft, he had no interest in society, and while charming and agreeable enough (out of financial necessity), he gave Kochno no help in raising cash. However, Madame Chanel adored him. He was, Bérard continued, entirely under the thumb of Vladimir Dimitriev, a demon-manager who had supervised his escape from the Soviet Union. This Dimitriev, an ex-opera singer, became a croupier at a gambling casino, then managed affairs for the ballet interests of Edward James. According to Bérard, Dimitriev was straight out of Dostoevsky and played Balanchine like a puppet. And so Bérard rambled on and on. Balanchine had only one lung, was drastically in love with Tamara Toumanova—half his age. Lengthily he delivered himself of the opinion that Balanchine was a depthless enigma, and I was hardly encouraged to make any further attempt to meet him. *"Enfin,"* Bérard said, *"il est un peu fou,"* cared about nothing—even the ballet—except for music, and was spending all his spare time taking piano lessons from an old Russian lady, a student of Rimsky-Korsakov.

Soon afterward, augmenting my condition of strained apprehension, Virgil Thomson and Maurice Grosser baited me with a broadside attack on my trivial behavior and my not taking whatever essential talent I might have more seriously. They instanced my awful mural in Harvard's Liberal Club, as well as my few portraits and still lifes, as evidence of real facility, which I felt was a quite false assumption. They could not know with what care, sweat, and anguish I drew or painted. However, they had decided that the role of impresario, toward which I appeared to be magnetized, was for the moment quite impossible for me—lacking, as I did, experience, position, or money. They thought that I had a "creative" rather than an "appreciative" temperament and that the one strong factor linking all my apparent preferences was the technique of painting. If I could claim expertise in any one sector it could later be transferred to the one for which I would find myself finally suited. At the present, I had no social adroitness and was far too apologetic for my lack of self-assurance. As an impresario, Virgil concluded, this would never do.

Perhaps as a field trip consequent on this lecture, I was taken to Pavel Tchelitchev's studio at 5, rue Jacques Mawas by Noel Murphy, the sister of the expatriate writer Gerald Murphy, who was having her portrait painted. Already there were the photographer George Platt Lynes, the novelist Glenway Wescott, and Monroe Wheeler. Gossip flared over the great Bérard-Tchelitchev feud. Tchelitchev claimed that Bérard had hired local stagehands and French dancers to sabotage his *Errante*. He was sure Tilly Losch's long, sea-green satin train had been deliberately stepped-on and torn during performance. She had stormed offstage, seized a practice train from her dressing room, and continued the performance to wild applause. Tchelitchev also gave a very interesting lecture on stagehands, without which nothing could be accomplished in theater. French stagehands were bribed to trick him, out of chauvinism, but German stagehands had the proficiency of surgeons. Around the room there were loose heaps of crumpled sketches overflowing from wastepaper baskets and Tchelitchev picked one up, handing it to me. I was too shy or slow in accepting it, for he remarked, "Oh, so it's not good enough for you." Monroe Wheeler seized it at once, thanked Pavlik, and smiled at me sardonically, as if I had quite failed to benefit from his prior advice.

By now I had become gloomy and depressed, and had not even received word from Romola Nijinsky at The Hague. No one appeared willing to see me or speak to me about the possibilities of classic ballet in America. I was lonely, impotent, dumbly waiting for something to flash like a beacon. Obviously, the activation of significant events needed some sort of cosmic budging. If I was to figure in any future, I decided it would be well if I patiently waited in static awareness, hoping lightning might strike.

At Tchelitchev's invitation, I went back again to his studio, this time for tea. He was extremely friendly, saw no need to hide his general ill-temper or exhaustion, and assumed a convincing manner of immediate intimacy. He was bored out of his skin working for snobs and amateurs. It had come to a pretty pass, he said, when ballet was the toy of dressmakers. Even the technical facilities of the Parisian theaters could not compare to those of Berlin. I tried to describe the amazing new stage of the Radio City Music Hall and the marvels that there might be caused to come into being. He said that it was, finally, not mechanics that were lacking but the very language of the dance itself. Toe dancing, classic ballet, was finished. Balanchine himself admitted the current academic dance was *kaputt*; but Tchelitchev allowed that Balanchine certainly had a gift for transforming movement and filling space with human bodies. And then Tchelitchev returned to the fact that he was sick to death of *scandales*, the intrigues of Parisian journalism and art dealing. The current atmosphere was unhealthy; everything was a retread or playback of an earlier epoch. Maybe a change would come from Germany or even America. But obviously Germany was no place to be in the present *crise mondiale*. Maybe, perhaps, New York . . .

Julien Levy, whose gallery was the first in New York to show Dalí, Tchelitchev, the Bermans, and Bérard, took me to Brancusi's studio. There stood in the middle of the room his all-but-finished "portrait" of Mrs. Eugene Meyer, magnificently monolithic in the hardest of black diorite. Brancusi's gramophone was playing. It had two needles, positioned slightly off center, playing jazz with what sounded like a split overtone. I saw a small plaster cast of his *écorché* stuck up on the top of a big armoire, and I asked him about the full-sized one in the academy at Bucharest. He was delighted that I knew about it and said that, as a young student, at first he had simply thought of copying Houdon's flayed figure, constructed from a skeleton already boned and wired. But Brancusi had been intending to teach himself and he told us he had actually dissected more than fifty cadavers, slowly able to conquer his extreme initial nausea. Standing around his studio were rounded-out stone pillars, cups for hemlock from which some giant Socrates might sip, but which were not yet hacked or smoothed. In their midst, Brancusi, clad in immaculate white linen cover-alls, looked and smelled like fresh baked bread: white thatch, white beard, white shirt, white neckerchief, the tiniest rim of nicotine staining his upper lip's moustache. He was an angel-man. Leaving his studio, which was so full of elegant accomplishment over intractable materials, such mastery derived from such profound study, I felt almost overcome by my failure to face a lack of my own possibility in Paris.

So, in the end, reeling away, I contrived to rejoin Romola Nijinsky at The Hague, where she had at least written, or re-written, five chapters of Vaslav's biography. As I read them impatiently, I realized that they were hardly inspired, and that it was my task to render them more readable. She was now full of the chance to arrange a charity benefit in London for Nijinsky's asylum care. But how to enlist the aid of the antagonistic ex-Diaghilev factions without losing the aid of Massine, Lifar, Kochno, and the others? She intended to gain the support of a committee of distinguished ladies—Lopokova (Lady Keynes); Lady Ottoline Morrell; Lady Juliet Duff—and she bade me proceed immediately to London to undertake all the arrangements under her name, while she would follow in a week. I knew none of these ladies, nor did I realize that, to a woman, they sided with Diaghilev in the split over Vaslav's marriage, holding Romola personally responsible for his insanity.

The Dutch guilder, still supported on a gold standard, was

threatening to fall off, with a disastrous effect on my own purse. Romola's horrible stepfather was still managing to keep her out of Hungary, away from her children—though she had hoped to complete her book at peace in Budapest. Meanwhile the costs of Vaslav's treatment and hospitalization increased, and there seemed no immediate solution. Although I was sorely troubled, I did as I was told, taking my contact with Romola as a step in an indicated fate to which there could only be assent for the moment. She, however, behaved with unwarranted cheerfulness and hope; this automatic response, which almost amounted to a talent, would keep her going for decades to come.

In London, I put up at Batt's Hotel, an edifice which within a few years was to disappear into the smoke and thunder of the Blitz. My father always stayed at Batt's on his trips to England. It had a particular charm for me as well, having been the longtime preferred base in England for colonial administrators on leave from Delhi or Cairo, mixed with a faithful clientele from Scotland and the home counties. I particularly liked the immaculate spareness of its large bedrooms and the webbed floor coverings of pristine rush, possibly split bamboo. This felt delicious under bare feet. Its matting was bound at its edges with thin, pale-green cordage which kept its straw lengths flat and fresh. I hoped the typescript of my small book, *Fokine*, might be serialized by A. R. Orage, then editing the *New English Weekly*. I had known Orage in New York, where he functioned as Gurdjieff's alter ego, and in London now he assumed for me the authority and support that Monroe Wheeler had been able to bestow in Paris, and through him I met a number of his team of critics. I was asked to have lunch at *The Criterion* and spoke to its editor, T. S. Eliot, as if I were going on with *Hound & Horn* without any interruption, although by this time I knew it no longer occupied me. I saw hardly anything of Bloomsbury, almost as if any renewal of my old enthusiasms in former summers might seem a lack of serious loyalty to whatever Balanchine might promise. Meanwhile I waited on the imminent arrival of Romola Nijinsky, since I could not summon up

courage to attempt to meet by myself any of her targeted
sponsors for the charity benefit. Finally, after almost two weeks,
she wired announcing she was coming. At the railroad station,
I waited with growing fury for her arrival on successively
emptying boat-trains. She did not appear, but back at the hotel
there was a telegram: no cash to pay for her bills at The Hague.
In a blind rage I dashed to the American Express to get enough
to send her.

I was compensated for all this by meeting a small circle of
new acquaintances whom I was able to join with an almost
instant, delightful, and surprising intimacy. Through Mr. Orage
I had met William Plomer, a South African writer whose poetry
I had already noticed. And through him, I found a friend in
Laurens van der Post, an acquaintance from Plomer's South
African youth. Laurens, for me, had an extraordinary animal
fascination, almost like a domesticated springbok or okapi.
Extremely sleek, fair-haired, almost always laughing or smiling
at everything and everybody, he spoke hardly at all but gave
off an aura of intense goodwill, generous sympathy, and delight
at being alive.

While in company he stayed silent, I found that when I
managed to be with him alone, he responded to my attraction
with the fullest of impersonal attention. He was a living encyclopedia of South African lore, and was able to describe weather,
landscape, color, and temperature as if it were the rehearsal
for a poetic narrative which he'd not yet committed to paper.
He guided me on an imaginary safari, punctuated by arresting
vignettes and vivid, picturesque, miniature lectures. Laurens
told me how once, in a jet-black electrical tempest, a shrieking
vulture that was trying to throttle a mortally poisonous black
mamba had dropped the snake onto the tin roof over Laurens's
bedroom. It slithered through an open window, and then out
into the veldt, off into the tall cone of a red ant-hill. I reveled
in the image of the endangered anteater's long snout and sticky
tongue, and so many other clear details of a weird Eden in
which Laurens seemed so perfectly framed. He had, for me,

the gift of a narrative bard, the treasurer of a wholly unsuspected but enchanted universe, and I spun like a top on the buzz of his related incidents. What was even more fascinating and provocative was that he seemed to have no particular personality of his own; he spoke as if with a disembodied recollection of his own youth. Laurens replaced all I'd once felt for Stephen Tomlin; and, as with Tommy, my eagerness was reciprocated by couth, distanced self-containment. For most of the remainder of my stay in London, I contrived to spend time with him almost every day—we enjoyed lunch, drinks, museum or book-shop visits, tea or drinks with Morgan Forster and William Plomer.

Kirk Askew, who ran the New York branch of the Durlacher gallery, and his wife, Constance, took me to the Alhambra for the première of the London season of the Ballets Russes de Monte Carlo under Massine. Edward James, very much present, preparing to launch his own *Ballets 1933* company, countered by announcing for the same night a fashionable *Serenade* concert with new French music and the first London hearing of Kurt Weill. This competitive calculation did not succeed, for the Monte Carlo dancers were triumphantly received. At the theater that evening, I noticed there was a considerable difference between the audiences of London and Paris. I had felt a cool, cliquish, snobbish, supercilious air considering itself inherently sophisticated at both the Champs-Elysées and the Châtelet, whereas the British at the Alhambra performances were frankly delighted by the dancing and responded enthusiastically, as if the performers' efforts were justified and worth generous, uncritical applause. There was as yet no national appetite for British ballet, but a public seemed hungry for it. I asked myself if I could compare this with a possible reaction in New York.

Arnold Haskell, a responsible journalist passionately de-voted to the arts, and perhaps the single professional critic of ballet in Britain at this time, took me to lunch with Balanchine's "baby-ballerina," Tamara Toumanova, and her redoubtable mamma. I was immediately suffused with the infinitely tangled *histoires* of the troubles and litigation with Colonel de Basil, the ex-cop, who was suing the Toumanovas for their desertion of the Monte Carlo ballets for the Edward James aggregation. De Basil had seized control of the Monte Carlo company, forcing Baron de Guinzbourg, its founder, to retire. He was trying to pressure the Toumanovas into a ten-year contract, which they viewed as penal servitude for life. And Tamarashka was already receiving film offers! What was there to do? Arnold Haskell stepped in, a knight in shining armor, calmly and pacifically saying, "Do not worry." In his hands all would be well. I had hardly considered so sordid an aspect of ballet-management before. It seemed incredibly messy, and I was rather disturbed by the apparent complacency with which Mamma Toumanova rehearsed the ins-and-outs of her trials. (Later, Haskell explained to me that ballerina-mothers were a special breed and had to be handled with the delicacy granted all artists.) But, as for me, what about Balanchine?

Mamma answered that he was planning a new ballet for Tamarashka, which would repudiate all transient, trendy *modernisme*. This would be a reaffirmation of the *danse d'école* of the eighteenth century and would surprise everyone with the rigors and elegance of a forgotten epoch. This hardly concurred with what Tchelitchev had told me of Balanchine's repudiation of the academy, but now I was becoming accustomed to the conflict of idioms, opinions, and players in the mysterious game of theater. I was strengthened by my proximity to the brink of Balanchine; at least I could begin to count on some resolution. Mamma Toumanova also explained that Balanchine was going to sign for a huge new work for Ida Rubenstein at the Grand Opéra and that André Gide was translating one of Pindar's Pythian Odes, which would be sung *a capella* by a boys' choir, as in ancient Greece. During all the gossip, Tamara was quite silent. But in response to Arnold Haskell's nudging, she affirmed that Balanchine had no wicked designs on her; they were simply good collaborators. He was an excellent dancer, a good partner; it was only because of his threatened tuberculosis that he was not known as a great dancer. When I was alone, I tried to strain the several elements of the general situation into some sort of sense, for now I knew that sooner or later I must meet Balanchine in the flesh, and had better be prepared.

One morning a few days later, I woke in my nice, cool room at Batt's Hotel, and rubbed my bare feet against the delicious straw matting. My toes were no dancer's toes, but, as part of me, they shared the properties of a general possibility which seemed to increase as I tried to formulate it. While I was shaving, Romola Nijinsky, who now had a room on the floor below me, burst in, dreadfully depressed. She would not have left Holland, except for my interest; she hinted at suicide. There was no use in trying to continue. The fight for Vaslav was hopeless. To hell with the ballet; I had better watch out or I would be as cursed as she had been.

I dressed fast and raced to find Arnold Haskell, explaining the crisis. He immediately took over, at once phoning the publisher Israel Gollancz, who asked to see as much of the manuscript of the biography as was available, and promised to read it over the weekend. (Gollancz ultimately, after much haggling during the coming months, accepted the book.) I bought a stout black spring binder but was rather dismayed to find the condition of Romola's typing was primitive and messy. Haskell said that was a proof of her sincerity; Gollancz would be quite familiar with an author's untidiness. As for the benefit for Vaslav, there seemed to be as many factions at odds here as in Paris—Edward James against de Basil; Maynard Keynes and Lopokova against Marie Rambert, Ninette de Valois, and Lady Ottoline. I silently hoped that perhaps Haskell might sort things out and, as if in response, he immediately told me he was meeting de Basil that very night with Tamarashka and Mamma after the performance at the Alhambra to clear up the contractual "misunderstanding," and avoid further litigation. Where that left Balanchine and his relationship to his favorite "baby-ballerina" couldn't be foreseen.

I ventured to speak about a proposal I'd been formulating

as a test ploy. The Monte Carlo company was preparing its first American season and I suggested to him that it might be a good idea to include an "American" ballet, with music by George Gershwin or Cole Porter. Haskell responded enthusiastically and promised he would suggest this to de Basil. I began to love Arnold; he was so transparently dedicated to the ballet, and when I made a gesture of thanking him, he turned away, his eyes almost tearful, and mumbled: "You never saw Nijinsky."

Very apprehensively, then, I squired Romola to the opening of Edward James's *Ballets 1933* season at the Savoy. I was worried as to how she might judge it, and whether or not, in a smaller theater than in Paris, with so many new English dancers, the première might be disappointing. It was not too bad. Toumanova danced like an angel and Tchelitchev's *Errante* with Tilly Losch had genuine success. Afterward, Romola said that Tamarashka was too big, too slow, not sufficiently musical, and should still be in school. In fact, as far as she was concerned, the whole evening had the aspect of a school graduation. To be sure, a few of Balanchine's *adagio* ideas in his supported duets were amusing, but the whole affair was a *salade russe*. During an entr'acte she left a note for Serge Lifar with the Hotel Savoy's concierge and then showed me the column behind which, twenty years before, she had hidden, watching Vaslav go down to dinner with Diaghilev. After the show, she took me backstage and I was introduced to Balanchine. He looked tired and haggard but Romola was sympathetic, complimenting him on making the scenery itself dance and his stage come alive, since he had few real dancers to work with. She also allowed that old Sergei Pavlovich would be pirouetting in his grave to see what had become of his Ballets Russes. I felt let down, and left Romola to come back to her room alone. Whatever, however, I felt about my singular, personal future meant nothing to her, yet I was still attached as if I was her keeper.

Shortly after, at a post-theater party at Kirk and Constance Askew's, the new English dancer Frederick Ashton spoke of his project for a ballet number in a new Cochran revue: it would concern the love of an orchid for a cactus. When I had drifted away from Ashton's enraptured group, the writer Elizabeth Bowen questioned me in some detail about Romola and her preoccupation with spiritualism. I was astonished to learn that Bowen, too, had known the trance-medium "Ma" Garrett, who had done some sort of research with Conan Doyle, and was not, she thought, entirely fraudulent.

Balanchine arrived with Diana Gould, one of his recently hired, native English dancers. After allowing things to settle down into individual personal groups, I managed to face him alone and then be seated, with drink, opposite. He began talking, saying he found it easier to make good dancers out of the English rather than the French, despite a lack of training and tradition. In Paris, too long a time was taken out for lunch; too much *vin rouge* and pastry; there had not been a great French dancer, girl or boy, for generations. The promising ones had to find careers in Russia. Nor had the Germans, Austrians, or even the Italians provided many notable performers. As for himself, he was scheduled to produce Beethoven's *Créatures de Prométhée* for the Grand Opéra. It was an orchestral score associated with a cult reputation but he felt it was not appropriate for dancing. Oh, he said, let Lifar have it to make an initial impression which the press might support. The music had never worked in a theater. At first Lifar had been a nice boy, with little training but a fine face and physique. But now as self-proclaimed heir of Russian male dancing he was spoiled and quite impossible to handle. He indicated down to the slightest degree how the choreography should frame him: had Diaghilev been around, this could never have happened.

I spoke of the Balanchine repertory I would so much like to see again, none of which was in current performance: *Barabau, Le Fils Prodigue, Le Bal, The Gods Go A-begging, Apollon Musagète*. But he said that one should be very slow to revive past work, and only after a decent interval had indicated a true value. *Le Bal*, for example, and *The Gods* too, were really only *pièces d'occasion*, run up quickly for the necessities of a weak season. Ballets existed as a breath, a mere memory, and there were sure to be opinions that revivals were never as good as debuts. Old ballets could seem laughingly *démodé* as, for instance, *Scheherazade*, now shabbily presented by the Monte Carlo company. Balanchine said he believed that the criteria of style changed from season to season, like the shifting waistlines of women's dresses. The vernacular of one decade faded for the next, and since fashion is a prime patron of the ballet, the up-to-date had its real significance. He kept using the adjective *"authentique"* or *"pas authentique,"* as if it had an ultimate criterion, qualifying what was possible to perform. I spoke such poor French that I probably grasped no more than half of what he intended, and imagined he noticed my failure to connect with an adequate response. But he went on expostulating, as if chiefly to himself.

This remained, even through later years, as my chief impression of him: never wholly discouraged, often depressed, absent as a tangible personality when not in actual labor onstage or in rehearsal. The classic dance was a concrete entity, almost a three-dimensional structure as he construed it. It must be reconstructed for service in our twentieth century, speeded up, its tempo accelerated, just as automobiles, once thought miraculous at sixty miles an hour, a mile a minute, now in the age of Sir Malcolm Campbell's "Bluebirds" were capable of almost five times that. Balanchine believed that ballet, as now taught, was at the mercy of petrified habit, chiefly instructed by retired dancers, seldom those of the first rank. In spite of this there had been considerable mechanical (and perhaps anatomical) progress in individuals. Today, Taglioni would seem inefficient compared to any well-trained technician like Danilova, Doubrovska, or his "baby-ballerinas." Most nineteenth-century dancers moved only on *demi-pointe*, without the snap and brilliance propelled by syncopation since Stravinsky and jazz. I had listened to this, as if to an oracle, and on reflection felt he must harbor some lurking curiosity about what I might ultimately propose, since my attention was genuinely rapt.

Back, alone in my room at Batt's Hotel, I tried to make sense of what Balanchine had meant for me to use—if such was the fact. I understood that Fokine, my previous basis for judgment, was no longer valid as a choreographer for the future. His taste was rooted in the aesthetics of Imperial Russia before World War I. Balanchine, despite his native origin, was a new sort of animal. I tried to define his particular role, which seemed at once that of repudiator and re-animator of the academic vocabulary. Stravinsky's innovation was an obvious companion and comparison, even if I was quite ignorant of any specific innovation. There was so much to digest, and although Balanchine had delivered an overwhelming bounty of suggestive indications—including hints that he might like to come to America, maybe with a group of twenty girls and five men, in a repertory of his own developed "modern-classicism"—he had made no sign that he cared to see me again.

In a tiny, magical bookshop devoted to books on ballet, Haskell introduced Romola and me to the owner, Cyril Beaumont, chronicler of the early Diaghilev years. Beaumont informed Romola that Serge Grigoriev, Colonel de Basil's *régisseur*, was trying to wreck plans for the Nijinsky charity gala, since it would be dominated by Lifar. I began to feel extremely restive, wishing to be free of all this in-fighting and trivializing gossip, which was not only harmful but added up to a waste of time and energy. It also competed with any future of my own, and proposed discouragement instead of open possibility. Local intrigue and scandal were far too complex for any innocent but ignorant American enthusiast to handle. Did such entanglement always attend the operation of theater, I asked myself. On the other hand, I wondered whether I could any longer afford a romantic attitude about sheer beauty and simple, selfless behavior in a world of markets and rivalries. I was an unappreciative freshman student in a postgraduate discipline but my choice was now to avail myself of actual immediacy, or count myself out.

However, despite anxiety approaching an agony of insecurity and doubt, some overriding instinct or dominant nerve of energy determined me to hold on, mainly to Romola, partly for her private need, perhaps even more so for my own half-acknowledged curiosity or hope. At least I was now in tenuous if direct contact with Balanchine; this was a reassurance that could not easily be kicked away. In the British Museum Library I pursued research to bolster the Vaslav biography, copying out for Romola's inclusion useful quotations from the musicologist Calvocoressi, the dance historian Léon Vallas, Debussy—an endless process. I had no training as an organized scholar, and was puzzled as to quality of reference, what might be useful or significant, and what might be merely a decoration. The manuscript, as read by any prospective publisher, would be in sore need of a great deal of editorial emendation, which I was not equipped to do. While Arnold Haskell was endlessly useful, I was worried and guilty that so much of what I had set down as fact was invention, deliberately incorrect, or tiresome. False or not, untidy as it may have been, it was the sole means to relieve Romola of her financial horrors, which might mean my freedom.

I began, quietly, to try to formulate for myself strategies as to how to get Balanchine to America, and what to do with him once he'd been landed. It could involve some kind of "educational" formula or "experimental" design, the establishment of a small model company which might be hired as a glamorous lecture-attraction, with myself as instructor. This could be built on, and I felt that sufficient interest would be shown for its novelty, particularly if it were presented as a serious, instructive event. Then there was the commercial theater; Fokine had mounted his own small numbers for Broadway revues, and Balanchine had worked well with Cochran in London. But I had no arrangement whatever with Balanchine, and so far had not been permitted to encounter Vladimir Dimitriev, his business manager, without whom, I had been universally told, no step could be taken.

I found a note from Romola stuck under my hotel room's

door: "Lots of interesting dirt. Am divorcing Vaslav to marry Serge Lifar. Gala benefit performance arranged for October 23rd. Karsavina, Spessivtsa, Woizikovski, Idzikovski all promise to dance: Duke of Connaught as royal patron." Later, at a long breakfast, she worried about problems involving the divorce, explaining that since she'd been married in wartime Argentina she lacked official documents. She seemed quite serious about this latest caprice, which sounded to me a combination of flagrant disloyalty and shameless madness. She claimed it was the only way she could bring herself back to the influential milieu with money and publicity which would secure Vaslav's maintenance. Also, far less crazily, she'd seen fit to open negotiations with the nefarious Colonel de Basil—a man full of "*Bolshoi cabotinage*," as she described it—about her proposal for her young daughter Kyra to dance in a "revival" of Nijinsky's unproduced *Mephisto Valse* with choreography by George Balanchine! This hit me hard. By October, I hoped Balanchine would be safe in America, educating a lecture circuit. Having arranged her worldly salvation, Romola then went off to church; she said her sins hung heavy over her, and I imagined she had some residual guilt for her dependence upon spooks or her notion of divorcing Vaslav. But, in the midst of her wild entanglements and drastic proposals, she was not exactly a fool, and seemed to be able to behave convincingly to those people who mattered most. In any case, I was still hooked.

Then, abruptly, as an auspicious signal, Balanchine invited himself to lunch with me, alone. He spoke of the nightmare of the *Ballets 1933* season paid for by Edward James, and of its operation in Paris and now at the Savoy. The difficulties came not from too little, but too much money, mostly misspent. James, he said, had no notion of order or control and would barely let Dimitriev act as a proper business manager. Meanwhile, James had slapped Lifar in the face, and was separating from Tilly Losch; clearly his real pleasure was not theater, but the drama of litigation. Things had come to such a pass for Balanchine that the vague promise of some odd American solution almost offered itself as salvation. The chaotic situation at the Savoy Theater allowed him to envision the projection of radical possibilities. Maybe, just maybe, there was the real chance for a New York adventure. Haunted by the lack of reality prompted by my closeness to Romola, I tried to explain to Balanchine the poverty of my own realistic position. But he seemed to prefer to take my disclaimers as modesty or discretion, which could even inspire a furtive, hopeful confidence. I realized our planning was artificial and unlikely, but hardly less promising than all the other elements which swarmed around our mutual needs.

The more we talked, the more specific were Balanchine's posited requirements. He would need his own team to found a school and a company. Absolutely necessary were Toumanova and her mother; hardly less so was Dimitriev. Then Pierre Vladimirov, the *danseur noble* who had followed Nijinsky at the Marinsky Theater, and Felia Doubrovska, his wife, still an important performer. The two could also teach and serve as the basis for a distinguished faculty. Then, there was Romola and the excitement her book would surely inspire. She would be an admirable hostess and could lecture with photographic documentation. Certainly, all this was possible, or impossible, as had been picturesquely proven by what theatrical history had seen fit to demonstrate over the last quarter-century. Balanchine swore that America had always been his dream since he had heard a jazz band as a schoolboy in Petersburg. His brief stint in Denmark had convinced him there was little chance for progressive work in Europe, what with the passive domination of the Paris Grand Opéra he'd helped, accidentally, to cede to Serge Lifar. He was now almost willing to gamble on a new continent. Romola would promise her dubious co-operation, with Vaslav's system of choreographic notation and what she could recall of his own ballets.

I was increasingly exhilarated by what he said, willing to suspend any negative judgment and to smother fright. Then Balanchine abruptly excused himself, intent on trying to find enough support to continue the season at the Savoy without the aid of Edward James, and perhaps with the appearance of Lifar as a surprising novelty. But before he went, he said he felt the need to explain to me why he'd been forced to quit the Monte Carlo company, and to found one of his own. It was not vanity, and he had lost much in the change, but he could not endure the oppressive tyranny of de Basil's sergeant-major, Grigoriev. Now de Basil was suing him for the breach of a contract which Balanchine said he'd never signed. Moreover, "Colonel" de Basil had called Balanchine a thief on account of Toumanova's defection. As for theft, Balanchine stated that de Basil, whose real name was Voskresensky, had been an ordinary policeman in Tiflis, and had no claim whatsoever to legitimacy as Diaghilev's successor. De Basil operated his troupe as if it were a police state.

While he spoke, I began to have a large and growing sympathy for Balanchine himself, not as an historic figure but as an individual, who, like others, depended on factors beyond his own extraordinary capacities, and whom perhaps I might have a real role in supporting. Perhaps it was this personal consideration, up until now quite lacking, that seemed to indicate my ultimate direction. An accumulation of self-confidence, almost amounting to a new peak of energy, enabled me to concentrate on a sixteen-page letter to Chick Austin, in Hartford, as a possible sponsor for a ballet school, a ballet company, and nothing less than an American renaissance of the arts through the collaboration of theater, music, and lyric poetry. At least, the museum held space for a studio and an auditorium for performances. Although the letter was fairly detailed and realistic in many respects, I did not venture into any guesses toward questions of money or maintenance. I knew little enough of the economic structure of Hartford, Connecticut, and its dependence on the great insurance corporations. Its Wadsworth Athenaeum was the oldest of American museums, Austin was the youngest of a new and volatile generation of museum directors, and I chose an optimistic style from which to project ambition, fate, ignorance, and something approaching passionate determination.

After I had finished, still at a peak of nervous tension, I went for a walk in Hyde Park to try to reach simplicity of mind again. There was a straggling parade of British Fascists, marching grimly along in columns of three abreast, since they had not enough men for military fours. I tried to soothe myself by isolating what one might recognize as the Fascist facial type, but failed. There were, among them, many good-looking working-class men and boys; the sight or threat of them did nothing to clear my head. Later, Romola made me take her to a séance conducted by the witch Garrett, with a few Hungarian hangers-on. A couple of metal picture frames bounced off a mantelpiece in the blacked-out room, but it all meant zero to me and led only to another sleepless night.

On the following afternoon, I spent from three o'clock in the afternoon until seven, just before curtain time at the Savoy, in my room at Batt's Hotel with Balanchine and Romola. Spread out on the cleanly swept, split-straw floor matting was a large map of the United States; I attempted to locate for them the distances from Hartford to New York City and beyond. There were towns with traditional interest in the arts, sites of museums and symphony orchestras, homes of possible patrons who might, somehow, at some future engagement, be sources of support. Balanchine spoke of his time in Copenhagen, and of how impossible as ballet music was Richard Strauss's *Josephlegende*, in which he'd been forced to make deep cuts, much against his principles. He spoke of other disappointments, fatalistically, which made me sad. While everything lay in a spectacular future, the tactile presence of the big map on the clear, fresh floor exuded an aura of comforting promise. One could not deny the affluence of our East Coast or its commitment to American culture. Why could it not be attacked on frontiers which already had been successfully conquered in the past against heavy odds? When I put away the map and Balanchine went off to the theater, Romola stayed behind. It was as if, with the map folded, the heart had gone out of my mirage. Romola commented on Balanchine's frailty and declared she knew his lungs were gone and he, too, would go within two years. This she had on the absolute authority of "Ma" Garrett, whose information was infallibly from "the other side." I undertook silence as a self-discipline, although I was broiling at her negativism, while she prepared to go off to a séance with two new Hungarian spiritualists who were investigating Mrs. Garrett. Again she hinted at suicide and bade me leave a full cocktail shaker beside her bed.

I had a shower, re-read the draft of my letter to Chick Austin, and went downstairs to the lounge-bar. In a corner, dressed beautifully in long white evening dresses, three debutantes up from the country had white ostrich plumes in their headbands, as if costumed for a ballet. They were perhaps coming from the photographer's, having been presented at court, but they seemed to have strayed from Balanchine's ballroom in *Cotillon*. Three muses, three harpies, or three fates? This abrupt entrance of a wholly poetical vision, their actual presence at so unlikely yet traditional an occasion, served as a cheering signal. The marvelous thing about existence was that it seemed to prove the validity of an historical process despite the opposition of the ordinary. Ballet as fact once again interposed itself, not as an adornment or an accident, but as a constant, valid, and worthy element, allaying, at least for the moment, my more feverish animadversions.

I felt able to present myself backstage at the Savoy after the evening's performance. Balanchine showed me a telegram offering him a job teaching in New York, with a further year's option. He looked worn, tired, and he coughed a lot, but said he would let me know the next day what Vladimir Dimitriev thought of all this. Whether or not he had discussed me with this shady figure, I could not tell. Balanchine seemed almost as confused as myself as to any next step. The London engagement was ending, and he certainly needed a restorative period. He'd mentioned that French friends in the country, near a village I only remembered afterward as named Negrepelisse, had invited Dimitriev, Toumanova, and her mother for a fortnight's vacation. Backstage was filled with friends and hangers-on. I was finally introduced to Dimitriev, a solid figure resembling a stocky, gray tiger, with hard eyes and perfect formal politeness. I didn't think he'd even bothered to allow me a once-over inspection, and I took this as a sign to retire without further words. Back at the hotel, my sense of failure was almost final. Further contact with Balanchine seemed cut for keeps, and I turned for consolation to Arnold Haskell. I also promised myself I must try again to find Laurens van der Post, who had been lost to me during my absorption in ballet business.

After a few days of relative ease with Romola, there blew up a trying *scandale* about cash. I was running short, and worried about how to explain my pressing needs to my father, who was still blissfully in complete ignorance of my summer's activity. I knew Romola was by no means extravagant but very insistent. Self-preservation stripped away what might have been the normal amenities of intimacy. At breakfast one morning, she took the trouble to tell me she had dreamed of us the previous night. We were driving in a Rolls-Royce runabout—straight to Hell—and were on the verge of a major discovery that human personality survived "the other side" (which we were fast approaching in the car). Of this she had absolute corroboration from a trance-session superintended not alone by Mrs. Garrett but by a new infusion of Hungarian spiritualists who were editing an encyclopedia of psychic science supported by Lord Rothermere. I had heard the likes of this too often before and I snapped.

At this rare show declaring a modicum of independence, she said that I had made her heart beat so fast that her life was endangered, and I'd better be careful or I'd be left with the unfinished manuscript of the Vaslav book, and all that might entail. Did I want to kill her? I had the impulse to do so, or at least to be rid of her somehow. But she was, in fact, as strong as a horse. However irritated I could become at her capricious or malicious provocation, a residual, coquettish level of sweetness almost apologized for what was, after all, a more or less instinctive histrionic habit, and I remained at her mercy. This made it easier to forget and forgive, but it reduced my morale to a kind of neurasthenic, repetitive tape-recording. At her most hysterical, she could manage diversions, temporarily relieving Arnold Haskell or myself from the burden of threatened disaster and reverting to a sensible tone, as if nothing had intervened. At this particular juncture, she swept off to a week in the country with Lady Una Trowbridge and Radclyffe Hall, from whose collaboration had sprung *The Well of Loneliness*— along with *Lady Chatterley's Lover*, one of the tendentious causes célèbres of the period. I urged her to stay in London and finish the manuscript. She giggled, tweaked my ears, cleaned out my wallet, and left me silent, on the verge of fury—and tears.

Virgil Thomson, who had come over from Paris for a few days, appeared with the disquieting news that Chick Austin in Hartford had gone forward with plans to produce his and Gertrude Stein's opera *Four Saints in Three Acts*, suddenly a possible competitor to my own balletic aspirations. I mentioned little of what had occupied me, and fortunately Virgil could hardly have imagined my private problems. I was relieved that he seemed to have slight interest in how I had managed life in London. He was very full of his own plans for the production of his opera, and counting heavily on Chick Austin's Hartford for its realization. I owed him, in essence, my experience of Paris, all my introductory apprenticeship into the immediacy of a post-Diaghilev world. Now I found myself, if not in a more or less morally treacherous position, at least a rival. It was a role I had hardly anticipated or desired, and which did nothing to enhance any singleness of purpose I was striving to attain. I almost decided to confess the dilemma to Virgil with entire frankness. But actually, what had I to put forward as even a halfhearted proposal which might imply that our aims were opposed? All I had to spill out were the net results of an overwhelming desire, and the frail contact I had been able to wrestle from it. So I explained nothing, and while this was cowardly, perhaps it was also the wisest way. In time to come, Virgil it should be who would compose *Filling Station*, our fledgling ballet's first truly American success.

At a meeting, arranged by Haskell, for the October Vaslav charity benefit, I found myself seated directly behind a lady whose presence was redolent of majesty yet whose face I'd not been able to see. She was clad in brilliant, shiny blue taffeta, and her *coiffure* looked like stiffened cobalt silk, the Ur-blue rinse. This was Madame Tamara Karsavina, whose autobiography, *Theatre Street*, sponsored by Sir James Barrie, had given the original impulse for Romola's book. Now she let a number of well-wishers express their several, often conflicting, opinions as to strategies best employed, then quietly volunteered to sign a public letter for publication in the *Times*, taking single responsibility for the gala performance and thereby bypassing the inevitable division of harmful rivalries which might be seeking a special advantage. The wife of a British diplomat, Karsavina was universally admired, and she exemplified the best of what was left in the battles over Diaghilev's inheritance.

A few days later, I received word from Romola's vacation retreat, bidding me to join her. She was filled with love, hope, and no hint of past displeasures. After worrying myself sleepless as to what I should plan, I decided I would join her, with the express aim of announcing my emancipation. However, I was still curious enough to try and cushion the blow, and so bought her a replica of her favorite loofah bath-sponge, which she had forgotten in Holland, a *flaçon* of *l'Aimant*, her favorite perfume, and six hard Green-H Venus pencils. On the cliffs of Birchington-by-the-Sea, I was able to transcribe her final chapter—"The Break with Diaghilev"—which she corrected and I handed over

to Haskell, who passed it on to Gollancz. This rather postponed
my proposed declaration of independence, which I now passively hoped might take care of itself without any urgency on
my part. I was learning to trust providence, or at least to count
as much on exterior destiny as on my own selfish and limited
capacities.

And the providential seemed to take account of my new
analysis. Back at Batt's Hotel, there was a telegram from Chick
Austin in Hartford in answer to my formidable letter. He had
gained promises from Eddie Warburg, Jim Soby, Philip Johnson, and Paul Cooley for at least three thousand dollars, which
he was depositing at my bank toward payment for Balanchine's
steamship fare. This was more than half of what I had budgeted
for transportation and a brief trial residence for Balanchine
and his populous *équipe*. I wired Balanchine at the Champs-
Elysées Theater, the sole address I had for him in France.
There was no response. A further cable from Hartford commanded: GO AHEAD IRONCLAD CONTRACT NECESSARY START-
ING OCTOBER 15 SETTLE AS MUCH AS YOU CAN BRING
PUBLICITY PHOTOGRAPHS MUSEUMS WILLING CAN'T WAIT.
I was in torment as to how I might tell Romola, but decided
that recklessness was required in my quest for Balanchine and
I must rush to France and search for him. I began to sense
that somehow I was now fatally aligned with a commanding
historical process. The succession of similar indications as
progressive steps forward seemed to project themselves into
my immediate future, as if I was on a mobile stairway and was
now unable to get off.

Yet, on the peak of such possibility, I also felt a pressing
need to cling to some shred of essentially private, basic level of
personal warmth. At Magg's bookshop I found the two-volume,
first English edition of *Moby-Dick*, the epic of deranged American searching, and on impulse I bought it as a farewell memento
for Laurens van der Post. The London evening of August 8,
1933, the day before I was to cross the Channel, Laurens and

I had agreed to have dinner with William Plomer, his friend Bernard, the guardsman, and Morgan Forster and his Bob Buckingham, a constable. Laurens arrived at the restaurant late with a bagful of bottles of South African wine. We'd already started on gin-&-bitters, good Gordon's gin to which an American under Prohibition was hardly accustomed. I found myself refreshed and jolly in the friendliness of this dispassionate company, and particularly warmed by the renewed immediacy of Laurens. Liquor helped to remove the overwhelming, imponderable burden of other grossly threatening worlds. I told myself I could banish the ballet and determine with a clear vision what would be healthy and correct for whatever existed of an essential me. Emotionally, I clung to the idea of continuous contact with Laurens, and the likes of his friends and theirs—my true, not my accidental preference, my real blood-tribe—without the egregious jungle rituals of dancing or theater.

It was a cozy celebration; we went on drinking until the bar shut. After a muzzy roundabout of goodbyes, I remember leaving half an Armagnac on the bar, but I must have been quite drunk, for Laurens saw that I could hardly get to my room without help and manfully supported me—much as the Englishman Metz had done years before in Fontainebleau on the night of my first meeting with Gurdjieff. Reaching my bed, I fell flat on my face, and I suppose that Laurens composed himself on the straw-matted floor. Paris retreated to the far end of a leafy-green tunnel as a black mamba shot from a vulture's yawn straight onto my tin pillow. I heard Laurens murmuring his "Zulu click" and told myself that I didn't absolutely *have* to go to Paris, did I? Sleep dropped its curtain, muffling any reply, and I swallowed oblivion.

I awoke with a panicky realization that I must catch a boat train for France in less than three hours. Laurens was gone, the room empty, the sun grandly promising the best of a fresh day, and streets below were already humming. I stretched my toes to touch the trim reassurance of the straw matting. Its immaculate texture felt almost like a springboard. Leaving

London would be leaping across a gap, drastic and final—
Boston, Cambridge, all my old certainties repudiated or fore-
sworn. For better or worse, I was abandoning Laurens and my
friends. I was alone now and I knew I must find Balanchine if
I was serious about anything . . .

Index

Index

Index

Index

Index

Index

Index

Index